The Red Thread

The Red Thread

The Passaic Textile Strike

JACOB A. ZUMOFF

Rutgers University Press
New Brunswick, Camden, and Newark, New Jersey, and London

Library of Congress Cataloging-in-Publication Data
Names: Zumoff, Jacob A., author.
Title: The red thread: the Passaic textile strike / Jacob A. Zumoff.
Description: New Brunswick: Rutgers University Press, [2021] |
    Includes bibliographical references and index.
Identifiers: LCCN 2020043346 | ISBN 9781978809895 (paperback) |
    ISBN 9781978809901 (cloth) | ISBN 9781978809918 (epub) |
    ISBN 9781978809925 (mobi) | ISBN 9781978809932 (pdf)
Subjects: LCSH: Textile Workers' Strike, Passaic, N.J., 1926. | Wages—
    Textile workers—New Jersey—Passaic.
Classification: LCC HD5325.T42 1926 Z86 2021 | DDC 331.892/87700974923—dc23
LC record available at https://lccn.loc.gov/2020043346

A British Cataloging-in-Publication record for this book is available from the British Library.

♾ The paper used in this publication meets the requirements of the American National
Standard for Information Sciences—Permanence of Paper for Printed Library Materials,
ANSI Z39.48-1992.

www.rutgersuniversitypress.org

Manufactured in the United States of America

Contents

Illustrations

Abbreviations Used in Text

ACLU	American Civil Liberties Union
AFL	American Federation of Labor
AFPS	American Fund for Public Service (Garland Fund)
AME	African Methodist Episcopalian
ASW	Associated Silk Workers of America
ATWA	Amalgamated Textile Workers of America
CEC	Central Executive Committee (of Communist Party)
CIO	Congress of Industrial Organizations
CP	Communist Party
DEC	District Executive Committee (of Communist Party)
ILD	International Labor Defense
ILGWU	International Ladies' Garment Workers' Union
IWA	International Workers' Aid
IWW	Industrial Workers of the World
NSDC	National Silk Dyeing Company
NTWU	National Textile Workers Union
SPC	Social Problems Club
TUC	Trade Union Committee (of Communist Party)
TUEL	Trade Union Educational League
TWOC	Textile Workers Organizing Committee
TWUA	Textile Workers Union of America
UCWCH	United Council of Working-Class Housewives
UFC	United Front Committee of Textile Workers
UMW	United Mine Workers of America
UPDW	United Piece Dye Works

UTW	United Textile Workers of America
YPSL	Young People's Socialist League
YWL	Young Workers' League

The Red Thread

Introduction

The Passaic Textile Strike
of 1926

In the winter of 1926 more than 15,000 wool workers in northern New Jersey went on strike. For more than a year, the workers—mainly immigrants, and half of whom were women—organized massive picket lines and braved arrest, harassment and police violence to organize a union and to reverse a 10 percent pay cut. Although known as the Passaic strike, workers in nearby Clifton, East Paterson (today Elmwood Park), Garfield, and Lodi also participated. Led by Albert Weisbord, a Communist who had recently graduated from Harvard Law School, the strike was the first time most Americans saw the ability of the fledgling Communist Party (CP) to organize thousands of workers in struggle.

In the 1920s, Prohibition, attacks on immigrants, racist violence, and the growth of the Ku Klux Klan as a mass organization marked a growing political conservatism. The Teapot Dome scandal laid bare the venal and corrupt nature of capitalist politics. In May 1924, President Calvin Coolidge signed the Johnson-Reed Act (better known as the National Origins Act) that limited immigration from southern and eastern Europe. Less than two years later, workers from that part of the world were in the vanguard of the fight to revitalize the labor movement. The strike captured the imagination of the labor movement, the left, and liberals. For a year the nation's eyes were trained on Passaic and surrounding cities. Although the strike was defeated, it exposed the soft underbelly of the Roaring Twenties. It gave a glimpse of the ingredients that would create such an explosive mixture less than a decade later: militant industrial unionism, dynamic and uncompromising tactics, political radicalism, and a creative use of culture and media to win public opinion.

The 1920s brought prosperity for capitalists and the rising managerial-professional class, but for many workers they were the beginning of the "lean years," presaging the Depression.[1] In 1919, according to the Bureau of Labor Statistics, 4,160,348 workers were involved in 2,665 industrial disputes. In 1926 the number had dropped to 329,592 workers participating in 783 disputes.[2] American capitalists waged an unrelenting war against the working class. Between 1919 and 1929, output per worker in manufacturing increased by about 43 percent while wages remained stagnant: in 1920 the average unskilled male manufacturing worker earned $22.28 weekly, a figure that by 1929 had risen by only 10 percent, to $24.40. Membership in the American Federation of Labor (AFL) plummeted from over 5 million in 1920 to 3.5 million in 1923, and then less than 3 million in 1933.[3]

The AFL leadership—first Samuel Gompers, and after his death in 1924, William Green—responded by seeking cooperation with management and eschewing radicalism. In 1923 the AFL convention in Portland unseated William F. Dunne, an elected delegate from Montana, because he was a Communist. Many unions purged anybody suspected of supporting the Communist Party or the Trade Union Educational League, the CP's trade-union arm. At the same time, several leading AFL bureaucrats were involved with the bosses-dominated National Civic Federation (NCF), including Gompers, AFL secretary Frank Morrison, and Matthew Woll (who became acting president of the NCF in 1926). Although industry was increasingly based on mass-production methods, with semiskilled and unskilled workers playing a larger role, the AFL remained focused on skilled workers.[4] The Passaic strike, led by Communists with a class-struggle perspective, challenged the pro-capitalist perspective of the AFL bureaucracy and ran counter to the retreat of the labor movement in the 1920s.

The Passaic strike captured the imagination of not just the New York area (the media capital of the country), but the nation as a whole. To take just two examples: the front pages of the *Helena Independent* in Montana and the *Montgomery Advertiser* in Alabama carried articles about the strike on February 10, 1926; later that month, papers in Alabama, California, Michigan, Missouri, Tennessee, and Utah (along with Ontario in Canada) ran a United Press article about the strike leadership.[5]

But why was the strike so important? The Passaic strike was not the most powerful strike of the period. The 170-day anthracite coal strike of 1925–1926 threatened to cut off the Eastern Seaboard's heat during winter as 150,000 miners shut down 828 mines belonging to 135 companies.[6] In 1927–1928, almost 200,000 bituminous coal miners, members of John L. Lewis's United Mine Workers (UMW), went on strike for months at the same time as the Industrial Workers of the World (IWW) led thousands of Colorado coal miners on strike.[7]

The Passaic strike was not even the only hard-fought textile strike of the period. In 1924, some 8,500 silk workers in Paterson went on strike. Police arrested Roger N. Baldwin, the head of the American Civil Liberties Union (ACLU), along with nine strikers.[8] The next year 2,200 cotton workers in Willimantic, Connecticut, struck the American Thread Company. For nine months the workers, under the leadership of the United Textile Workers (UTW), faced 1,700 scabs protected by state police. The Willimantic strike ended in a defeat.[9] Nor was the Passaic strike the only strike at this time in which the Communist Party played a leading role. For seventeen weeks, from February to June 1926, some 12,000 furriers in New York City under the leadership of Communist Ben Gold went on strike, winning a wage increase, a forty-hour week with overtime pay, and an end to subcontracting, among other terms. Then from July through November, 40,000 New York City cloakmakers in the International Ladies' Garment Workers' Union went on strike, under Communist leadership. (The cloakmakers' strike lost.)[10]

These strikes suggest an underlying militancy and discontent among American workers, even in the quiescent 1920s. Even though these strikes were important, none of them transcended the immediate issues involved to symbolize the greater class struggle between labor and capital. None offered an alternative vision for the labor movement as a whole. The coal strike in 1925–1926, while impressive, was a rearguard action by a union on the defensive. The coal miners lost, and by the end of 1926 more than 61 percent of coal miners were working without a union contract. The 1927–1928 anthracite strike was also a disaster, and the Colorado strike lost after police killed eight miners. The UMW—the largest union in the AFL—had lost 200,000 members since 1922 and, in the words of Lewis's biographers, "was in a headlong race to oblivion."[11] Unlike the AFL, the syndicalist IWW had sought to organize unskilled workers, but the coal strike was its last gasp, many of its best militants having been won over to the Communist Party.

In contrast, the furriers' strike was victorious and the Communist leaders in the New York needle-trades unions had a radical vision. But the internecine battles of the garment unions—often fought in Yiddish between Socialists and Communists—did not resonate for most American workers. Furthermore, the tens of thousands of workers involved in the strike worked in scores of subcontracted workshops, making it difficult to personify the abuses of the bosses.

The Passaic strike drew on a tradition of struggles of textile workers in northern New Jersey, most famously in the Paterson strike led by the IWW in 1913. The Paterson silk workers—mainly skilled Italian and Jewish workers who toiled in hundreds of competing shops—represented a previous age of labor struggle, and by the 1920s the silk industry in Paterson was already entering terminal decline.[12] In contrast, Passaic's wool workers had more in common with mass-production workers in the automobile and steel industries than with their skilled neighbors in Paterson. Wool and worsted production was done around the clock in a handful of large mills by unskilled, immigrant workers. Ownership of the mills was concentrated in the hands of a few large companies—mostly connected to the German textile industry. To keep out unions, mill management used espionage, company unions, and domination of local politics. In this concentrated power of the bosses the wool workers faced larger obstacles than did their counterparts in Paterson, but at the same time, once they went on strike, they wielded more power.

The strike's location amplified its importance. Passaic is outside of New York City, but within the metropolitan area. Passaic is—geographically and culturally—part of the mainland United States, and the nation could better relate to events in a midsize industrial city than in the island of Manhattan. The advances that New York City unions made in the early 1900s for unskilled and women workers, particularly in the needle trades, did not extend across the Hudson and Passaic Rivers. But even if many Passaic workers never ventured into New York City, the wool industry was connected to the city because its main customers were in the New York City garment trade. The powerful needle-trades unions in New York, with their Communist and Socialist traditions, rallied to the Passaic strikers. And Passaic is only a commuter train ride away from New York, the nation's political and media center; mill owner Julius Forstmann lived in a mansion in Manhattan's Upper East Side. Reporters, photographers, activists, lawyers, and politicians visited the strike (and often returned home in time for dinner), increasing its impact. Papers ranging from the *New York Times* to the *New York Evening Graphic* covered the strike.

Location alone did not make the strike important. What made the Passaic strike unique was that in many ways it was *not* unique. The low wages, poor conditions, ethnic divisions, company hostility, and state repression, and the hostility of the AFL leadership that the woolworkers confronted were shared with millions of mass-production workers throughout the country (some of whom faced even worse conditions). The Passaic strike highlighted these common issues, while demonstrating that workers could struggle against them. This points to the main difference between the Passaic strike and the other strikes of the period: the Passaic strikers' success in winning support and solidarity from the broader labor movement and among radicals and liberals—what Michael Goldfield has labeled "associate power."[13]

Leadership was key to the strike's distinctiveness and power. Weisbord and other Communists focused on building strong picket lines and building workers' power, in contrast to the AFL's focus on seeking cooperation with the employers or their government. What distinguished the strike's leadership was not their view of the strike zone, but their broader vision. Passaic became nationally important because Weisbord and other Communists in its leadership *made it* nationally important. In a pamphlet about the strike, Weisbord wrote: "The real importance of Passaic is there are many Passaics. America is virtually built on Passaics, not only in the textile industry, but in every fundamental industry in this country.... The monstrous exploitation, the terrible brutality that characterizes Passaic characterizes them all. The struggle of the Passaic workers, therefore, symbolizes the sufferings and determination not only of these workers, the million unskilled and oppressed workers in the textile industry, but the twenty-eight million in the other industries the country over."[14]

In many scholars' views, Communist politics were a straitjacket on militants in the labor unions, forcing them to put the "party line" above the interests of the workers.[15] This was true later (especially during the Second World War when the CP supported a no-strike pledge), but in the United States, in 1926, this was not yet the case. The Communist Party and its publicity machine—including the *Daily Worker*, foreign-language publications, pamphlets and books, speakers and agitators, even a movie—imbued the Passaic strike with an importance that it would not have had otherwise. Communists in other countries wrote articles on the strike.[16]

In the Communists' eyes, the Passaic workers were not just fighting for their own interests; they were fighting for the entire working class. "Organize the Unorganized" became a central slogan. If the wool workers could prevail against the anti-union textile barons, then workers in other mass-production industries had a chance to organize as well. The silk, cotton, or coal workers were no less determined to defend their wages and working conditions than were the workers in the Passaic wool mills. The main difference was that the Passaic workers had a leadership that not only was determined to win the strike, but saw the Passaic workers as symbolic of workers throughout the country.

Rather than narrow the focus of the strike, the Communists expanded its influence. They brought the strike to well-known liberals and radicals, who took up the cause of the New Jersey wool workers. Elizabeth Gurley Flynn, a veteran from the IWW's battles (including textile strikes in Lawrence, Massachusetts, and Paterson in 1913) and a famous labor radical, threw herself into the strike. She spoke at numerous rallies—sometimes more than one a day—and helped ground the Passaic strike in a tradition of labor militancy. Through her, radical journalist Mary Heaton Vorse became immersed in the strike, editing the strike bulletin and publishing articles and eventually a book on the strike. Liberals like attorney Frank P. Walsh, economist W. Jett Lauck, and Rabbi Stephen S. Wise became active in building support. Norman Thomas, a Presbyterian minister, journalist, and Socialist Party member, supported the strike. Roger Baldwin, the ACLU's founder, supported the strike, and his organization defended the strikers.

The key to this situation was the Communist Party. The CP was founded in 1919 when left-wing members of the Socialist Party split from their parent party, determined to forge a Bolshevik-style party in the United States. As John Reed, a founder of the new party put it, the October Revolution shook the world, making the struggle for workers' power concrete and attracting support in the factories, mines, and mills even in distant North America. The

CP began its life with broad sympathy among workers and leftists, enabling it to recruit key labor leaders like William Z. Foster in the early 1920s.

Soon, however, Red Scare repression, the AFL leadership's hostility toward Communism, and mistakes by the Communists themselves led to the CP's becoming isolated from the organized labor movement in the 1920s. The Passaic strike was key in gaining Communists respect among in the broader workers' movement, demonstrating that Communists could competently lead a strike. In the mid-1920s the Communist Party was riven by factionalism. Although many of the strike leaders, including Weisbord, supported the faction of C. E. Ruthenberg and Jay Lovestone (against Foster), during the strike supporters of all factions worked together, hinting at the potential strength of the party.

By the late 1920s, amid defeats in the revolutionary movement in Europe, the CP became thoroughly Stalinist, subordinating its fight for a workers' revolution to the current needs of the Soviet leadership. In 1928 James P. Cannon and supporters of Leon Trotsky's Left Opposition were expelled for their opposition to Stalin's rejection of the need for international revolution in the guise of building socialism in one country; the following year, Jay Lovestone and supporters of Nikolai Bukharin's Right Opposition were expelled. In the mid-1930s, under the leadership of Foster's former protégé Earl Browder, the American CP used its considerable influence among workers and intellectuals to support the New Deal capitalist reforms of Democratic Party president Franklin D. Roosevelt. In 1926, while Stalin was becoming more powerful in the Soviet Union, the American Communist Party still had not become fully Stalinist. The cynicism and reformism that marked the later 1930s had not taken over the party.[17]

The importance of the Communist Party in the strike has hindered understanding of the strike. The aura of romanticism around the Industrial Workers of the World contributed to an outpouring of books about the Paterson strike. Despite the contemporary hatred toward the IWW, from today's academic perspectives the IWW belonged to another epoch, safely past— converted, to paraphrase Lenin, into harmless icons robbed of revolutionary substance. In contrast, there is no similar romanticism around the Communist Party, since for much of the twentieth century the Communist Party was vilified. Many of the same eastern and central European communities that supported the strike in Passaic became resolutely anti-Communist after the Second World War. There was little public historical memory of the strike or its Communist leadership: many people in the area confuse the Passaic and Paterson strikes. In contrast, even though the wool industry left Passaic long ago, the mill owners still cast a shadow; the public library is named after Julius Forstmann (on land he donated). Nor did the Communist movement itself want to analyze the strike in more than a cursory manner, because doing so would require grappling with the differences between the party in the 1920s and the 1930s—that is, the rise of Stalinism. Many of the people active in the strike, including Weisbord, were expelled with Lovestone in 1929 and became bitter enemies of subsequent Communist leadership.

Weisbord wrote and spoke extensively about the strike, to an extent that some have seen as egoistical.[18] Until his death in 1977 he accentuated his own role in the strike and downplayed the role played by other Communists or the party as a whole. Another early Communist who wrote about the strike was Benjamin Gitlow, a leader of the Communist Party since its founding in 1919. Gitlow, who had briefly worked as a cutter in the garment trades, was in charge of the party's work in the clothing industries and involved in the early stages of the strike (although he soon was drawn into the furriers and then the cloakmakers strikes in New York). Gitlow, too, supported Lovestone and was expelled from the CP in 1929, but by the late 1930s he became an anti-Communist. In his autobiography, *I Confess* (1940), Gitlow regaled his reader with sordid tales of sex and corruption, depicting the Passaic strike (like everything else the early CP did) as a cynical ploy.[19]

While Theodore Draper was researching his two books on the CP in the 1920s, he corresponded with James P. Cannon, then the leading Trotskyist in the United States, but previously a leader of the CP. Cannon's correspondence—published as *The First Ten Years of American Communism* (1962)—provides key political insight into the early CP. Even though he recounts discussions in the leadership about the Passaic strike, Cannon was not centrally involved in the strike (and it is not clear that he visited Passaic during the strike).[20]

Mention must also be made of Vera Buch Weisbord's memoirs, *A Radical Life* (1977), which contain a chapter on the strike.[21] Vera Buch was a founder of the American Communist Party who moved to Passaic during the strike and became romantically involved with Albert Weisbord, eventually marrying him. Like all memoirs, hers suffer from the passing of time; because Vera Weisbord followed Albert Weisbord out of the Communist Party and through all his subsequent political turns, her memoirs are colored by her later politics. Like Gitlow and her late husband, Vera Weisbord had a political ax to grind, and at times the book reads like it is trying to settle old scores. As a whole, though, it is thoughtful and incisive. Nonetheless, the memoirs of one person involved in the strike cannot tell the entire history of the strike.

Historians have not ignored the Passaic strike. Most studies of the labor movement and radical politics in the 1920s include an obligatory discussion of the strike. Some of these, of course, are more insightful than others.[22] What is lacking is a synthetic attempt to analyze the development of the strike from start to finish, placing it in historical context. There have been two attempts to give a broad overview of the strike. The first is a collection of primary sources published fifty years after the strike, edited by University of Minnesota historian Paul L. Murphy with David Klaassen and Kermit Hall.[23] This book contains many excerpts drawn from a variety of sources. The second is a documentary radio program, "Passaic on Strike," produced by the New Jersey Historical Commission and NJN Public Radio.[24] Both of these are well done and would be useful for a general audience or a university (or advanced high school) classroom. Neither one is, or pretends to be, a scholarly assessment or analysis of the strike.

There have been several unpublished academic studies of the strike, beginning when the strike was still in people's memory.[25] Among these is Morton Siegel's 1953 meticulously researched doctoral dissertation.[26] Siegel's work has held up remarkably well for a sixty-five-year-old unpublished dissertation, but his study was written before many archival sources were available. Siegel's dissertation was written before there was a synthetic history of the Communist Party, and therefore much of the work is concerned with outlining the history of the Communist Party, something that Theodore Draper's two-volume study of the CP rendered unnecessary.[27] Together, these new sources allow today's historian to get a more complete picture of the strike—especially the role of the Communist Party—than was possible when Siegel wrote his dissertation.

The most recent work on the strike was David Lee McMullen's biography of Ellen Dawson, a mill worker who became active in the strike and the Communist Party.[28] McMullen painstakingly and masterfully shifted through archival and newspaper sources to reconstruct Dawson's early years in Britain, her life in Passaic, her role in the Passaic strike and subsequent Communist efforts in the textile industry, her expulsion from the Communist Party in 1929, and her later life. By necessity the book deals with the strike, but McMullen does not make the strike itself the central focus of his work. As a result, there are important aspects of the strike that McMullen does not examine.

The present study differs from these works in several ways. It is based on research in the archives of the Comintern, as well as the papers of participants in the strike efforts such as Mary Heaton Vorse and Alfred Wagenknecht, together with sources such as the papers of Rabbi Stephen S. Wise, attorney Frank P. Walsh, and the records of the American Civil Liberties Union and the American Fund for Public Service. My research is also grounded in contemporary newspapers and journals from New Jersey and New York City. When I began researching the strike, looking at these papers required sitting in front of the microfilm reader for hours at public libraries or sorting through clippings that were part of archival collections; by the time I finished the research, many of the papers were digitized and available in searchable databases.[29]

Perhaps more important than the use of new sources is how the present work approaches the strike. Almost all writers about the strike come from a perspective of anti-Communism. In contrast, as readers of my previous study of the Communist Party in the 1920s will be aware, I am sympathetic to the politics of the early American Communists, as they struggled to apply the lessons of the Bolshevik Revolution and the Communist International to American soil and forge a party that would be able to lead such a revolution here. The Communist Party committed errors (these are discussed in this book), but its essential strength must be recognized: the Communists believed that even at the height of the Roaring Twenties, capitalism was a doomed system that needed to be replaced through the mobilization of the working class, culminating in a workers' revolution. Taken with the subsequent Sacco and Vanzetti campaign, the Passaic strike offers a glimpse of the potential strength of the Communist Party in the 1920s, before Stalinism and factionalism gutted the party politically.

Organization of This Book

It is my hope that after reading this book, the reader will have an understanding of the origins, development, and conclusion of the strike. As I researched this book, it became evident to me that understanding the context and impact of the strike required more than a chronological narrative. It is necessary to understand the development of the area's textile industry, the Communist Party, and the broader political and economic condition of the United States in the 1920s.

Chapter 1 describes the origins of the Passaic wool and woolen industry, organized as an American outpost by German companies in the late 1800s, as a result of high protective tariffs. Paterson's silk workers were famous for their militancy, but Passaic's wool workers remained unorganized.

Chapter 2 examines the beginning of the strike, the efforts of the United Front Committee (UFC), and the strike's spread through the wool mills in the Passaic region. Chapter 3 examines the role of Weisbord and the CP in the early stages of the strike, and how Communists propelled the Passaic strike to become nationally important. Chapters 4 and 5 look at how the strike leadership tried to broaden support for the strike. Weisbord and other Communists sought to mobilize the power of other textile workers—in the first instance, the silk workers in nearby Paterson.

While the Passaic strikers had limited success in attracting support in the labor movement in March 1926, they did gain the support of several prominent liberals in New York City, including Walsh and Wise. Chapter 5 examines these liberal supporters' attempts to pressure liberal congressmen to investigate conditions in Passaic and force the mill owners to negotiate.

Chapter 6 examines government repression and the workers' response. The united front built by the CP helped sustain the Passaic strike while highlighting the party's organizing and political capabilities. Chapter 7 describes efforts to build relief and solidarity with the strikers. These efforts included providing food and clothing to strikers to help them brave a long, cold winter without pay, and helped frame the strike as emblematic of the struggle of the entire working class.

Chapter 8 examines the role of women in the strike, and the failure of the strike leadership to deal with this question head-on. This chapter also examines the role of young people in this strike, including the Young Pioneers and the Young Workers' League. Chapter 9 examines how the United Textile Workers took over and ended the strike. Unable to continue the strike, the UFC joined the UTW, who then proceeded to settle with the mills piecemeal and failed to achieve a union contract. Chapter 10, the concluding chapter, looks at how the strike affected the workers of Passaic, the wool industry of Passaic, the Communist Party, and the labor movement as a whole. While the strike presaged the labor battles of the 1930s, Passaic remained a non-union town until the 1940s.

This does not exhaust the areas of the strike worth researching, but it does allow the historian to place the strike in historical context and tell its story.[30] This book is aimed at several audiences, which are distinct although they may overlap—including scholars and students of labor and working-class history, the textile industry, or northern New Jersey, as well as those who study the Communist Party. I also hope that residents of the Passaic area today will find this book helpful in understanding the events that took place almost a hundred years ago and made Passaic "Hell in New Jersey."

More broadly, since I began working on this book in 2016 there has been an upsurge in labor struggle: hundreds of thousands of teachers, hotel workers, automobile workers, copper mine and smelter workers, and others have gone on strike for the same issues that motivated the textile workers almost a century ago. The wool industry will most likely never again be so important in the United States—and almost certainly not in New Jersey—but the lessons of Passaic remain relevant: not just the need for militancy and solidarity, but the importance of building mass picket lines and refusing to back down in the face of government and police repression, and an understanding that workers and employers do not share a common interest and that victory can be won only through mobilizing the workers' own power, not relying on support from politicians from the capitalist Democratic or Republican Parties. Just as the Passaic strike came to symbolize the determination of the working class to struggle in 1926, it is my hope that this long-ago strike inspires future struggle.

1

Passaic, New Jersey

Today, 90 Dayton Avenue in Passaic, New Jersey, is one of many light-industrial parks in the northern part of the Garden State. The Passaic Industrial Center's forty-one buildings totaling 1.64 million square feet on thirty-one acres were sold for $10 million in 2013. It has easy access to State Route 21, and from there Manhattan or Newark. This location most likely explains its recent use by various criminal organizations: in March 2018 the New Jersey State Police alleged that the site was the headquarters for a gang of criminals who stole tractor trailers, and in November 2015 the police claimed the park was home to New Jersey's largest "synthetic marijuana" factory. Only what is carved above the main entrance—"Botany Worsted Mills"—indicates that this site, built in 1894, was one of the largest textile mills in the United States.[1]

In the nineteenth century, foreign-made wool and worsteds dominated the American market. In 1890 the Tariff Act, championed by Ohio Republican congressmen (and future president) William McKinley, imposed high tariffs on imported wool to protect the American textile industry. Tariffs on woolen and worsted cloth averaged 100 percent in the 1890s, with some cloth being taxed at 150 percent. Worsted imports to the United States were cut in half, and production in the United States soared from about $20 million worth of worsted goods in 1859 to some $300 million in 1909. Wool imports plummeted, from being almost 23 percent of all wool consumed in the United States in 1889 to being less than 2 percent in 1919. To avoid these tariffs, Belgian and French textile capitalists opened plants in Woonsocket, Rhode Island, while German companies invested in plants on the Passaic River in New Jersey. The wool and worsted companies' profitability depended on high tariffs that shielded them from foreign competition—even though the companies themselves were foreign-owned.

Like silk companies in the 1880s, wool companies were drawn by the area's access to water, labor, raw material, and markets. The first Passaic wool company was Botany Mills, established in 1889 by Paul Rudolf Eduard Stöhr (later Americanized to Stoehr), born in Eisenach in 1846. Botany was controlled by Stöhr's family firm, the Leipzig-based Kammgarnspinnerei Stöhr & Co., which the *New York Times* later called "the most noted in the German wool industry."[2]

Christian Bahnsen followed suit in 1890. Bahnsen, a Dane who had migrated to Germany before settling in the United States, was the American agent of Ernst Friedrich Weissflog, a large wool manufacturer in Saxony. Bahnsen called his company Gera Mills, in honor of Weissflog's home city. In 1904 the same group founded the New Jersey Worsted Spinning Company in nearby Garfield. In 1909 the two companies, with three mills between them, were combined.[3]

Julius Forstmann (born in 1871), the sixth generation of a German wool-manufacturing family, moved from Essen to Passaic in 1903. His great-grandfather established Forstmann und Huffmann in 1803, and the company had been exporting wool cloth to the United States since 1853. One hundred years after its German namesake was founded, Forstmann and Huffmann was organized in Passaic. In time, Forstmann and Huffmann would open plants in Passaic and Garfield. By 1926, there were 2,000 workers who sorted, spun, and wove wool at the Garfield plant, and then 1,000 workers finished the wool at the Passaic plant.

Forstmann, a spokesman for his industry on a local and national level, was well integrated into the American capitalist class. After living in Passaic, the Forstmann family moved to East Seventy-First Street on the Upper East Side of Manhattan in 1922, sharing the block with steel-magnate Henry Frick and Robert Chesebrough, the inventor of Vaseline. Forstmann remained head of this company (eventually renamed the Forstmann Woolen Company) until he died in 1939.[4]

The Textile Industry in Paterson and Passaic

By 1915 at least one-fourth of New Jersey's workers toiled in the textile industry, which encompassed a variety of specializations based on product and cloth. The New Jersey textile industry was dominated by firms in the Paterson-Passaic district, and included Clifton in Passaic County and East Paterson—known today as Elmwood Park—Garfield, and Lodi across the Passaic River in Bergen County. In the 1920s about 311,000 people lived in these cities. Paterson, some twenty miles from Manhattan and with a population of about 135,000, provided silk; Passaic, fifteen miles from Manhattan and with a population of about 65,000, provided wool; Lodi, fifteen miles from Manhattan

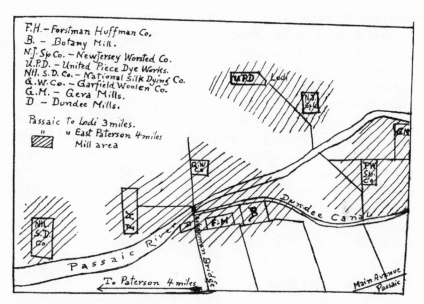

F.H. – Forstman Huffman Co.
B. – Botany Mill.
N.J. Sp Co. – New Jersey Worsted Co.
U.P.D. – United Piece Dye Works.
NH. S.D. Co. – National Silk Dying Co.
G.W. Co. – Garfield Woolen Co.
G.M. – Gera Mills.
D – Dundee Mills.

Passaic to Lodi 3 miles.
  "   " East Paterson 4 miles
        Mill area

Map of strike zone in Albert Weisbord's pamphlet, *Passaic*. Wool and worsted mills employed tens of thousands of workers in Passaic, Clifton, and Garfield, while silk dye mills employed thousands of workers in Lodi and East Paterson (today Elmwood Park). (Courtesy People's World.)

and with a population of about 10,000, dyed textiles. Wool and woolen mills were in Clifton and Garfield, while dyeing was also done in East Paterson. Additional mills of various sorts were scattered throughout Passaic, Hudson, and Essex Counties, forming a textile archipelago.[5]

Silk production in Paterson had always been decentralized, with many smaller mills instead of a handful of larger companies. Male workers—skilled and ready to strike—dominated the Paterson silk industry. The predominance of small shops contributed to the willingness of workers to go on strike, although it undercut their ability to form durable unions.[6]

In silk dyeing, by contrast, the trend was the formation of larger companies. In the late nineteenth century, silk production became more specialized and companies outsourced dyeing: in 1902, twenty-two silk-dyeing firms in Paterson employed almost 3,500 workers. The next year two large dyeing companies merged to form the United Piece Dye Works (UPDW), which employed 1,225 people. In 1908 six dyeing companies, in Paterson and Pennsylvania, merged to form the National Silk Dyeing Company (NSDC). After the UPDW (with its main plant in Lodi) purchased two smaller dyeing companies in 1912, the UPDW and the NSDC dominated the country's silk dyeing.[7]

As the silk industry in Paterson declined, the dye industry grew. The UPDW had nearly $20 million total assets and net profits of almost $2.8

million in 1926. By the mid-1920s, there were 10,000 dye workers in the Paterson area. The work was dirty and dangerous, involving boiling pots of dye.

In 1917 a newspaper noted that there had been two explosions in ten days at the Lodi UPDW plant. Shifts were long, often at night. One UPDW worker in 1926 called the dye house "the worst room in the mills" and added he worked fifty-five hours a week for 51 cents an hour.[8]

Most of the dye workers were Italian immigrants, mainly from Sicily. A few hundred Black workers toiled in the dye mills as well—which underlined the dangerous and dirty nature of the job, since Black workers were confined to the worst positions in northern industry. Almost all of the workers were men. Dye workers struck less often than silk weavers. According to labor historian Steve Golin, "the strikes that did occur tended to be big—and they tended to be violent." They had struck in 1890, 1894, 1902, 1905, and 1913. By 1926 the dye workers had a tradition of bitter struggle, and bitter defeat.[9]

The Growth of Big Wool

The late foundation of the American wool and worsted industry meant that—in contrast to wool and worsted production in Europe and silk production in Paterson—production was concentrated in large, productive companies with advanced machinery. In the United States as a whole, between 1869 and 1914 the average number of workers per wool mill doubled. The number of wool companies fell by a quarter in the first fifteen years of the twentieth century, while the number of workers rose by a quarter. The number of power mills increased more than 16 percent in this same period.[10] The woolen industry was horizontally and vertically integrated. A writer described Forstmann and Huffmann's operations in 1910: "Controlling the entire processes of woolen and worsted manufacture—buying the wool in the primary markets, spinning the yarn and weaving, dyeing and finishing the cloth in its own mills—the company has succeeded in turning out fabrics of the finest quality, recognized as equal in all respects to the best imported goods and fully sustaining the reputation enjoyed for over a century by the parent firm in Germany."[11]

A handful of large companies dominated Passaic, each employing thousands of workers. These companies were part of international concerns. In 1926, Botany Consolidated Mills (the product of the merger of Botany and Garfield) controlled two German textile groups that in turn had thirty affiliated companies in Germany, Hungary, Czechoslovakia, Italy, Latvia, and the Netherlands, employing thousands of workers. This concentration meant that a well-organized strike would wield immense power—and face a well-organized opponent.[12]

In the interwar period, textile production in New England and the Mid-Atlantic moved southward. Between 1920 and 1930, according to census figures, fifty-five New Jersey silk mills closed or moved out of state, eliminating almost 11,000 jobs. During the same period, North Carolina, South Carolina, and Georgia hired new workers to increase their numbers of workers in textile and silk by average of 30 percent. Pennsylvania, Texas, and Tennessee—where textile workers were not organized—also saw an increase in textile jobs.[13]

By 1910, 52 percent of Passaic's workers were immigrants. In 1920, of some 64,000 people living in Passaic, more than 23,000 were foreign-born, and fewer than 9,000 were native-born of native parents. In Clifton, Garfield, and Lodi, 32 to 37 percent of the population was foreign-born, with many Polish, Russian, Ukrainian, Czech, and Hungarian immigrants; almost 10 percent were Jewish immigrants, and almost 8 percent were Italian. Immigrants from Germany, Holland, and the British Isles (including Ireland) together constituted about 15 percent of the immigrant population, many of whom were skilled workers.[14]

Unlike Henry Ford and other industrialists who saw "Americanization" of their employees as a way to ward off unrest, the mill owners in Passaic opposed the assimilation of their workers, viewing a divided workforce as a bulwark against unionization. The mill owners opposed plans to teach workers English. According to Weisbord, "The bosses were afraid of the Bolshevism and unionism following if the workers should all speak the same language—English."[15] When Alice Barrows Fernandez, an investigator for the Bureau of Education of the United States Department of the Interior visited Passaic in 1919 to observe how immigrants were taught English, the wool companies viewed her as a threat and spied on her.

In 1910, 55 percent of immigrants in Passaic did not speak English. Nearly a quarter of immigrants above the age of ten were illiterate in any language; a decade later, more than 40 percent of foreign-born women did not speak English. Even among working Polish women who had been in the United States a decade or longer, nearly 65 percent did not speak English. "One often feels a stranger in Passaic because one speaks English," recalled Justine Wise, a social worker who worked in the mills in the 1920s.[16]

Passaic was an immigrant city, but immigrants were excluded from political power. The mill owners dominated local government, so there was no need to incorporate immigrants into politics, as in cities like Jersey City run by political machines that needed immigrants' votes at election time. Nor, unlike Paterson, did local politicians and civic leaders feel the need to allow the workers a certain amount of political influence. "The political bosses were the mill owners," one study concluded. In 1919, of more than 80,000 Passaic residents, only 5,000 were registered to vote. The mill owners looked down on the workers with patrician disdain. Many of the immigrant workers were Catholic, while mill owners like Julius Forstmann were Lutheran. When Forstmann's younger son later married a Catholic, Forstmann disowned him, with the admonition: "Where we come from, the Protestants walk on one side of the street, the Papists on the other." The social divisions in Passaic were reflected in its geography. Immigrants were concentrated in the areas around the mills, while nearly half of the city was occupied by only 10 percent of the population.[17]

Women workers played a larger role in the wool and worsted industry than in Paterson's silk mills. Men held skilled jobs, including supervisors and technicians, loom fixers, and mechanics. Women held less skilled jobs, including wool sorters, scourers, and machine operators. Men dominated weaving itself, but there were some women weavers. Women mainly handled the yarn and prepared it for cloth construction but were joined by less skilled men. Ninety-five percent of bundlers, menders, and cloth inspectors were women, whereas men constituted a similar percentage of cloth dyers and pressers.[18]

The Labor Movement in Passaic

The labor and socialist movements were weak in Passaic. Building trades and hosiery workers were the only unionized workforces. The Socialist Labor Party and the Socialist Party had Passaic branches for decades, but these never obtained many votes. The United Textile Workers of America (UTW), affiliated with the AFL, organized few wool workers. For the most part, the UTW was a federation of skilled crafts, focused on skilled, male, and native-born workers of English, Scottish and Irish descent. This is one reason the UTW never organized more than 3 percent of all textile workers in the United States through the 1920s, and almost none in the worsted and woolen trades. As one scholar put it in 1922, "Although theoretically it is an industrial union, as it claims jurisdiction over all workers in the industry, its spirit and, for the most part, its methods, are those of the old craft unionism." During the Passaic strike, Thomas F. McMahon, president of the UTW, told Congress that 90 percent of the union's members were skilled workers.[19]

Only radicals, such as the Industrial Workers of the World, were willing to try to unionize the wool workers—often as an extension of struggles in Paterson. When thousands of Paterson silk workers struck under the leadership of a dissident IWW faction in March and April 1912, the strike spread to Passaic and Garfield; the central demand was for a uniform daily wage. The superintendent of Botany declared, "We have never dealt with unions and never will." In April, forty policemen and sheriffs' deputies attacked a strike rally that included more than a hundred women. The events of 1912 set a pattern—the mill owners, in fear of outside organizers, encouraged police violence, which fueled hostile coverage of the strikes in out-of-town newspapers.

Divisions between two IWW factions, and the companies' hard line against unions, defeated the strike. Botany, Gera, and Forstmann mills fired suspected strike leaders. This defeat underscored the weakness of radical groups in Passaic: local workers would follow radicals in struggle, but these groups did not have deep support among workers. The next year, when the Chicago-based IWW led the more famous Paterson silk strike, Passaic workers remained at work.[20]

The First World War and Passaic

Between 1914 and 1919, the value of wool and worsted production tripled. This gave workers more power. In 1916, workers at Forstmann's mill in Garfield struck against piece rates and demanded a minimum $14 weekly wage. The strike spread to twenty-five factories in the Passaic area, including several unrelated to wool production. The strike cut across ethnic divisions, and included women workers. Workers organized daily mass meetings, and defended their strike by publicizing the names of scabs and throwing red pepper at them. After six weeks, workers at Forstmann and Huffmann returned to work, on the promise of 20 percent wage increases and better conditions. Returning workers walked out again when they discovered that, despite the agreement with the company, six strikebreakers were still employed.[21]

One result of the 1916 strike was the formation of the Industrial Council of Passaic Wool Manufactures, known as the Wool Council. Julius Forstmann was its first chairman, Hans E. Stoehr (treasurer of Botany) was its vice chairman, and J. Frank Andres (former editor of *The Journal of Commerce*) its secretary.[22]

The Wool Council served as a united front for the capitalists against their workers. According to its constitution, the Wool Council sought to "establish and maintain an Employment Bureau to provide its members with competent employees." Given the German background of the mill owners, and their continued links to the German textile industry, it seems likely that they were influenced by the formation of employers' associations (*Arbeitgeberverbände*) to defeat a textile workers' strike in Crimmitschau in 1903–1904. A closer inspiration was the Silk Association of Paterson, founded in October 1913 to combat unionism.[23]

Writing in the July 1917 *Bulletin of the National Association of Wool Manufacturers*, Andres noted that "work was started almost immediately in equalizing the rates of wages for various occupations in the mills." The Council sought to reduce the "very large" turnover among mill workers, and eliminate "the flow of labor from one mill to another, because the pay for different classes of work was reported to be more remunerative." Key to this was the "employment bureau through which all applicants for work in the mills were to be cleared." Workers applied to the Council's bureau, which gave suitable workers cards to take to the member mills. Andres emphasized: "No applicant for work in any of the member mills can get in the mills without the card which is issued by the Employment Bureau.... [T]he statements made by every newcomer are investigated by employees of the Bureau."[24]

No doubt, many workers appreciated the 10 percent pay increase and bonuses of $10 to $25 per worker that the Wool Council implemented in late 1916. But the system that Andres described soon became an elaborate network of espionage against workers to weed out dissatisfied or radical employees. When an unemployed Paterson silk worker answered an advertisement in a New York paper for silk workers, a detective agency called him for an interview in Lower Manhattan. They told him they were searching for a spy to send to Passaic "to investigate the sentiment of the workers toward the employer, what they say is unsatisfactory in the shop, their attitude toward radicalism, Bolshevism and such things." The Wool Council spied on Alice Barrows Fernandez, the investigator from the Bureau of Education, when she visited Passaic in 1919.[25]

The First World War highlighted the fact that Germans (or German Americans) still owned and managed the mills. As a Justice Department report put it after the war, these plants "have always kept their distinctly German organization, both to executives and employees." The government accused the Passaic woolen mills of selling wool to Germany for military uniforms while neglecting to produce clothing for American soldiers and making large profits selling to civilians.[26]

In late March 1918, A. Mitchell Palmer, alien property custodian, seized six companies' mills, together worth $70 million. "The cumulative effect of these Government measures," Palmer predicted, "will, it is believed, separate forever the woolen business in this country from the domination, if not complete ownership, of the Woolen Cartel of the German Government." Prominent capitalists or politicians were made directors of the firms, and any earnings were to go toward purchasing Liberty Bonds.[27]

In April 1918 the government set up the National War Labor Board to adjudicate labor disputes. In general, the government accepted higher wages and better conditions to ensure labor peace and continued production. Conditions remained abysmal for workers. A report by Florence Kelley for the National Consumers' League in 1917 described one plant that the government had seized during the War:

This great plant, although clean and well kept, was notoriously lacking in provisions for the welfare of its workers. Light and ventilation were shocking, many rooms lacking windows and depending for air and light on high skylights....

Because of the massing of machinery in large rooms, the noise was deafening, particularly in one huge room filled with gilling and combing machines. No seats were provided. The workers were crushed under the combined strain of noise, heat and constant standing. Women at lunch time sat on the floor, too exhausted to eat. There was no lunch room. A foreign woman, when asked about the flushing of the primitive vault "toilets," answered simply, "The water,

Julius Forstmann, the sixth generation of a German wool-manufacturing family, emigrated to Passaic in 1903. Forstmann and Huffmann's two plants employed 3,000 workers in Passaic and Garfield at the time of the strike. United States National Archives.

she stink!" There were no dressing rooms and the investigator watched women and girls changing to their street clothes in the workroom where men were constantly walking about.

This disregard for comfort and health of the workers and failure to supply their most elementary needs contrast sharply with a care for the quality of product and for mechanical efficiency unequalled elsewhere.

Such conditions contributed to high rates of tuberculosis and other lung ailments such as bronchitis, pleurisy, and emphysema.[28]

In December 1918, Palmer oversaw the sale of several plants, no doubt with the goal of "Americanizing" their ownership. But Christian Bahnsen regained control of Gera Mills, and bought New Jersey Spinning Company for good measure. After the Supreme Court upheld the seizure of Botany Mills in 1921,

Colonel Thomas W. Miller, Palmer's successor as alien property custodian, used the government's ownership of 88 percent of Botany's shares to effect a reorganization of its board of directors. The new board included Colonel Charles F. H. Johnson, a Passaic real estate executive who had served in the military during the war. Johnson convinced president Warren Harding to not sell the mill, and as director, regained control of Botany for Max W. Stoehr, the son of the company's founder. Forstmann and Huffmann, Botany, and Gera remained in the hands of the families that had founded them. By this time the American wool industry was facing declining demand after the war and increased foreign competition. Only protective tariffs kept the industry profitable. Companies sought to lower wages to improve their competitiveness.[29]

After the First World War there was an upsurge in textile unionism, including in Passaic. In February and March 1919, and again in July, Passaic wool workers struck for shorter hours and higher pay. These strikes continued the earlier pattern: workers followed radical leadership and displayed great militancy despite police and company violence and red-baiting. The workers won reduced hours and a significant pay increase, but the mill owners fired militants and refused to negotiate with the union.[30]

The Amalgamated Textile Workers of America (ATWA) arose of such struggle, led by A. J. Muste, a radicalized former Calvinist minister, and inspired by Sidney Hillman's Amalgamated Clothing Workers of America. The ATWA eschewed the conservative, craft-based unionism of the UTW, and advocated an industrial union that organized men and women, immigrants and native-born. One of its organizers was Robert W. Dunn, a recent Yale graduate who went on to become active in the ACLU and then the Communist Party. In late 1921 Muste and the ATWA helped organize the Federated Textile Workers Union, which grouped together several unions outside of the UTW. In its short existence in Passaic, the ATWA posed enough of a threat to the mill owners to cause some of them to improve conditions in an effort to undercut the union. Forstmann and Huffmann and Botany provided housing for a small number of (mainly skilled) workers, and in May 1920 the companies raised weekly wages by $3 for adults and $2 for children.[31]

As part of this effort to undermine the ATWA, Forstmann and Huffmann's personnel manager established a company union, the "Representative Assembly," the same month. The assembly contained 106 members, half elected by the workers and half directly chosen by management. Workers could not bring complaints before the assembly without management's approval. Despite its veneer of workplace democracy, the assembly was, as Dunn put it, "a nest of stool pigeons and spies." According to one worker who had served as a representative: "Workers have refused to be elected as representatives and on several occasions voted for famous race horses for their 'representatives!'" Management took notes on what workers said and how they voted in this committee and fired workers seen as malcontents or who pushed grievances. Workers rejected the company union.[32]

Women in Passaic

In 1920 the National Consumers' League published a pamphlet about the city by Agnes de Lima, *Night-Working of Mothers in Textile Mills*, and two years later the Women's Bureau of the Department of Labor published another pamphlet, *The Family Status of Breadwinning Women*. In Passaic, men could not support a family on mill wages, and women toiled in the mills to make ends meet and worked at night to be able to be with their children during the day. In 1923, there were 1,308 women in Passaic County who worked overnight—compared to none in Bergen or northern Hudson Counties. Although the silk mills in Paterson ran twenty-four hours a day, women silk workers did not work at night.[33]

Women workers reported backaches, headaches, chest pains, and varicose veins. They appeared "beaten and dragged down," even when young. Pregnant women continued to work until days before giving birth. Some women gave birth in the mills' toilets.[34] An article in the July 1920 *Survey* highlighted the poor living conditions in Passaic: "In casual visits we found a woman mill worker's family of seven living in three tiny rooms, two of which were unventilated and pitch dark. An Italian girl who works in the Botany Mills was living with a large family of brothers and sisters in the basement of a tumbledown frame house."[35] By the 1920s, infant mortality in Passaic was as much as 50 percent higher than in the rest of New Jersey, and the death rate of adolescents was 28 percent higher.[36]

The Passaic wool companies opposed any limits to women's hours, cynically highlighting that without this work their families could not survive. The Passaic Industrial Council, dominated by the wool companies, defeated a measure in 1922 to limit night work by women, even though the bill enjoyed wide support from the public and from the Democrat and Republican Parties.[37]

By the mid-1920s the Passaic wool industry remained profitable, but it faced difficulties. Workers worked long hours in poor conditions and faced significant hardship. Previous attempts or improve their lot through unionization had failed in the face of police repression, company espionage, and AFL indifference—the same obstacles that millions of workers throughout America faced.

2

The Strike Begins

In April 1925 Justine Wise, a recent Barnard graduate, created a scandal. The daughter of Stephen Solomon Wise, a prominent liberal rabbi in New York City, she had used her mother's maiden name to work first at a Passaic cotton mill and then at Forstmann and Huffmann. When Forstmann and Huffmann discovered her true identity, they fired her, and she found herself blacklisted from all the other mills. She detailed her experience with the mills' espionage system and blacklist, long hours, and low pay. The Passaic mills were not unique in spying on workers and trying to eliminate undesirable employees; but Wise helped personalize and emphasize this common practice.[1]

One of Wise's sources reported how the police worked with the companies by arresting supposed troublemakers: "When you see in the paper someone arrested on a minor charge you can guess that he's a union man. Then the sentence will be suspended and he will be told to get out of town on that suspended sentence." A former employee at the Forstmann and Huffmann mill recalled: "When you're laid off you never know why. I was laid off a year ago.... Lots of men have told me at different times they were laid off on account of the list."[2]

In 1926 John Sherman, a detective for the Wool Council, reported that "if you steal, or get drunk, or don't come in on time," a worker would be blacklisted. "And of course you are kept out if you are an organizer, or want to make a union, or if you are a trouble maker." Sherman added that the Council had "detectives inside and outside the mills."[3]

The Wise scandal did not come at a good time for the Passaic wool mills. The mills were profitable. For the seven years ending on December 31, 1923, total profits for Botany (the only company with public books) averaged $3 million annually, according to radical accountant Stuart Chase. In December 1924, when Botany Mills issued 40,000 additional shares of stock, its president, Max W. Stoehr, announced: "Botany Worsted Mill has never had an unprofitable year." Despite these high profits, in 1925 the companies sought to drive down wages even more. Since the end of the war, changes in fashion and the rise of competing types of clothes (especially those with new synthetic fibers) led to frequent overproduction and fluctuating prices. The companies feared foreign competitors who were more efficient and paid their workers less than in the United States. Republicans' high tariffs—most recently the Fordney-McCumber Tariff (1922)—helped keep the industry prosperous in early 1923, but soon the market crashed and 1924 was marked by severe economic depression.[4]

Workers in Passaic did not share their bosses' prosperity. According to the union, before the strike 47 percent of workers were paid less than $1,000 per year, and 71 percent were paid less than $1,200 per year. Conditions were horrible. In May, "J.T.," a sixteen-year-old mill worker, reported that he had dropped out of school two years earlier to help his mother, a Botany worker, provide for his four young sisters. He added: "My father died of consumption at the age of 27. He was working in the Botany Mills when he became sick and later died. I am working in the same mill now and the way the conditions are it looks I am going to die in the same damn way."[5]

Colonel Johnson Wages War against Workers

The Passaic mill owners disagreed on how to respond to the decline in the industry in 1925. Colonel Charles F. H. Johnson, the vice president of Botany, insisted that a wage cut was necessary for prosperity in the industry, but Julius Forstmann feared that a cut would cause labor unrest. Botany Mills and Garfield Worsted quit the Wool Council over this disagreement, although they claimed to quit in protest of the spying exposed by Justine Wise. Their departure left only a rump Wool Council of Forstmann and Huffmann and New Jersey Worsted Mills. In June, Botany laid off 900 employees in their weaving department, and planned wage cuts. A wage cut by wool manufacturers in New England in July prompted scattered strikes, including 3,000 members of the UTW in Pittsfield, Massachusetts, who struck from August 16 to September 1. After an arbitrator kept the cuts there, Johnson must have decided that he could brave any action taken by the workers in Passaic.[6]

On September 25, 1925, the 5,275 workers at Botany Worsted Mills and the 925 workers at Garfield Worsted Mills found the following attached to the mills' gates: "Notice—Owing to the action taken in other textile centres several months ago, and on account of general market conditions, a reduction in wages of about 10 per cent. will take effect beginning Oct. 5, 1925. All overtime will be paid at time and 10 per cent. instead of the present rate."[7] This sign kicked off what became the Passaic textile strike.

Gustav Deak, a Hungarian American worker, and several coworkers approached the UTW to fight the cut.[8] When the UTW leadership refused to help, Deak and his coworkers organized the United Front Committee of Textile Workers (UFC) to fight the wage cut. Helping them was Albert Weisbord—who worked in the silk industry in Paterson. Weisbord was a Communist; Deak probably was also. (It is not clear when Deak joined the CP.) Weisbord had organized another UFC in Hudson County to lead a silk workers' strike in North Bergen.[9]

By January the UFC in Passaic grew to a thousand supporters. On January 25 Deak and the committee met with Colonel Johnson. According to the *Daily Worker*, Johnson tried to bribe Deak to abandon the strike. When that failed, he fired Deak and other committee members, prompting Deak and the UFC to call a strike. Weisbord claimed that Botany wanted to "provoke a premature strike, crush it ruthlessly and thus prevent any resistance or unionization for years to come." Morton Siegel, in his study of the strike, concluded that Johnson's unwillingness to compromise was a factor in making the strike so bitter and protracted. Johnson was confidant Botany could weather this strike just as the company had defeated earlier strikes.[10]

There was little reason to see the strike as more than a local incident doomed to fail.[11] The industry magazine *Textile World* mentioned the strike only in passing in its January 30, 1926, issue, and the *New York Times* gave the strike little attention. "They quit, and we recognize them as people who have left their jobs," Johnson warned. "If they do not return to work tomorrow morning, we will take immediate steps to have their places filled." He blamed the strike on outside agitators. Passaic chief of police Richard O. Zober sent twenty-five policemen to protect strikebreakers.

The strike soon grew. On the second day of the strike, January 26, the strikers' ranks doubled to 8,000 workers, according to the UFC. On Wednesday, January 27, the strike's third day, 600 to 700 workers walked out of the Garfield Worsted Mills. Johnson announced that Botany would eliminate its night shift, supposedly to lessen the need for twenty-four-hour police protection of the plant. On Friday, January 29, as temperatures plunged to 4°F (−15.5°C), 350 workers at Passaic Worsted Spinning Company walked out. Three hundred workers at Gera Mills joined the strike on February 2, even though their employer had not cut wages. The city called all Passaic policemen into strike duty and canceled all police vacations. Even before the strike spread to their company, fifteen foremen at Gera mills were sworn in as special officers with the power to make arrests.

The next day Weisbord led a demonstration of 7,000 to 10,000 strikers, including several women with baby carriages. Workers carried placards:

"If We Have to Starve, We'll Not Starve While Working"
"To Buy an Overcoat, We Have to Save Half a Year"
"Give Us an American Standard of Living, You 100 Percenters"
"The Wages of Sin Are Death. The Bosses Are the Sinner"
"The United Front of Workers against a United Front of Bosses"
"Mill Owners—Open the Books and Let Us See the Profits."

The strikers demanded the reversal of the 10 percent wage cut, time-and-a-half overtime pay, and reinstatement of the fired UFC leaders.

By early February it was clear that this strike was large—and not going away. The strike kept growing, to 15,000 workers on strike by February 4 according to Weisbord, and the UFC soon claimed some 6,000 members. Amid ice and slush, the picket lines outside Botany and Garfield mills grew to 1,000 people. "12,000 Workers Demonstrate in Passaic Streets: Ranks of Strikers Increase as Strike Spreads" was the headline in the Communist Party's *Daily Worker*. A committee of one hundred workers, with Weisbord at their head, coordinated the strike and organized daily strike meetings. The strikers increased their demands—making them "more aggressive," said Weisbord. They now demanded a 10 percent wage increase, the return of money lost through the previous wage cut, overtime pay, a forty-hour workweek, more-sanitary conditions, recognition of the union, and no discrimination against union members. The mills belittled the strikers' concerns and attacked the strike as being led by professional agitators. Johnson dismissed the strikers, claiming they "were well taken care of," well-dressed, and well-fed.[12]

Slightly before the 2:30 P.M. shift change on February 6, strikers prevented scabs from entering the Botany, Garfield Worsted, and Passaic Worsted Spinning Co. mills. The *Passaic Daily News* reported: "The largest crowd of pickets that has yet gathered at the New Jersey plant.... The police were not strong enough to fully protect all the workers [i.e., scabs]." On February 7 some 20,000 workers from all the struck mills marched in a procession more than a mile long.[13]

The next day, February 8, Clifton chief of police William J. Coughlan threatened strikers: "Get back to Passaic. Get out of Clifton." In Garfield, police arrested UFC leader Felix Penarisi, who was sentenced to a month in jail. Penarisi was probably the first person arrested, but he was certainly not the last. The police chiefs of Garfield, Clifton, and Passaic began coordinating their efforts and made all the policemen in the three cities available. This did not faze Weisbord, although he told the *Passaic Daily News*, "We have learned the police have cleaned their riot guns." Raising the specter of the 1919 strike, he predicted a "general strike of all mill workers"—some 20,000 workers in the Passaic area. The next day Clifton police attacked 1,500 strikers—half of them girls and women—preventing them from crossing the Ackerman Avenue Bridge from

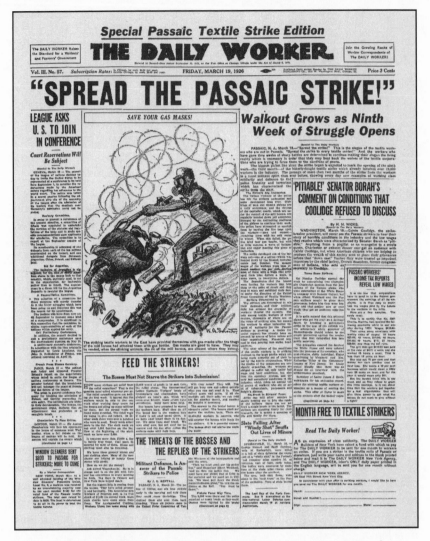

Front page of *The Daily Worker*, March 19, 1926. Communist Party newspapers and magazines, in English and other languages, built solidarity with the Passaic strike, emphasizing that the entire working class should support wool workers' struggle. (Courtesy People's World.)

Garfield en route to the Forstmann and Huffmann plant in Clifton. In this "Battle of Ackerman Bridge," police arrested two women and two men.[14]

The *Passaic Daily News* later published an account from a witness of the police riot:

> I saw coming through the River Road a line of strikers walking peacefully, two by two. . . . I saw Chief Coughlan of Clifton and his men with clubs, give a signal to the police of Garfield, who were stationed at the corner of Outwater

Lane and River Road, also with clubs. As soon as the strikers started to turn the corner to cross the bridge into Clifton, Coughlan and his men who were stationed on the corner of the bridge ran to meet them. Garfield police ran and met the Clifton police and the readers will know what a chance those strikers had against a hundred or more police with clubs. . . .

The clubs struck right and left. Women carrying little babies were battered, women were walked upon, women were put through plate glass windows and the poor defenseless strikers had to take that for walking on a picket line. . . . All this could have been avoided if the three cities had Mayors who were not controlled by the mill owners.[15]

Colonel Johnson declared that Botany's mills were open for business, and workers who remained on strike would lose their seniority and benefits. The *Passaic Daily News* estimated that strikers had already lost $400,000 in wages. Landlords and merchants began complaining of losses. Police had given injunctions to more than a hundred strikers. And a heavy blizzard hit on February 10.[16]

On February 14 the Board of Commissioners passed "An Ordinance concerning Disorderly Persons." This ordinance (three pages long in the official ordinance book) focused on cockfighting, illegal gambling, public drunkenness, nude swimming, and similar activities. However, Article 8 gave the police broad powers to arrest "any person who shall in any place in the City of Passaic make, aid, or assist in making any improper noises, riot, disturbance or breach of the peace or who shall behave in a disorderly manner, or make use of obscene or profane language, or who shall indecently expose his or her person, and all persons who shall collect in bodies or crowds for idle or unlawful purposes."[17]

By this point the major features of the strike could be seen. The police, acting in tandem with the local courts, attempted to use violence to break the strike. The mill owners struck a hard-line pose, refusing to negotiate or recognize the legitimacy of the strikers' grievances. And above all, thousands of mill workers, at least half of them women, struggled in the face of economic hardship, police violence, scorn from the mill owners, and freezing weather.

The UFC made a special effort to bring out Forstmann and Huffmann workers. Forstmann had not cut wages, and the management favored a more paternalistic style instead of Botany's brazenness. When presented with UFC demands in early February, Forstmann management convened the "Representative Assembly," or company union. This laid bare the nature of the company union as a tool against the workers, and stoked workers' anger. The Forstmann and Huffmann workers joined the strike in mid-February, underlining how the strike tapped into long-standing grievances among Passaic workers.[18]

Upset at this threat to their power, the mill owners and city officials increased the violence, trying to break the strike. To just take one week: On Monday, February 15, Frank Lasseck—a thirty-year-old striker from Gera Mills out on $500 bail in Clifton—was put on trial in Passaic for calling office workers at the struck plant "dirty rotten scabs"; Jack Rubenstein, an eighteen-year-old Communist from New York, and twenty-one-year-old Bela Varga were arrested for trying to prevent strikebreakers from crossing a picket line; on Tuesday, February 16, four strikers and two organizers were arrested; Jacob Bentall, representative of the *Daily Worker*, was issued a summons in Garfield for making "verbal attacks" on the police department at a meeting (he was cleared of charges).[19]

On Thursday, February 18, six strikers were arrested as 200 picketers blocked the entrance to the Forstmann plant to prevent 1,200 strikebreakers from returning from lunch. On Friday, February 19, the police raided Neubauer's Hall, which the UFC was renting as their headquarters. After a strikebreaker claimed to have been attacked by two strikers who ran into the hall, Passaic police chief Zober sent twenty-five policemen to disperse the 1,500 strikers who had just finished listening to Weisbord.[20]

By March the Passaic strike was nationally known. In the first month of the strike, the *New York Times* ran ten articles about it. The Communist Party's *Daily Worker* ran almost daily articles about the strike, as did the New York City tabloids and New Jersey newspapers. The New York *Progresso Italo-Americano*, an Italian-language paper with almost 90,000 readers daily, covered the strike. The daily Spanish-language *La Prensa* published frequent translations of wire service articles on the strike. The *New-York Volkszeitung*, the oldest German-language daily in the United States (and whose editor, Ludwig Lore, had been expelled from the Communist Party the year before), ran regular articles about the strike. Newspapers throughout the nation featured the strike, often on their front pages.

The strike proved a divisive issue in local politics. Many local merchants opposed the strike and pressured Passaic mayor John McGuire to get the strikers to return to the mills. McGuire refused to issue such a proclamation but did appoint a citizen's committee to try to end the strike. However, the mayor made a return to work by the strikers the precondition to such "negotiations"—something that Weisbord dismissed.[21]

On February 25, Weisbord and Penarisi—president of the UFC at Botany Mills—came to a Garfield city council meeting with 300 strikers, filling the chamber to capacity. Although the meeting had been called to try to resolve the strike, the lack of company representation made this futile. But the presence of Weisbord and the UFC turned the meeting into a debate on the strike itself. The *Passaic Daily News* called this "one of the liveliest and most exciting [meetings] ever held in the history of the city." Garfield mayor William A. Burke, who was a white-collar worker at the Botany Mill, and city recorder Judge Richard Baker denounced the strike. But several city councilman were sympathetic to the strike. Two put forward a motion "requesting that the citizens and taxpayers of Garfield support the strikers in their fight, financially and morally." Another motion requested that Baker be more lenient on the strikers. Weisbord suggested a motion that city police not be stationed in halls

Gus Deak (left foreground) with a striker in a gas mask. When Botany Worsted fired
Deak, one of the founders of the United Front Committee, in January 1926 for protesting
wage cuts, this prompted the start of the strike. American Labor Museum/Botto House
National Landmark.

where strikers were speaking. Weisbord also suggested that the City Council
establish a relief fund for strikers, and that the city's department of education
establish relief kitchens for strikers.

Weisbord certainly knew that such resolutions would have no practical
effect: the mayor opposed them and they exceeded the authority of the City

Council. But the meeting did expose the city government's servility to the mill owners, and it demonstrated the deep polarization caused by the strike. In response, Baker red-baited Weisbord and declared to him: "The quicker you get out of this vicinity, the better I will like it." Instead, it was Burke and Baker who stormed out of their own meeting—to boos from the crowd.[22]

Both sides dug in. Weisbord promised to bring 2,000 strikers to the picket lines, while the Passaic police announced they had 300 policemen plus mounted officers at the ready.[23] The demonstration on March 3 was larger than predicted. As some 3,000 strikers and supporters gathered on the border between Clifton and Passaic, police from both towns attacked. According to the *New York Times*: "Men, women and children were struck this evening by motorcycles which, guided by patrolmen, cut wide circles on sidewalks and zigzagged up and down the street. Groups of strikers fled, some knocking each other down in their scramble to get out of the way of the motorcycles and the patrolmen who followed them, brandishing clubs." Adding to the chaos, the Clifton chief of detectives, Anthony Batello, ordered his men to "get all the cameramen." The police smashed two movie cameras and six still cameras—worth $3,500 in total—and beat six photographers.[24] By attacking strikers—including many women and children—and reporters from the most important media center in the country, the police guaranteed hostile press coverage. As in the 1950s, when the rise of television exposed the brutal repression of civil rights activists in the American South, the rise of tabloid newspapers—emphasizing photographs, headlines, and sensation over the more pensive or ponderous broadsheets—publicized the treatment of workers in Passaic. By early March the struggle of the Passaic workers against company hostility, police brutality, and the indifference of AFL leaders became emblematic of the struggle of all workers.

3

The Communist Party and the Start of the Passaic Strike

During the strike, C. E. Ruthenberg, head of the Communist Party (CP), observed, "It is no secret that our Party initiated the movement among the Passaic workers." Communist Party member Anthony Bimba, in his *History of the American Working Class* (1927), underlined that in Passaic, "for the first time in the history of this country a strike was conducted on a large scale under communist leadership." Despite the importance of Communists in the strike, few of the strikers were Communists and Communism was not the cause of the strike. As the American Civil Liberties Union (ACLU) put it in a report, "The real issue is wages and living conditions. The mill owners are attempting to divert attention from the wage question by shouting 'Communism.'" The report stressed that "Communism is not being taught. . . . Certain of the leaders of the strike do not deny that they believe in Communism, but in the meetings, the speakers make a positive effort to hold the thought of the strikers to their fight for wages and collective bargaining as against its being diverted to such extraneous topics as communism." Workers, the report emphasized, "do not even know what communism is, and are not interested in it for a moment. They want their union and their wages."[1]

The Communist politics of the strike's leaders were crucial in the strike's development. Only Communists were willing to organize the wool workers in the first place. The established labor movement, especially the American Federation of Labor (AFL) and the United Textile Workers of America (UTW), looked at the largely female, immigrant, and unskilled wool workers as incapable of being organized, but the Communists saw the workers' plight as central to the working-class struggle against capitalist exploitation. The perspective of the AFL and the UTW was constrained by what was "realistic" under capitalism. The Communists' vision was based on replacing the entire profit system with one based on workers' rule and the principle of production for use and not profit. These differing political programs shaped how the AFL and the Communists approached the strike.

Communists proved themselves to be credible organizers, mobilizing tremendous national and international resources and dedicating an untold number of hours to the strike. As James P. Cannon, a leading Communist, wrote in 1930 (after having been expelled from the CP for his support for Leon Trotsky), "By their services and skill the Communists led the workers with a moral authority that needed no mechanical manipulation; moral authority, which, in the final analysis, is the rock on which real leadership is based."[2]

Besides leaders like Gus Deak and Albert Weisbord, the CP provided an apparatus to build the strike and raise support and solidarity. Martha Stone Asher, a high school student from Brooklyn and a member of the Communist youth group, recalled decades later that "the party assigned people to go to Passaic and encourage the workers, whose concerns were primarily economic and not political, to take strike action in their own defense."[3]

Most important, the CP brought to Passaic a political framework. For Communists, the strike of wool workers in Passaic was part of a greater struggle of the working class against capitalists. Communists strove to make this strike, unlike its contemporaries, emblematic of labor struggle in the 1920s. They offered a vision of class struggle that most of the AFL leadership lacked. More than a decade earlier, Bolshevik leader V. I. Lenin wrote about strikes in Russia: "Only the defenders of the bourgeoisie and its excessive profits can sneer at the demand for a 'rise.' But the workers know that it is the *widespread* character of the demand for a rise, it is the *comprehensive* character of a strike, that has the greatest power to attract a multitude of new participants, to ensure the strength of the onslaught and the sympathy of society, and to guarantee both the success of the workers and the national significance of their movement."[4] Echoing Lenin, Weisbord asserted that "the real importance of Passaic is that there are many Passaics. America is virtually built on Passaics, not only in the textile industry, but in every basic and heavy industry in this country."[5]

The other side of Communist involvement was that the mill owners and their allies tried to make Communism, and not the poor conditions of the workers, the central issue. In late March, Monsignor Thomas J. Kernan, rector of St. Nicholas Church in Passaic, echoed this in his homily during mass: "These leaders are radicals and Communists, who do not care one way or another in whose favor the strike is settled, but are using it only to bring about a revolution of the people."[6] Mill owners used Communist involvement as a

Advertisement in *Workers Monthly* for pamphlet by Albert Weisbord about the strike. (Courtesy People's World.)

pretext to refuse to negotiate with the strikers. The United Textile Workers and the AFL refused to assist the strikers for the same reason.

While it is common to point to the strike as an early attempt of the Communist Party to lead labor struggle, most historians have not studied the CP leadership's role in the strike, or Weisbord's relationship with the CP during the strike. Until the archives of the Communist International were opened in the 1990s, historians lacked access to the necessary sources. Communist writers, presumably with better access to party sources, have avoided these topics as well. This is partly because many who were in the leadership of the strike—especially Weisbord—were expelled from the CP in the late 1920s, and examining the strike would require that the CP and its sympathizers honestly grapple with its early history, something they have resisted. William Z. Foster's 600-page *History of the Communist Party of the United States* (1952) deals with the strike in three paragraphs. The party's role in the strike is reduced to the following: "The official head of the strike was Albert Weisbord, a weakling; but the main strength came from the Party backing."[7] An unsuspecting reader would not realize that Weisbord was a member of the Communist Party during the strike (and Weisbord is not even listed in the book's index).

On the sixtieth anniversary of the strike, Arthur Zipser wrote an article for the *Daily World* explaining how in Passaic "the Communist Party became involved in a major strike struggle for the first time." In the article's last column, Zipser allowed that "CP member Albert Weisbord became the official leader of the strike," but added: "he proved more able at making speeches than at planning strategy" and credited a list of "party stalwarts" who "were thrown into the breach."[8] The last volume of Philip Foner's history of the American labor movement (1994) dealt with the strike in more detail, but its treatment of the CP's role is still problematic (for example, confusing the United Front Committee and the party's broader trade-union arm, the Trade Union Educational League).[9]

This chapter traces the role of the CP in the first portion of the strike. While Weisbord was central to the strike, the CP as a whole—from its highest leadership body, the Central Executive Committee (CEC), on down—paid attention to and collectively made decisions about the strike. Further, while much of the leadership of the strike, including Weisbord, supported the dominant Ruthenberg-Lovestone faction in the CP, all of the CP's factions worked together in the strike. Passaic was the Communists' first trial by fire. The strike demonstrates the strengths—and limitations—of the Communist Party in the mid-1920s.

The Communist Party

The CP was born in the summer of 1919, after left-wing dissidents split (voluntarily and by expulsion) from the Socialist Party. Concentrated in more than a dozen semi-autonomous language federations, these left-wingers united to support the Bolshevik Revolution and oppose what they saw as the Socialist

Party's reformism. They were divided by political and ethnic background and political perspectives; for several years there was no one American Communist Party but only hostile underground groups, each claiming to be the *real* Communists in the United States. The authority of the Bolsheviks—who, amid the devastation of the First World War, had led the first successful socialist revolution—recruited more people to Communism than the activities of these groups. Early recruits included members of important unions like the garment trades in New York City or coal miners in Illinois and Pennsylvania, and non-union workers. Many of the foreign workers who joined the early CP brought traditions of struggle from their native countries.

Soon incessant factionalism, Red Scare repression, and the hostility of the trade-union bureaucracy decimated the membership of the CP. Only at the insistence of the Bolshevik-led Communist International (Comintern) did the competing groups form one united party in 1921 (officially called the Workers' Party but referred to here as the CP). Soon after this the CP emerged from the underground as the Red Scare receded.

The history of the CP in the 1920s is beyond the scope of this study.[10] Although the Bolshevik Revolution was popular among much of the labor movement—including leaders like William Z. Foster, who joined the CP in the early 1920s—the party was often politically disoriented and isolated. In 1923–1924 the party tried to cash in on a perceived upsurge in populism and tailed the farmer-labor movement. This threatened to eliminate the party's focus on the working class in favor of populism. When much of the farmer-labor movement coalesced around Wisconsin Republican senator Robert La Follette, many Communists wanted to support him until Leon Trotsky instructed the party to stand its own candidates and oppose La Follette. The Comintern's directive prevented the party from liquidating itself into a non-working-class movement, since much of the labor movement supported La Follette, but left the party isolated. Nonetheless, despite a large turnover of members, the party's membership stabilized. In 1922 the unified Workers' Party counted some 12,000 dues-paying members; by June 1925 there were 14,500 members, with more than 3,500 in New Jersey.[11]

The party divided into three factions. One was led by C. E. Ruthenberg, a former left-wing Socialist from Cleveland and a party founder, along with Jay Lovestone, a former Socialist youth leader from New York City. John J. Ballam and Benjamin Gitlow, prominent in the CP's textile work, were former Socialists who supported Ruthenberg. Another faction, led by Foster, enjoyed wide support, especially among union members. A smaller group, also including many unionists, supported Cannon, a former organizer for the Industrial Workers of the World (IWW). These groups had originally cohered in 1923 in response to the party's farmer-labor and La Follette maneuvering, but by 1925–1926 their original political differences had diminished. Instead of principled struggle over the line and tactics of the party, factionalism devolved

into organizational maneuvers to gain and maintain leadership without sufficient political clarity.

Such factional warfare came to the fore during the Fourth Communist
Party National Convention (held in Chicago in August 1925), where the
Comintern (through what it called a "parity commission") disregarded the
opinions of the membership and supported the Ruthenberg faction's central
leadership while putting Foster in control of trade-union activity. The heavy-
handed intervention of the Comintern reflected the Stalinization of the
Comintern; in the party's early years, the Comintern had provided crucial
assistance, but in the post-Lenin period it increasingly sought a pliant leadership in the U.S. CP that supported Stalin's leadership in Moscow. In 1925–
1927 the American party was still in an intermediate period in its Stalinization.
Both factionalism and Stalinism (and their relationship to each other) are
beyond the scope of the present book, but they form the backdrop of the CP's
intervention into the strike.[12]

By 1926 Ruthenberg's faction was in the leadership of the CP, but Foster's
faction, which controlled trade-union work, sought to dislodge it. When the
strike broke out, most of the factions' leaders were in Moscow trying to win
support from the Comintern leadership. This distance created a partial shield
for the Passaic strike, preventing it from being completely sucked up into the
factional vortex, and keeping the Comintern leadership from paying too
much attention to the strike. (The strike also coincided with the British General Strike, which presumably meant that much of the Comintern's limited
English-language capacity was not focused on New Jersey.)

Albert Weisbord and Communist Leadership

Weisbord was born in 1900 in New York City of "poor Russian-Jewish parents." During his childhood, his father graduated from operating a newsstand
to running a coal distribution business to owning a small textile factory.
Weisbord later claimed that his father fired him for trying to organize a union
in his factory. Weisbord enrolled at City College in New York, the "proletarian Harvard" that had earlier graduated several leaders of the Ruthenberg
faction.

Although he claimed to have joined the Brooklyn Socialist Party while in
high school, at City College Weisbord focused on chess, warranting several
mentions in the newspapers. An article in the *Brooklyn Eagle* describes how,
against an opponent, Weisbord "played the dangerous Evans Gambit and
obtained a slashing attack" and "established such an advantage that a win was
conceded to him." In the Evans Gambit, white sacrifices a pawn but obtains
control of the center of the board; the play requires aggression and quickness—
some might say recklessness. While the play can devastate an unwitting opponent, a more prepared player can successfully defeat it.[13]

During the strike, one New Jersey newspaper observed that Weisbord "talks two vernaculars—one of the student, the other of the masses. Despite his education, he seldom talks over the heads of the ordinary workers." Asher was more measured: Weisbord "was a very charismatic leader of the strike. People were taken with him, and appreciated his qualities. People close around him did not all share those feelings, but everybody recognized that he was the established leader" of the striking workers.[14] Other leading Communists were more blunt, often describing Weisbord as arrogant and an egomaniac, especially after the strike—when Weisbord developed around him a sort of cult that emphasized his own role and downplayed other Communists.[15]

After graduating from City College in 1921, Weisbord enrolled at Harvard Law School. He was active in the Socialist Party, becoming a member of its National Executive Committee and national director of the Socialist youth group, the Young People's Socialist League (YPSL). In his greetings to the YPSL national convention in December 1922, Weisbord wrote: "We have still before us the tremendous problem of attracting to our standard the distinctively American young working man and woman. We have barely scraped the surface of the Trade Union section. We have been completely lost to the unskilled worker."[16] At this convention the Federal Bureau of Investigation became aware of Weisbord, whom a confidential informant later called a "fanatic who has real organizing ability." In November 1924 Weisbord quit the Socialist Party and joined the Communists. The *Daily Worker* printed his letter on the front page. The Communist leader in Boston was John J. Ballam, a founding member of the party, a supporter of the Ruthenberg faction, and the leader of the party's work in the textile industry. After Weisbord joined the Communist Party, the *Daily Worker* quoted Ballam: "I have a high regard for his personal integrity and revolutionary purpose and I am convinced that comrade Weisbord can be of the greatest service to our party and the American working class."[17]

More than fifty years later, Weisbord wrote that upon joining the Communists, he decided to "immerse [himself] in the working class" by working at a textile mill in Massachusetts. He observed that much of the country's industry was centered, not in large cities like Boston or New York, but in surrounding "industrial villages" like Lawrence, Massachusetts, or Paterson, New Jersey. After receiving his law degree, Weisbord, under Ballam's supervision, organized United Front Committees of textile workers in Massachusetts and Rhode Island. He also joined the Ruthenberg faction.[18]

In 1925, after separating from his wife, Weisbord moved to Paterson and joined the silk workers' union. According to his own account, Weisbord contacted Bert Miller (the party name of Benjamin Mandel), a former teacher who was the party's organizational secretary for the New York area. In his pamphlet *Passaic Reviewed* (1976), Weisbord claimed that Miller, a fellow Ruthenberg supporter, "knew very little about" his new position, and "was astonished at my desire to plant myself in the 'sticks' and said he would help me in what way he could."[19]

He claimed that by the time of the Passaic strike he "was well-prepared for the coming struggle, infinitely better than the leaders of the Communist Party, which party I dragged by the hair into the fight, against the snarling will of its leaders who finally succeeded in treacherously stabbing it to death." In his telling, the Communist Party was "infantile, faction-ridden, Russian-dominated" and "completely untested in workers' organization and struggle." He added: "Even though I was a member of the party at the time, I received no help from them at the time."[20] Years after the strike, Weisbord downplayed the role of other Communists, including Miller and Ballam, ignored how the strike reflected long-standing collective discussion within the party, and de-emphasized his connection to Ruthenberg's faction.

The leadership of the Communist Party had prepared for a New Jersey textile strike months in advance—although most likely in Paterson, where there had been a silk workers' strike the year before. The transfer of Weisbord—a protégé of Ballam with experience in the New England textile industry—was an attempt to intersect militant textile workers. Weisbord's original emphasis was not the wool industry, but the silk industry.[21]

The CP had a *fraction* in the silk workers' union—a group of members who acted to carry out the day-to-day work of the party under direction of the leadership. Article 17 of the CP's constitution, adopted in the fall of 1925, mandated that "in all non-Party workers' and farmers' organizations ... where there are at least two Communists, a Communist fraction must be organized for the purpose of increasing the influence of the Party in applying its policy in the non-Party sphere."[22]

In October 1925 members of the fraction wrote a document, "Proposed Basis for Left Wing Program in the Associated Silk Workers Union of Paterson," denouncing "the intellectual bankruptcy of the leadership of the union and ... their false policies." The document demanded: that the union "organize the unorganized—especially the poorest paid"; amalgamation of textile unions and "one industrial union of textile workers" that would be "a united front of the workers against the united front of the bosses"; the formation of a labor party; and that "women and young workers [be] brought into full union activity."[23] The United Front Committee's demands during the Passaic strike echoed this perspective.

The minutes of the CEC's Trade Union Committee indicate that the party leadership followed and directed its members' activities in the trade unions. For example, the minutes of the January 4 meeting contain motions on unions in the building trades, the food industry, marine transport, railroads, the needle trades, the printing trades, as well as the textile workers' union.[24] During the strike, the CEC Trade Union Committee, as well as the textile commission, regularly met to discuss the Passaic situation. This underlines the *collective* nature of Communist work. It is likely there was no functioning Communist fraction in the Passaic wool mills before the strike.[25] It is not clear when Gustav Deak joined the Communist Party, but it possible he was the only Communist in the wool mills when the strike started. The Passaic strike underline the fact that, for the Communists, dynamic organizers and supporters sent in from outside the industry could not substitute for a base within the workforce. Even after months of struggle, the Communists still had only a small number of supporters among wool workers. This made it difficult to maintain a party presence in Passaic after the strike ended.

This should not obscure Weisbord's role. Cannon, who was not fond of Weisbord, recalled thirty years after the strike that organizing the workers and leading the strike in Passaic "was pre-eminently Weisbord's work." He added: "It is true that he worked under the close supervision and direction of a party committee in New York appointed by the national party leadership in Chicago. But it's a long way from committee meetings in a closed room, off the scene, to the actual leadership of a strike on the ground."[26] Weisbord's role was made even more important by the fact that during the Passaic strike, Communists were involved in two New York City needle-trades strikes, the Furriers (March through June 1926) and the ILGWU Cloakmakers (July 1926 through February 1927) that required the attention of many of the same people as the Passaic strike, especially Gitlow.

Communist Organizing in Northern New Jersey

Northern New Jersey was not virgin territory for the Communists in the mid-1920s. New Jersey was part of District 2, comprising the New York metropolitan area. The district had its own organizer (for most of the strike, this was William W. Weinstone, a leading member of the Ruthenberg faction), political bureau, and executive council. Below the executive council were city central committees (CCC) overseeing individual branches. In 1924 there were some 120 branches in District 2, comprising 2,500 members. Most were in New York City's four main boroughs (not Staten Island). Nonetheless, by 1924 there were city central committees in Hudson County, Essex County, and the cities of Passaic, and Paterson, and party organizations in Middlesex (Perth Amboy), Union (Elizabeth and Linden), and Mercer (Trenton) Counties. In turn, each CCC oversaw the work of several units, often divided by language and geography.[27]

The most important northern New Jersey city for the party was Newark, where Communist activity among eastern European immigrants went back to 1919. In 1923 the Communist Party opened offices in Newark. Communists were active in the furriers' union and other local unions, including among mainly Greek restaurant workers.[28]

In Paterson in 1924 there was an English-language branch (10 members), a Jewish branch (45 members), a Polish branch (5 members), and a Ukrainian

James P. Cannon, a former organizer in the Industrial Workers of the World and founder of the Communist Party in the United States, organized the International Labor Defense in 1925 as class-struggle defense organization. In 1928, shortly after this photo was published in the *Labor Defender*, Cannon was expelled from the Communist Party for his support to Leon Trotsky's Left Opposition. (Courtesy Communist Party U.S.A.)

branch (8 members). In 1924 in Passaic—where the first Communist group was organized in 1919—there was a German branch (11 members) and a Jewish branch (18 members). Fewer than half of the branches in District 2 submitted reports for any month, so it is likely that there were other ethnic branches in the area.[29] In any case, in 1925 the Communists felt confident to try to stand candidates for governor and other state offices, as well as mayor of Union City. (George Perlman, the party's gubernatorial candidate, received 591 votes—out of more than 900,000 total votes—concentrated in Bergen, Essex, Hudson, Middlesex, and Passaic Counties).[30]

The Passaic strike reflected the party's perspective in the textile industry.[31] This work began in Boston under Ballam's direction. New England's largely immigrant textile workers had a history of militancy (as shown in the 1912 Lawrence strike led by the IWW) but were largely still unorganized in the 1920s. According to a report by Ballam, "in February 1924, the Workers Party created a United Front Committee of Textile Workers" in Lawrence, consisting of representatives of the UTW and Francophone, Italian, Russian, Armenian, Lithuanian, and German-speaking fraternal organizations, and other workers from the mills.

The UFC's goals were the organization of the unorganized, "the amalgamation of all existing textile unions into one powerful industrial union . . . based upon the shop committee and the mill as the unit of organization," and "a congress of Textile Workers and the establishing of a National Textile Bureau." In turn, the UFC organized the Lawrence Textile Union, which, Ballam stated, "is independent of the United Front Committee and sends its delegates and supports it financially." Ballam added that within the UFC and the Lawrence Textile Union, Communists "are organized as a fraction under the discipline of the Party and the direction of the District Executive Committee."

Like everything in the party at this time, the UFC had factional significance. Ballam's report implies that the UFC was organized in counterposition to the Trade Union Educational League (TUEL), Foster's pan-union organization that strove to win militant workers to revolutionary principles. Several times Ballam described the TUEL in New England as moribund and "a useless appendage to the Party" that was "withering away because it has no present function" for aiding Communist work in the labor movement. By the spring of 1925 there were six United Front Committees organized in the Massachusetts textile industry, under the broad leadership of Ballam.[32]

In New Jersey, the party's textile work seems to have arisen out of the party's extensive work among the needle-trades unions in New York City. The Foster-led TUEL needle-trades section played a prominent role in a silk workers' strike in Paterson in the fall of 1924. That November, Foster wrote to Charles Zimmerman (a Ruthenberg supporter in the International Ladies' Garment Workers' Union in New York City) mentioning a "plan to reach out to other centers to organize the silk workers" in Paterson. Minutes from a February 1925 District Executive Committee (DEC) meeting authorized "a committee to mobilize the entire Paterson membership for work in the silk industry." Several reports by Miller indicate Communists had been paying attention to the Paterson-Passaic textile industry since 1925.[33]

By the fall, Weinstone, a Ruthenberg supporter, became the leader of District 2. The new district leadership stepped up the campaign in Paterson and Passaic; Weisbord was an integral part of this. As early as October 15 he is mentioned in this role in a report by Bert Miller; on October 23, at a meeting of the district leadership, Weinstone proposed that "Weisbord leave his job and devote himself to the situation" and be made a party functionary. Two days later the DEC minutes noted that both Paterson and Passaic "have become active under the textile situation." The report added: "Weisbord has been sent into Paterson and Passaic districts in order to exploit the textile situation. He has gone to work there in the mills." It is possible that Weisbord volunteered to move to New Jersey, but rather than acting on his own, Weisbord was an agent of the district leadership with the mandate to resolve problems in the local branches and prepare a strike.[34]

The Lead-Up to the Passaic Strike

The *Daily Worker* in the six months before the Passaic strike was full of articles on the textile industry. The paper carried several articles by Weisbord about poor conditions in the Rhode Island textile mill where he was working. In August and September, the paper ran notices about a textile workers conference, sponsored by the "General Amalgamation Committee," to be held in New York. New Jersey representatives were expected to attend. (It is not clear if this conference took place, or if it accomplished anything.)[35]

In early October the *Daily Worker* carried a small notice (datelined Philadelphia) announcing the wage cuts in Passaic. In late October the paper carried a one-paragraph article noting that some 380 Passaic silk workers were striking. Then, on October 29, the *Daily Worker* carried two articles by Weisbord, both datelined Paterson. The first mentioned that Weisbord "has taken charge of the strike" at the Passaic Worsted Spinning mill; the second denounced the leadership of the UTW and the Association of Silk Workers of Paterson for their opposition to class struggle and hailed a Communist leader in the needle-trades unions. The next day, an article by Louis Kovess, editor of the party's Hungarian journal, predicted a "rebellion brewing" in the Passaic mills. In late October, Kovess and leaders of other language federations, along with Weisbord and Benjamin Gitlow, held a meeting of more than a hundred people to organize a united front committee. The *Daily Worker* announced there would be future meetings, with speakers in Italian, Hungarian, Polish, and "Slavic." On November 6 an article, "Passaic Mill Workers Organizing the Fight against the Wage Cut," asserted: "In case the weavers do not organize, they will suffer a wage cut and starvation they never had before."[36]

Behind the scenes, the district leadership and Weisbord continued preparing a strike. As one report put it on October 25: "[The] District Industrial Committee has drawn up a policy for situation in Paterson and Passaic. District has put a representative in the field. Party branches of the textile areas have been mobilized to help. Several strikes in Passaic and West New York have developed. Our comrades taking an active part. Organization campaign started in Paterson. . . . Aiming toward a broad united front campaign."[37] On October 31, after the Botany mill fired Deak and other militants, Miller wrote to Ruthenberg listing eighteen steps that the party was taking in Passaic. He ended his letter: "It is planned to do organization work of this character with a view toward a strike sometime in December." The correspondence indicates, contrary to Weisbord's later claims, that the party's leadership expected a strike and had discussed Weisbord's work.[38]

A reading of the *Daily Worker* indicates that the party continued to organize in the Passaic area. In November 1925, Communists in Paterson met to commemorate the Bolshevik Revolution, as did their comrades in Bayonne, Jersey City, and Newark. A series of articles by Kovess urged organizing the unorganized and struggling for better conditions and wages. At times running as a TUEL column, these referenced a committee dedicated to amalgamating the textile unions.[39]

The first battle in Weisbord's war to organize the New Jersey textile workers was fought, not in Passaic or Paterson, but about fifteen miles away in Hudson County. On October 24, some 250 workers under Weisbord's leadership struck the Hillcrest Silk Mills in North Bergen against wage cuts, increased hours, and increased work demands. The Hillcrest strike was a dress rehearsal for the Passaic strike several months later. Immigrant workers—this time largely Italian—braved police violence and intimidation. The company obtained court injunctions against picketing, and Weisbord was arrested twice for disorderly conduct. The workers were organized into a United Front Committee of Textile Workers; the party-aligned International Labor Defense mobilized to support the workers; and veteran radicals built solidarity. Alongside Weisbord, Elizabeth Gurley Flynn and Carlo Tresca spoke at a mass rally in December 1925. Although the strikers remained steadfast in the face of government repression and an attempt by a local Catholic priest to end the strike, the strike was lost when management relocated the mill to North Carolina.[40]

During the Hillcrest strike, Weisbord kept abreast of the situation in Passaic and Paterson while engaged in the battle in North Bergen. In late December 1925 the *Daily Worker* carried an announcement: "We have elected textile workers employed in the mills here to become worker correspondents and send the *Daily Worker* regularly articles on conditions in the Passaic textile mills." It was clear that a strike was imminent: On Christmas Eve the paper carried an article by Art Shields, "Paterson Textile Strike Makes a United Front to Strike for the Eight-Hour Day January 4."[41]

On January 4, three weeks before the Passaic strike began, the Trade Union Committee (TUC) formed a Textile Committee to coordinate the party's work in the industry. The minutes of the January 4 CEC meeting indicate that on the eve of the Passaic strike, Communists saw work among Passaic workers as part of a broader textile campaign encompassing Hudson

County and Lawrence. While the Communist leadership was paying attention to the Passaic situation, they did not expect that it would explode into
such a massive strike in less than a month.[42]

The Passaic strike, although not caused by the Communists, reflected long-
standing Communist efforts, including sending Weisbord there. None of this
undermines Weisbord's role in the strike. It also does not mean that his sense
of isolation was not legitimate. Weisbord was the transmission belt between
the Communist leadership and the strikers. As Cannon indicated, it was eas-
ier to make decisions in New York than to implement them in Passaic. Even
during the strike—when he was no doubt aware of the attention paid to the
strike by the party leadership—he complained: "I am all alone except for
speakers."[43]

Communists and Dual Unions

One disputed issue between the factions was the age-old question of "dual"
unions: Should Communists focus on work within the AFL, which remained
the largest trade-union federation despite its pro-capitalist leadership? Or
should Communists try to organize new radical, militant unions? Lenin, in
"Left-Wing" Communism: An Infantile Disorder (1920) argued that Communists must work within the AFL because refusing to do so would leave Communists isolated from the labor movement. Based on this perspective, Foster
joined the CP, after playing a leading role in the 1919 steel strike, and built
the TUEL, a pan-union opposition group that sought to unite class struggle
around a socialist perspective. The TUEL advocated the amalgamation
of craft unions into industrial unions and the organizing of unorganized
workers.

What did opposition to dual unions mean when the AFL leadership
refused to organize unskilled workers in mass-production industries such as
the Passaic wool mills? How could militants push for "amalgamation" when
there were no AFL unions to unite in Passaic's wool mills? Foster addressed
this in his pamphlet, *Organize the Unorganized*, published shortly before the
Passaic strike. He acknowledged that it might be necessary to form new
unions, but argued that Communists should strive to have these join the AFL
as soon as possible: "In spite of our most urgent desire for unity with the general labor movement, we will often, under these circumstances, be compelled
to form independent unions. But . . . we must from the outset follow a program for the affiliation of these unions to the A.F. of L. We must be keenly on
our guard not to get into a dual union position, by declaring against the A.F.
of L. in principle or by permitting an open warfare to develop against it." Foster acknowledged that "often these [AFL] leaders will propose such terms of
affiliation as to make their acceptance tantamount to the sacrifice of the interests of the workers." But he stressed "that greatest danger that the left wing

confronts in such situations is the persistent dual union tendency to pull away from the old unions and to establish new and independent organization[s] which isolate our forces from the main body of organized workers."[44]

This transformed the original tactical objections to organizing dual unions—that it divided the labor movement and isolated Communists from organized workers—into a principle that the AFL should have a monopoly on the labor movement. Furthermore, there was a contradiction at this policy's core: it recognized that militants outside the AFL would have to organize workers whom the AFL bureaucracy refused to organize, but it confused union organization with AFL membership. It did not allow the possibility of militants—much less Communists—organizing the unorganized outside the graces of the AFL. Whatever its theoretical weakness, Foster's perspective reflected the weakness of the party in the working class. Regardless of the whether it would be principled to organize new unions, there was the question of whether it was possible, and Foster had few illusions about the relative strengths of the CP and the AFL.

Ruthenberg's faction was less fixated on avoiding dual unionism and, because most of its leaders were intellectuals with little experience in the labor movement, more optimistic about the party's chances. The Ruthenberg leadership sought to lessen Foster's role in trade-union work, replacing leading Foster supporters with their own supporters (particularly Gitlow) and absorbing the TUEL into a broader Communist front in the unions.[45] As part of Stalinization, the Comintern leadership sent mixed signals, supporting Foster's trade-union perspective while supporting Ruthenberg's party leadership.

In the lead-up to the strike, the UFC collected dues and issued membership cards. Foster's supporters objected, and Ruthenberg's supporters defended Weisbord, who continued his work. Still, the UFC and Weisbord's work continued to be contentious at the highest levels of the party leadership. In early November, Weinstone reported to Jack Johnstone, "We are now proceeding with the formation of Mill Committees and organising the workers into the United Front. Headquarters have been established in Passaic and all regular steps taken—stationery, etc.; membership books, etc., are being issued." He advocated "one big national drive" and stressed that it was "absolutely necessary that the Massachusetts and Rhode Island, as well as Philadelphia sections should be ready to join in the movement."[46]

This appeared to go too far for Ruthenberg, who objected that this appeared to be "organizing some sort of new union in the textile region."[47] Weisbord argued that the UFC must organize workers:

> What to do with those who are being pressed now and are unorganized and where other unions will not or dare not enter the fields. In that case the United Front Committee . . . ceases to become a mere propaganda body. It then enters

into the actual organizing of workers and gets all workers, say on strike in a particular mill, into a mill council, gets the council to pay dues to the Central Bureau of the United Front Committee of Textile Workers and conducts their strikes [sic] for them. At the same time there is made an attempt to broaden the strike and the movement wherever possible.

Weisbord noted that the UFC should press for amalgamation of the textile unions, but "if after all our efforts there will be no convention to discuss amalgamation, then we must keep these affiliated [mill-based] bodies. We shall not go into an area where another union has already stepped in but we must be prepared to organize the workers in such an industry where about 95 percent are unorganized. Constantly we must state our purpose is the formation of One Union in the Textile Industry and to Amalgamate all forces." Ruthenberg responded that Weisbord's plan "smacks very much of a dual in union in spite of all we may say to the contrary."[48]

A week later Miller wrote to Ruthenberg, defending the UFC. He noted that "it is only because such a state of terrorism exists in the mills that an outside force must take the initiative." Indeed, Miller proposed that the party redouble its efforts in the textile industry, and that Weisbord be made "National Textile Organizer and should travel from one textile center to another during the next few weeks or so." In a report several days later, Miller argued that it was "necessary to do away with the formal and mechanical conception of Comrade Foster and his group on the whole question of dual unionism." More than 80 percent of all workers—especially the unskilled—were unorganized and the AFL bureaucracy was not interested in organizing them. Thus, Miller continued, "We will have to exert pressure through the existing unions and also from the outside."[49]

On November 25 Ruthenberg wrote to Miller, shifting his position. Noting that "the work being done by Comrade Weisbord has the full endorsement of the CEC," Ruthenberg signaled a more flexible approach: "While we cannot at all times say that we will not form a new union in the textile industry, we must first make the effort to unite some of the many existing unions and use these as the basis for the organization campaign." Ruthenberg's letter gives an indication that Comintern pressure had contributed to the shift in his views. "The general policy you are following in the textile [industry] is . . . in line with the resolution of the National Convention." He added that this policy "was subject to considerable debate in the Parity Commission, but was adopted with the support of Comrade Green [Gusev]."[50]

The correspondence indicates that leading Communists continued to debate the issue—and that the discussion divided along factional lines. In early December 1925 Miller wrote to Ruthenberg complaining that Johnstone "was here this morning and he said definitely that the C.E.C. is opposed to the policy being followed by Weisbord in the New Jersey Textile district" because it was dual unionism. "He wanted it stopped at once, altho he has a very hazy idea of what he wanted us to do." Miller asked for "written approval of the work being done, and authority to go ahead." Ruthenberg responded that "the statement by Comrade Johnstone which you report . . . is too sweeping a statement." Instead, the "only decision of the Trade Union Committee . . . was that the individual members are not to be affiliated directly to the United Front Committee." By this time, in any case, the work in the textile industry in northern New Jersey had already led to one strike, in Hillcrest, and was about to result in another, in Passaic. On December 21 Weisbord wrote to Miller, indicating that the UFC had organized almost 900 mill workers in Passaic.[51]

In late December the party's CEC held a plenum that discussed the organizing work. In his report, Ruthenberg mentioned that "the United Front textile committee developed the plan of organizing the workers in the mills in mill councils with the view of using these organizations as a club in the campaign for amalgamation of the textile unions." While the UFC had issued membership cards and collected dues, Ruthenberg explained, this was not dual unionism because the UFC "could not issue individual membership cards and thus in a measure take the form of another union." Foster supporters attacked this policy, but the CEC approved Ruthenberg's report.[52] When the strike began in January 1926, the party leadership had not yet resolved these issues, but meanwhile Weisbord continued organizing what amounted to a union.

Communists in the Early Strike

Unlike many strikes where the leadership keeps workers in the dark, the UFC kept workers informed and involved. Each department of the struck mills elected a delegate to the UFC's General Strike Committee, which met daily. At the height of the strike, this committee had 200 delegates; these were picket leaders who organized rank-and-file workers in their divisions. The strike zone was divided into five main areas that met to discuss the strike. There were regular mass meetings to vote on important strike decisions. The leadership of the strike fell to a smaller executive committee of ten to twelve organizers. Several members of the executive committee were members of the Communist Party, including Weisbord, Alfred Wagenknecht (a founding member of the CP in charge of relief), Gustav Deak (a Botany worker), and Lena Chernenko and Jack Rubenstein (young Communists active in the picket lines).[53]

Foster and Lovestone and other key elements of the CP leadership were in Moscow in early 1926 for meetings of the Executive Committee of the Comintern, but the resident leadership—particularly Gitlow—followed the strike closely.[54] A TUC meeting on February 3, a week into the strike, passed a motion to "inform the United Front Committee in Passaic that in this strike they must not function in any way as a union." The meeting also voted for a motion in favor of "broadening out the strike" such that the strikers "be hooked up" with the Federated Textile Workers or the Associated Silk Workers, two non-AFL textile unions.[55]

The TUC discussed the textile industry at its meeting a week later. The motions again speak to a desire to both extend the strike and to involve established unions. One motion spelled out the CP's general perspectives in intervening in the strike at this stage: "That a meeting be held with the representatives of the textile unions, composed of strikers and representatives of the textile united front committee for the purpose of bringing them officially into the strike, or bringing the mill committees into the union at the same time, preserving the shop committee as the unit. That they support the demands of the strikers, carry on [an] intensive campaign to broaden the strike and to organize the unorganized."[56] Three days later, on February 13, the Textile Committee of the CEC met. One motion postponed the planned textile conference—scheduled for the next week—"in view of the fact that no preparations have been made." The motions indicated that "the questions of the role of the Party was discussed." The committee "decided that as the strike support was being broadened the role of the party should be brought more and more prominently into the strike situation" including "efforts . . . to give wide circulation to the party press" as well as "Communist speakers . . . introduced in some instances as members of the workers party" and "publicity . . . given to the role played by the party in relief work." The motion concluded that, "The Party should hold meetings of its own to which meetings the strikers are to be invited an[d] an effort made to enroll the best elements among the strikers into the party." The meeting also passed a motion outlining what type of statement Weisbord should make in response to announcements of a proposed settlement.[57]

The next TUC meeting was on February 17. It focused on trying "to get some union to come in on the strike." The committee had the perspective of organizing a national conference of textile unions and trying to get a union to organize the Passaic workers and assume control of the strike.[58] In mid-February 1926 the Comintern Executive Committee held its Sixth Enlarged Plenum in Moscow. In his speech to the meeting, Grigory Zinoviev attacked the AFL for its conservatism, citing a Ruthenberg supporter's quip that the federation was "the labor aristocracy of the labor aristocracy." The meeting passed a resolution declaring that "secessional movements and formation of parallel trade unions should not be instigated or encouraged in any form."[59]

At a meeting of the CEC Textile Committee on March 3, Weisbord reported that Passaic Worsted was ready to agree some of the strike demands for better conditions and overtime pay, but balked at union recognition. This indicates that the strike was having an effect on employers, but it also indicates that the UFC was acting like a union, whatever motions Communists had passed. Beyond this, Weisbord's report and the discussion underline that while Weisbord had great responsibility, the CP leadership made important decisions collectively. On March 11 the Political Committee noted that "the comrades in Passaic request five or six organizers," and the minutes indicate that at least two Communists were being sent, indicating that while the party leadership did not lead Weisbord on his own, it also did not have the resources to back up the strike that he requested. This pattern was repeated throughout March. The Textile Committee and the TUC discussed and made decisions about almost all aspects of the strike, from publicity to defense work, from approaching other unions to meeting with liberal sympathizers. Weisbord was neither left on his own nor taking matters into his own hands, but acted as an agent of the party leadership.[60]

4

Bringing Passaic to the
Labor Movement

By the end of February the strike had grown to more than 10,000 workers. The workers refused to give in, and the companies refused to back down. Textile production was not crucial to the U.S. economy or national security, and consumers could still wear last year's wool coat while they could not burn last year's coal. This lessened the Passaic workers' power, but gave the strike more breathing room. At the same time it encouraged the mill owners to try to wait out the strikers on the hope that hunger and misery would force them back to work.

To defeat the mill owners, the strikers needed to mobilize forces beyond their own ranks. The Communists threw themselves into the battle as organizers and in building relief efforts. Though the CP was crucial, it could not substitute for broader support, because there were more strikers in Passaic than Communists in the United States. Communists sought to bridge the gap between the size of the Passaic strike and their own smallness by seeking support among organized labor, radicals, and liberals. In the process the CP broke out of its isolation.[1]

Communists used the strike to gain an audience among workers, stressing the need for class solidarity and a fight to organize unorganized workers. This message resonated with many rank-and-file workers but not the leadership of the American Federation of Labor (AFL) or the United Textile Workers of America (UTW). While the mainstream labor movement was anti-Communist, in the 1920s many radicals and liberals with links to the labor movement—including former IWW leader Elizabeth Gurley Flynn, Italian

American anarchist Carlo Tresca, ACLU founder Roger N. Baldwin, or Socialist Party member Norman Thomas—became active in the strike.[2]

In turn, these leftists helped obtain support from liberal reformers—including politicians Robert La Follette Jr., Robert Wheeler, and William Borah; religious leaders such as Rabbi Stephen Wise and Reverend John Howard Melish; journalists such as Frank U. Kellogg; attorneys like Felix Frankfurter, Frank P. Walsh, and Samuel Untermyer, and economist W. Jett Lauck. As historian Carmen Brissette Grayson wrote, "Reformers who converged on Passaic or who took up the workers' cause read like a Who's Who of American liberalism in the 1920s."[3]

The American Federation of Labor and the Passaic Strike

The United Textile Workers of America, the AFL union in the textile industry, had long seen the Passaic wool workers as impossible to organize. In reality, the UTW found it almost impossible to organize *anybody* in the 1920s: with only seven organizers, the union could count no more than 5 to 10 percent of textile workers in the country as members. It claimed jurisdiction over all textile workers, but the UTW was in spirit closer to a craft union than a modern industrial union. Skilled workers constituted 90 percent of the UTW's membership.[4]

From 1902 to 1922 the UTW organized, on average, less than 1 percent of all wool and worsted workers nationally. The small UTW local in Passaic, Branch 17, claimed about a hundred members—sixty knitters and forty helpers and other workers—in a city with more than 15,000 textile workers. Almost every issue of the UTW's *Textile Worker* (including during the strike) carried advertisements from Botany Mills, Gera Mills, Forstmann and Huffmann, and United Piece and Dye Works. The Passaic mills subsidized the UTW through such advertisements, and the UTW in turn left the mills unorganized.[5]

Despite the UTW leadership's hostility to Passaic workers, the Passaic mills' poor conditions meant the UTW could not oppose the strike once it began. Thomas McMahon commented in his column in the February 1926 *Textile Worker*: "The workers in the mills of Passaic were justified in striking against the hardship they were forced to suffer and endure. It is foolish to think that workers will strike in the middle of winter for some fancied grievance, or for the sake of being on strike." The cause, McMahon observed, was not only a reduction in wages, "but also the horrible abuses the workers were forced to accept at the hands of officials (petty and other), during the past several months." But McMahon's "support" was designed to show the mill owners the value of the UTW and the AFL in maintaining class peace and keeping out radicals. Given that the Passaic workers were unorganized, he stressed, "The enemies of organized labor will be hard put to find excuses to place these outbreaks on the shoulders of the leaders of the American Labor

Movement." The same issue carried a letter by James Starr, a vice president of the UTW, who sneered at the strikers. "A strike is now on in Passaic, N.J., called by the people who go by the name of 'The United Front,' which was born in Moscow, and fathered for some time by A.Z. Foster [*sic*]."[6]

In March McMahon again claimed sympathy with the strikers for the "abuses and wage reductions" they faced, but stressed that "the workers in Passaic were not, and are not now, members of the United Textile Workers of America, [and] therefore cannot be in any way connected with the American Federation of Labor."[7] McMahon told the *Passaic Daily News*, "There is no center in the industry in a more pitiful condition than that at Passaic today, but the United Textile Workers cannot help until the workers agree that they want a regular organization like the American Federation of Labor to lead them, rather than a communistic or socialistic group."[8]

McMahon complained to Elizabeth Gilman, of the Christian Social Justice Fund, that "the Passaic strike is not a legitimate trade-union strike, but is being conducted by representatives sent from the Communist headquarter[s]" in Manhattan.[9] But it was the UTW's hostility to organizing the wool workers that left the field open to the Communists to begin with. McMahon's attitude came down to the following: first, the UTW did not organize the "unorganizable" wool workers; when the workers went ahead and formed a union anyway, McMahon denounced them for not being members of the UTW. Only by turning their backs on the people who were willing to help them organize, and joining the UTW, which had refused to help, would the wool workers earn the right to UTW support. McMahon's only consistent message was that he wanted nothing to do with organizing the wool workers.

McMahon denounced the UFC as an "outlaw union" reminiscent of the IWW. He urged UTW members to donate money to the Passaic Central Labor Union, affiliated with the AFL, which promised to collect and distribute relief independent of the United Front Committee. Starr, for his part, blamed the UFC and the workers themselves for the dire situation in Passaic. According to him, the UFC had sabotaged an ongoing AFL organizing campaign, and had "appealed to the passions" of the workers with "promises . . . that are impossible to fulfill." Communist involvement in the strike made it impossible for the mills to negotiate. "I am willing to admit," Starr wrote, "that I have no use for this type of organization." Starr predicted that the UTW would organize a union in Passaic—*after* the strike.[10]

Despite such hostility from their leadership, many workers in AFL unions supported the strikers. When strike supporters invited AFL unions to a meeting in Newark in late March to raise funds for the strike, Henry Hilfers, head of the New Jersey Federation of Labor, complained that the AFL and the UTW "were not consulted or asked to take part in any conference prior to the strike, or advised of any decisions that were reached." Thus, Hilfers added, "for the A.F. of L. or any of its affiliated organizations to inject themselves into the strike now could not find any good coming from it."

Hilfers echoed Starr's claim that the AFL had tried to organize the Passaic workers for more than a decade, but that the "the textile workers had . . . proved themselves absolutely indifferent or antagonistic." This situation meant that "Passaic and vicinity, and the textile industry in particular, have proved a fertile ground for all kinds of radical movements and organizations, which has split the workers in that industry into three or four organizations and has left the vast majority unorganized." Hilfers concluded: "Organization of all the textile workers in one union affiliated with the American Federation of Labor is their only salvation."[11]

Left to their own devices, the AFL leadership was happy to bemoan the fate of the Passaic workers while not doing anything to help them.

The UFC's Attitude to the AFL

Communists, however, pushed the issue, hoping to bring the AFL into the strike or, barring that, expose the AFL leadership's strikebreaking role. On March 20 the Political Committee passed a motion that the UFC send a letter to William Green "stating that they are sending a delegation to discuss ways and means . . . of enlisting the complete moral and financial support of the trade union movement of the Passaic strike" and "to assure complete cooperation with the AF of L."[12]

Less than a week later, on March 25, Weisbord sent a letter to the executive council of the American Federation of Labor. Weisbord advocated "the unification of all the existing labor forces in the textile industry to fight the campaign of wage cuts, to increase wages, shorten hours, and to organize the million unorganized textile workers into a powerful union." The letter continued:

> We call upon the executive council of the American Federation of Labor . . . to use its experience, prestige and power to establish the unity of all existing labor organizations in the textile industry in a campaign to end wage cuts and organize the industry. . . . We pledge ourselves that if such a move is made we will do everything in our power to achieve such unity through the American Federation of Labor. . . . The United Front Committee of Textile workers is not a dual organization. It does not desire to set up an organization distinct and apart from the American Federation of Labor.[13]

Hilfers told the *Passaic Daily News* that the letter was a sign of weakness and proved that "the Passaic strike had 'gone over Weisbord's head'" and that the leader was crying for help." Hilfers denounced the UFC as similar to the IWW and whined that the UFC had not sought the advice of the AFL before the strike. If they had, Hilfers claimed, "I would have told him that the time was most inopportune, workers on short time in midwinter, with a condition of over production existing and with the owners having all the advantage."[14]

The UTW rejected aiding the Passaic strike. A spokeswoman for the UTW headquarters in New York made it clear that to gain AFL recognition, the textile workers needed to desert the UFC: "We will give no recognition to the United Front Committee or any other labor organization not connected with the American Federation of Labor. If the textile workers of Passaic, independently, desire to affiliate with the United Textile Workers of America, their application for a charter will be considered, but we cannot recognize the United Front Committee."[15]

Several days after Weisbord's letter was sent (and printed in the *Passaic Daily News*), Green claimed that the AFL had not received it, and claimed ignorance about the UFC. Thus Green and the AFL leadership did nothing about the strike, which was finishing its ninth week. They repeated their promise to send organizers to Passaic *after* the strike. The AFL could not equivocate forever; in late March, Green wrote a curt note to Weisbord, emphasizing that only the UTW had an AFL charter to organize textile workers. While the AFL opposed the wage cuts that had sparked the strike, Green explained, the federation would not work with the UFC.[16]

On April 7 the Communists' Textile Committee voted that Weisbord should withdraw from the committee negotiating a settlement if this would facilitate a settlement, and that the negotiation committee should accept an offer to become a local in the UTW. The Textile Committee decided that the minimum demands of the strike were union recognition and a restoration of the initial wage cut. Later in April, Weisbord wrote to McMahon. Seizing on comments by Green about poor conditions in Passaic, the letter noted that the UFC was "glad to hear that the American Federation of Labor has taken this position and supports us in this struggle." The letter proposed "a conference with the officials of your organization with the purpose of establishing greater [unity] among all Textile workers." McMahon declined to get involved in the strike. When the UFC proposed that five of its members, including Weisbord, meet with the UTW, McMahon replied that "any further outside conferences would be hurtful on the principle that 'too many cooks spoil the broth.'"[17]

Attempts to Spread the Strike to "Silk City"

In early March the *Passaic Daily News* reported that Weisbord predicted that if the Passaic strikers could hold out for another month, silk workers in Paterson, and then textile workers in Providence, Lawrence, and Philadelphia, would walk out. The Passaic strike could spark "the organizing of 300,000 wool and worsted workers and 350,000 cotton workers" throughout the nation. According to another New Jersey paper, Weisbord hoped that the

New Jersey strike would lead to one million textile workers striking and forming a strong and united textile workers' union. This specter scared the Paterson mill owners. In early March the *Paterson Morning Call* warned that "the strike in the textile industry in our sister city down the Passaic seems rapidly reaching a stage where there is likely to be a serious outbreak, especially with foreign agitators active in keeping the strikers up to fighting pitch."[18]

Weisbord and the UFC appealed to the Paterson-based Associated Silk Workers of America (ASW). The ASW, whose origins went back to the IWW, split from the UTW after a strike in 1919 because of that union's conservatism. In December 1924 the union led 13,000 workers on strike, dealing with police violence and company resistance. The ASW had a reputation for militancy; many silk workers in Paterson, facing the rise of non-union "cockroach shops" and the exodus of jobs to non-union areas in Pennsylvania and the South, sympathized with the wool workers' struggle.[19]

In mid-February 1926 the ASW donated $1,000 to the Passaic strikers' relief fund. The union leadership did not want to extend the Passaic strike, especially if it would give the Communists more authority. The CP played a prominent role in the 1924 strike (stoked by newspaper fear-mongering) and Weisbord was a member of the ASW. In early March, Fred Hoelscher, secretary and treasurer of the ASW in Paterson, dismissed reports of the silk workers joining the strike as "bosh."[20]

The UFC sought to bring out silk dye workers. About 85 percent of national silk dyeing was concentrated in the Paterson-Passaic area—employing some 13,000 men, women, and children. The work—some of the dirtiest of textile work and not unionized—was concentrated in several large companies. The United Piece and Dye Works (UPDW), the largest dyeing and finishing company in the county, had 7,000 workers in plants in Lodi and Paterson.[21]

Most of the workers at the Lodi plant were Italian, but there were also 400 Black workers. According to the UFC, workers in the Lodi plant earned 25 to 45 cents per hour, with the majority earning between 30 and 40 cents per hour. They worked sixty-five-hour weeks and often collapsed of exhaustion. "Rest rooms, wash rooms, garment closets or lockers, [or] lunch places are unheard of in the dye-houses," the Federated Press reported during the strike.[22]

Weisbord wrote to Hoelscher, proposing to extend the strike to the UPDW's two Paterson mills: "We do not wish to call a strike in Paterson over the heads of the Associated Silk Workers. . . . The United Front Committee of Textile Workers would be glad to form a united front with the Associated Silk Workers for organizing the workers in these mills." Weisbord predicted, "This is going to be the foremost textile strike this country has ever seen." In what newspapers called an "invasion," on March 10, between 3,000 and 4,000 strikers and supporters picketed the UPDW plant in Lodi, convincing 400 workers, or about 10 percent of the workforce, to join the strike.[23]

Within days about 40 percent of the UPDW workers in Lodi were on strike, demanding a 25 percent wage increase, union recognition, time-and-a-half overtime pay, and a forty-four-hour workweek. Theodore Boettger, UPDW president, refused to negotiate with the UFC and claimed that he would not shut the plant. The ASW executive committee met for more than two hours to discuss Weisbord's proposal, but did not make a decision. The Bergen County authorities were more decisive: county prosecutor Archibald C. Hart sent twenty-five detectives, a justice of the peace, and three interpreters to Lodi and instructed them to not be "too technical" in arresting strikers.[24]

Soon 200 workers at the National Silk Dyeing Company in East Paterson—a third of the mill's workforce—joined the strike. "The strike in that mill was spontaneous," Weisbord told the Communists' textile committee on March 13. "They came to us, and asked us to organize them." When the silk dye workers joined in early March, the number of strikers reached its high point.[25]

On March 14 the UFC set up picket lines outside the National Silk Dyeing Company's plant. Bergen County sheriff George P. Nimmo threatened massive arrests of strikers. The next day, as 1,000 strikers marched from Garfield to East Paterson, Nimmo's officers arrested Jack Rubenstein, Thomas Regan, and Frank Sarno. Within an hour of being arrested, Rubenstein was sentenced by a justice of the peace to ninety days in county jail for disorderly conduct—the longest sentence so far in the strike—and Regan and Sarno were sentenced to thirty days.[26]

As the strike against the UPDW heated up, Weisbord met with Hoelscher and asked for the silk workers union to help organize dye workers.[27] Two weeks later Weisbord proposed "joint action with the Associated Silk Workers and the establishment of a joint office by both organizations." Weisbord pledge that the UFC would support any organizing drive by the ASW among the silk dye workers, but added: "If on the other hand the Associated Silk Workers does not wish to participate in any way in this drive, then the United Front Committee will organize alone and if necessary open an office in Paterson for that purpose. The understanding will then be that the Associated Silk Workers may join us in the United Front."[28] In response, Hoelscher and other ASW representatives visited the silk dye workers' picket lines in Lodi, but refused the UFC's offer for joint work. Hoelscher claimed that "because of the slump in the silk industry, this would be a poor time to call a strike" in Paterson." On a narrow economic basis, Hoelscher's view was rational: On March 27 the UPDW laid off 40 percent of its workforce, citing a decline in orders.[29] Yet once the battle had been joined, Hoelscher's attitude meant standing in the way of the strike.

The UFC approached textile workers in New England, no doubt keeping in mind that textile workers in Plymouth and Pittsfield, Massachusetts, and Woonsocket, Rhode Island, had recently struck against similar wage cuts. Two Passaic strikers and Communist leader Ella Reeve Bloor addressed a meeting in Lawrence in early March. Joseph Salerno, a leader in the 1919 strike, announced that the Italian Cooperative Workers association pledged $10 a week to the Passaic strikers, and that the group's members were prepared to call a sympathy strike if such a course "seemed advisable."[30]

On March 26, Bloor organized a meeting in Boston that drew seventy-five representatives from local unions. A leaflet from an organizer of the Cloth, Hat, Cap, and Millinery Workers' International Union stressed that if the Passaic strikers won, it would halt the attacks on workers nationally, but if they lost, workers in other textile centers would be targeted. Several days later at another meeting in Boston, Robert Dunn declared that due to Bloor's work, several thousand textile workers in Lawrence were eager to strike. In mid-April, sympathizers in Lowell demonstrated against "Police Terror in Passaic." The leaflet, signed by the UFC in Passaic, urged workers in Massachusetts: "Don't do any Passaic work" and "stop the bosses from doing scab work in your mills."[31]

The hopes that silk workers would strike faded after late March, although Weisbord never gave up hope. On May 24 Weisbord announced that the United Front Committee planned to organize the 10,000 unorganized silk workers in Paterson, and the *Textile Strike Bulletin* regularly ran a column about Lawrence.[32] But with hostility from the textile unions' leaders, this seemed like rhetoric, not a plan.

The Battle Heats Up

In addition to allies in the labor movement, Weisbord and the UFC sought sympathetic liberals and radicals, especially in New York City, to help sway public opinion. Between the Progressive Era and the New Deal, New York City remained home to many liberals who were sympathetic to organized labor, even as they supported capitalism overall. After massive strikes of garment workers in 1909 and 1910 and the Triangle Shirtwaist fire a year later, trade-union leaders and middle-class reformers sought government intervention against rampant exploitation. In New York, Democratic Party machine politicians had a closer relationship with labor leaders and middle-class reformers than in New Jersey, where organized labor was weaker and trusts and large corporations were more powerful. These reformers wanted to make capitalism more fair, not smash the entire system, but were willing to work with Communists on specific issues, such as during strikes.[33]

An important liberal who supported the strike was Stephen S. Wise, who was the rabbi of Manhattan's Free Synagogue and a leader in the liberal Jewish community. Wise was a prominent progressive reformer who sympathized with the labor movement, going back to campaigning against child labor while living in Oregon in the 1890s. Among the labor causes he had supported were the McNamara brothers (two leaders of the iron workers union arrested on charges of bombing the building of the anti-union *Los Angeles Times* in 1910); the Triangle Shirtwaist fire victims in 1911; and striking steelworkers in 1919.

Amid the growth of strikes prior to the First World War, Wise, along with Paul U. Kellogg, lobbied the president to appoint a commission on industrial relations, a committee eventually headed by attorney Frank P. Walsh. Wise was an early supporter of the ACLU and was willing to anger powerful men: in 1911 Wise, the invited speaker at the annual meeting of the New York Chamber of Commerce, denounced labor abuses to an audience that included Andrew Carnegie and J. P. Morgan.[34]

Wise had a personal connection to the strike: in the fall of 1924 his daughter, Justine, caused a stir after working under cover in Passaic with a friend and remained in touch with workers and supported their strike. Rabbi Wise was also drawn into the strike through his affiliation with the ACLU. On February 24 he wrote to A. J. Muste, the head of Brookwood Labor College and a former leader of the Amalgamated Textile Workers, for information on the strike. The same day he asked Harvard Law professor Felix Frankfurter for information on Weisbord: "He has done a remarkable thing in getting things started in Passaic. He cannot win the strike without handing it over to the organized forces."[35]

Wise's note to Frankfurter highlighted that even though Communists, radicals, and liberals formed a united front for a common cause, this was an unstable, temporary alliance divided by class. As Marxists, the Communist

Communist Party leader J. O. Bentall speaking at rally in support of Passaic strikers in Union Square in Manhattan in 1926. American Labor Museum/Botto House National Landmark.

Party saw strikes as exercises in class struggle that would one day lead to the destruction of capitalism itself and liberate workers. Liberals and progressives saw strikes as symptoms of unrestrained capitalism that underlined the need to make capitalism more fair and reduce class conflict.[36]

Stephen Wise's Attempts to Settle the Strike

In pursuit of his strategy of "handing [the strike] over to the organized forces," Wise approached McMahon, the head of the UTW, and Sidney Hillman, head of the Amalgamated Clothing Workers. Wise found McMahon "indifferent" and "dilatory," but Hillman promised to appeal to William Green. Two days later Wise telegraphed his daughter: "Long Satisfactory talk [with] Green[.] He will try to initiate action."[37]

Weisbord was less sanguine about Green's support. Referring to a possible meeting with the UTW leadership, Weisbord wrote to Wise that "the Central Bureau of the United Front Committee would be glad to cooperate with any organization that wishes to aid us in the struggle and carry it forward to victory." Weisbord stressed that the UFC leadership would negotiate with the UTW only if the union supported the strikers' demands and "has decided to back up our relief work." Then the UFC "be very glad to consider the question of affiliation."[38]

Wise convinced Green to force McMahon, Hilfers, and two AFL organizers to meet him at his home. But this meeting was futile. "McMahon situation hopeless," he cabled his daughter. This convinced Wise that there was little hope of the UTW's helping the strike. After consulting with Hillman, Wise proposed to Weisbord that he organize a five-member committee "that under no circumstances can be considered radical or Communist" to negotiate on behalf of the strikers. Wise suggested ten possible liberal politicians or public figures as members of the committee.[39]

After discussion in the CP's Textile Committee, Weisbord agreed to Wise's proposal on the conditions that the committee "give full and unequivocal support to the demands of the strikers," that strikers accept the committee members, and that the strike committee approve any terms before they were agreed upon. The next day, March 5, a committee offered to mediate the strike. The committee consisted of Wise along with four others: John Lovejoy Elliott, of the Ethical Culture Society in New York; Paul U. Kellogg, the editor of *Survey*, the nation's leading social work journal; and the Reverend John Howard Melish, of Trinity Episcopal Church in Brooklyn,. The four were well-known New York City liberals who had worked together for decades advocating social reforms and supporting labor unions.[40]

The Committee issued a statement to the strikers offering to serve "as your representatives in these negotiations, which we are prepared to offer to initiate in the event of your acceptance of our offer." They declared the strikers' demands "just and righteous" and stated they were "deeply grieved" by "the ruthlessness with which you have been treated by the police of your city." They noted that the mill owners refused to negotiate with the strikers "on the ground, real or alleged, that you are not regularly organized within the ranks of labor, and that your leader is a man of radical political views." They added that, in regards to this charge that Weisbord was a radical, "we have learned after careful investigation that, whatever his political views may be, he has scrupulously avoided the injection of these into the situation in which you find yourselves under his leadership." While the mill owners claimed to be willing to negotiate with the AFL, the committee argued that the owners opposed any union.[41]

After Weisbord and the UFC accepted Wise's offer to resolve the strike, the rabbi and his committee wrote to the mill owners to arrange a meeting. The mill owners did not even formally reply. They had no desire to surrender managerial control over their businesses, and there was insufficient political pressure to force them to. The owners claimed that the strike was an illegitimate Communist stunt. Botany's Colonel Johnson complained about the strikers' "policy of terrorism" and claimed that there was no strike "in the commonly accepted sense of the term." Instead, he insisted, "there is a Communist demonstration, led by professional Communists, not for the purpose of helping the workers of Passaic, but to use the words of their organ, to give the textile workers a 'schooling in revolution.'"[42]

Wise recalled that trying to deal with the mill owners "did more to take me over into radicalism than any experience of a lifetime."[43] Although Wise's efforts at mediation accomplished little in the short run, they helped consolidate liberal support for the strike and served to get an element of the labor leadership to become more interested in the strike.

5

Enter the Politicians

Rabbi Stephen Wise and other progressives and liberals saw the Passaic strike as exposing the worst elements of unfettered capitalism. In this view, the workers' willingness to follow Communist leaders underlined their desperation, and the need for outsiders to intervene. The key to ending the strike, in their eyes, was to pressure the government to step in. By exerting enough public pressure, they hoped to create a fairer capitalism that treated workers better, on the model of the "protocols of peace" in the New York garment industry more than a decade earlier. These liberals were neither "dupes" of the Communists nor secret supporters: instead they thought that the best way to undermine support for the Communists was to improve industrial conditions.

The Communists, on the other hand, saw Passaic as emblematic of the capitalist system itself. So long as the capitalist class controlled the productive wealth of society and made profits by exploiting the working class, class struggle was inevitable. They wanted the strikers to win through mobilizing their own power, and believed that a victory would help raise class consciousness among the nation's workers. Neither Democratic nor Republican politicians—representatives of capitalist parties—would serve the workers' interest, they reasoned. The capitalist state—the police, the prisons, the military, and the court system—could not be reformed to serve the interest of the workers; at best, fear of workers' militancy could prod the government to enact reforms that would be reversed as soon as possible.

Despite these differences, Communists saw Wise and his cohort as useful (if temporary) allies because they could build support for the strike in milieus closed to Communist appeals. Similarly, Communists were willing to negotiate with political leaders. They did not have illusions that such liberal allies or government officials could bring justice for workers, since both served the capitalist class. Instead, they believed that any solution would depend on the workers' strength on the picket line and reflect the workers' power on the ground.

This chapter explores attempts by government officials in New Jersey and Washington to intervene in the strike, and the liberals' and Communists' roles in these efforts. Starting in March there were three overlapping attempts at government intervention: by Governor A. Harry Moore; by president Calvin Coolidge's secretary of labor, James Davis; and by several congressmen. The Democratic governor and Republican labor secretary sought to break the strike, whereas the congressmen framed their efforts in more sympathetic terms. In each case, Weisbord and the UFC were willing to negotiate, but not to demobilize workers before victory.

Early Attempts at Negotiations

Calls for local politicians to settle the strike quickly arose, especially from local merchants who felt an economic pinch. In early February, several merchants appealed to Passaic mayor John H. McGuire to urge the strikers to return to work pending arbitration. McGuire refused to negotiate with the strikers until Weisbord left town, but appointed a citizen's committee to explore solutions. Over the course of the strike, the Passaic Young Men's Hebrew Association, Lodi's Sons of Italy, and similar groups tried to resolve the strike, without success.[1]

In late February, Weisbord and Felix Penarisi—president of the UFC at Botany Mills—led 300 strikers into a Garfield city council meeting, which had been called to resolve the strike, and filled the chamber to capacity. The mill owners did not attend, and the presence of Weisbord and the UFC turned the meeting into a debate on the strike itself. The *Passaic Daily News* called this "one of the liveliest and most exciting [meetings] ever held in the history of the city." Garfield mayor William A. Burke, a white-collar employee of Botany, and city recorder Judge Richard Baker denounced the strike, but others were more sympathetic.

Two city councilmen put forward a motion "requesting that the citizens and taxpayers of Garfield support the strikers in their fight, financially and morally." Another motion requested that Baker be more lenient on the strikers. Weisbord suggested a motion that that city police not be stationed in halls where strikers were speaking. He suggested that the City Council establish a relief fund for strikers, and that the city's department of education establish relief kitchens for strikers. Baker red-baited Weisbord and warned him: "The quicker you get out of this vicinity, the better I will like it." Instead, it was Burke and Baker who stormed out of their own meeting—to boos from the crowd. The meeting exposed the city government's servility to the mill owners, and the deep polarization caused by the strike.[2]

On Saturday, March 13, Weisbord and a delegation from the United Front Committee met with attorney Frank P. Walsh, seeking his help to get a congressional investigation and arrange a meeting with Coolidge. Walsh had fought anti-labor laws and advocated pro-union policies within the Democratic Party and was one of the few prominent attorneys who represented labor leaders. He had been chairman of the U.S. Commission on Industrial Relations (the Walsh Commission) during the Taft administration and, during the First World War, co-chairman of the National War Labor Board with former President Taft (the Taft-Walsh Board). He had visited Soviet Russia in 1922, and in the same year helped defend William Z. Foster, who had been arrested in a raid of the underground Communist Party in Bridgman, Michigan.[3]

"In the conference with Walsh," Weisbord reported back to the Communist textile committee, "Walsh treated us very well. . . . He had his mind made up before we came." Walsh agreed to help the Passaic strikers for no charge. He was able to draw on his connections, including economist W. Jett Lauck, the ex-secretary of the National War Labor Board. Walsh agreed to travel with the strikers to Washington, D.C., Weisbord recalled, "and to present our case, and to demand an investigation." Walsh also "arranged that our Committee should see and interview with President Coolidge, and request him to appoint a Committee on Investigation."[4]

The Secretary of Labor Tries to Break the Strike

Earlier in the strike, two representatives of the Department of Labor had traveled to Passaic to secure a settlement. When these efforts failed, according to a report, the agents "finally recommend[ed] to the department that an invitation be extended to the employers to confer with the Secretary of Labor and the Director of Conciliation for the purpose of devising an agreement on a tentative proposal which might be acceptable to all those involved in the controversy." On March 15, representatives of the mill owners met with James J. Davis, the U.S. secretary of labor.[5]

Davis proposed that the workers should return to the mills without an agreement. *Then* the mill owners would meet committees of workers elected from each of the mills' departments and provide "redress" for all grievances. Any remaining disagreements would be decided by a tripartite committee with one representative each chosen by the mill owners, the workers, and the Department of Labor. There was one other condition: "Organizer Weisbord and all outside influences are to be ignored." The mill owners agreed to this plan, which would have allowed the owners and the government to outflank the strikers.[6] The next day the *Passaic Daily News* reported that Labor Department officials had confided "that if the strike leaders will step aside the Bureau of Mediation and Conciliation could effect a settlement of the strike within forty-eight hours." Davis emphasized that the mill owners continued to refuse to meet with Weisbord. The strike headquarters did not comment.[7]

The delegation from Passaic attempted to see President Coolidge on Tuesday, March 16. Everett Sanders, the president's secretary, met with the strikers for fifteen minutes, but told them they would never see Coolidge and directed them to the Labor Department. Weisbord's reaction was printed in the papers: "We read in the papers every day that [Coolidge] sees Charleston dancers, opera singers and people of all kinds and descriptions, yet he would not see us who want to recite to him the wrongs of 16,000 wage workers."[8]

The specter of the strikers meeting with Coolidge startled the mill owners enough that the next morning the general counsel of Botany Mills sent a telegram to Sanders, denying all the strikers' accusations and underlining "that [the] strike is communistic in origin and purpose."[9]

On March 17 the Passaic delegation met with Secretary Davis for two hours. The delegation rejected Davis's plan and reiterated the strikers' original demands. They demanded that the mills agree to pay a "living wage . . . to be that which has heretofore been determined by the United States Department of Labor itself." Once this was achieved, they promised that the workers would return to work. Within three days they proposed that the strikers and the mill owners each pick a representative to negotiate the other terms "so that the principle of collective bargaining through representatives freely selected may be preserved." The proposal continued, "These two representatives shall be empowered to adjust all points in dispute between the mill owners and the workers, and in the case of disagreement shall have authority to select an impartial referee to the end that any remaining disputed points may be equitably adjusted." The strikers authorized Walsh to represent them "in any negotiations, investigations, or hearings in regard thereto." Davis and the Department of Labor seem to have lost interest in the strike once it was clear that the strikers were not going to capitulate, and the owners refused to deal with Weisbord and the UFC.[10]

Lobbying Congress for an Investigation

On Monday, March 15, the delegation from Passaic went to Senator William Borah's office and met with Borah and Senators Robert La Follette Jr. and Burton Wheeler. These three were the remaining progressive giants in the Senate. Borah, a Republican from Idaho, was the chairman of the Senate Foreign Relations Committee; La Follette, a Republican from Wisconsin, was a first-term senator elected to take the seat from his father who had died a year earlier. Wheeler, a Democrat from Montana, had run for vice president on the elder La Follette's Progressive Party ticket in 1924.

The three opposed what they saw as corrupt moneyed interests. But they eschewed working-class-based politics and were anti-Communist. Borah had prosecuted IWW leader William Haywood in 1907 for the murder of a former Idaho governor, and opposed the closed shop. The delegation sought (in the words of the *Passaic Daily News*) "the creation of a Federal Commission on Industrial Relations with sweeping powers to hold summary hearings in the great industrial centres [*sic*], beginning in the textile centres of New Jersey." The effort to get a congressional investigation—which Lauck coordinated in Washington—was designed to publicize the poor conditions in Passaic and pressure the mill owners to settle.[11]

Besides Weisbord and Walsh, the delegation included Mary Heaton Vorse and Katherine G. T. Wiley, executive director of the New Jersey Consumers' League. Each struck mill sent a representative. All were U.S. citizens, except one who had completed his "first papers," the first step in the naturalization process. The workers showed the senators their pay envelopes, indicating weekly wages between $11.50 and $20.45. Only one worker had earned $1,100 the previous year. When a senator asked about the role of Communism in the strike, Walsh replied: "If there is any textile worker in Passaic who would like to overthrow the government, nobody is serving him better in this respect than his employer. The answer is in the pay envelope."[12]

The UFC hired counsel in Washington to lobby for an investigation of the textile industry. On March 18, Walsh telegraphed Edward N. Nockels, secretary of the Chicago Federation of Labor, requesting that he "send as many telegrams as possible from labor leaders and organizations" to Illinois Republican senator William B. McKinley, the chairman of the Committee on Manufacturers, urging Congress to investigate the strike. The next day Nockels replied to Walsh that the Chicago Federation of Labor and a dozen other labor organizations had wired McKinley.[13]

On March 19, Wisconsin congressman Victor Berger, the only Socialist Party member in the House, introduced a motion calling for the House Committee on Interstate and Foreign Commerce to investigate the strike. The resolution highlighted low wages in the mills and police repression against the strike, noting that "brutal assaults have been made upon these workers by police officers and other city officials." Congressman George N. Seger, a Republican from Passaic, defended "the good name of Passaic as well as that of neighboring cities" from "unenviable notoriety and unjust criticism." Seger complained that "the picture newspapers don't report the news, they make it up."[14]

Colonel Charles F. H. Johnson disputed Berger's claims. But he supported a congressional inquiry, which, he hoped, "would reveal that the strike was 'Communistic in instigation,' the strikers have used massed picketing to intimidate workers and cause attacks on law and order, and that efforts are being made to involve the whole textile industry." Johnson sent a telegram to Representative Seger denouncing the strike as "designed to propagandize the communist attack on the industry and government of this country." In response, Weisbord described accusations of Communism as a diversion from the conditions in the Passaic mills.[15]

In Passaic, on March 18, the day after the strikers rejected the secretary of labor's plan, there was an hour-long clash between strikers and police. Weisbord cabled New Jersey senators Edge and Edwards along with La Follette, Borah, and Wheeler: "Passaic Police cassocks [*sic*] have brutally assaulted orderly strikers this afternoon," describing the attack.[16]

Sidney Hillman, the head of the Amalgamated Clothing Workers, telegraphed Borah urging him "to use influence to bring about an investigation of the working conditions and prevailing wage scale in the textile mills of the Passaic district of New Jersey." Norman Thomas and the ACLU sent similar cables. Walsh redoubled his efforts to lobby Congress. Lauck began working on "a thorough survey of conditions both of wages, housing conditions, working conditions, police outrages, threats of deportations, undue sentences, etc." Walsh hired Pauline Clark "to present the case of the strikers together with the material already on hand to as large a number of senators as possible before the hearing."[17]

Senator Edge's response was to ignore Weisbord's telegram, saying "I will not recognize this outside agitator." Senator Edward I. Edwards, a Democrat from Jersey City, replied to Weisbord, using the concept of states' rights to shield the violation of strikers' rights. He declared that he "firmly believe[d] that to allow the Federal Government to intervene would be a serious mistake" and "a denial of New Jersey's prerogative to settle their own domestic affairs."[18]

On March 20, Senator La Follette introduced a resolution calling on the Committee on Manufacturers to investigate the strike, including low wages, police violence, and attacks on the rights of strikers. Senator Edge—who had received a $1,000 donation from Julius Forstmann for the 1924 election—objected to the accusations against the mill owners and authorities in New Jersey, and asked for an investigation into "the real inception of the strike." Edge repeated the mill owners' assertion "that this strike is engineered, that this strike has been incited, that this strike is now being managed, by representatives of the Communist Party in this country." He opposed federal interference in the strike, pointing out that Governor Moore, a Democrat, did not think it was needed.[19]

Senator Edwards echoed this argument. He accused "the present leader of the strikers" of being "a foreigner and not a citizen of this country" and "not even a citizen of the State of New Jersey." He warned that "as long as the Passaic strikers . . . are willing to permit outside agitators to come to New Jersey for the purpose of creating dissension and incipient revolution," they "must be ready and willing to accept the consequences." (Weisbord responded by calling Edwards "a plain out and out liar," and pointed out that he was born in the United States, and had lived in New Jersey for the past year.)[20]

Over the next weeks, strike supporters attempted to corral the progressive senators into pushing for an investigation. Liberal and labor leaders sent telegrams to Borah supporting an investigation. Senator Borah dismissed attempts to red-bait the strikers. While sympathetic, neither Wheeler nor La Follette seemed optimistic or enthusiastic, especially because several senators on the Manufacturers Committee—including its chairman—opposed an investigation.[21]

In late March, by a vote of six to two, the Senate Committee on Manufacturers deferred action until Edwards could visit Passaic to investigate the strike. Instead, Edwards soon traveled to Paterson for three days and refused to enter Passaic. When the *New York Daily News* asked Edwards if he had spoken to any strikers, the senator replied: "No, and you can put that in double faced type—no; and I will not talk to them as long as Weisbord is at their head." In response, two men and two women strikers picketed Edwards' home in Jersey City. "Senator Edwards See Us—We Are Real Passaic Strikers," one sign read.[22]

Attempts to get the Senate to take up the strike dragged on through April.[23] On April 20 the Committee met for six hours in closed session to discuss the strike, but deferred any decision. Edwards continued his red-baiting, blaming the strike on Communist agitators funded by Russian money and asserted that the strike would be easily settled "if Albert Weisbord, professed Communist, and some twenty other 'Red' lieutenants, were driven out of Passaic today, and entirely eliminated as one of the serious factors in the strike situation." He appealed to nativism and anti-Jewish racism by calling Weisbord "a young Jewish man, born in Brooklyn."[24]

Local Attempts to End the Strike

Local politicians continued to try to end the strike. On March 11 the mayor named a "Committee of 26," composed of merchants, doctors, lawyers, and Rotarians. Weisbord wrote to local religious leaders, trying to get them to intervene into the strike. In response the Reverend George Talbott of the First Presbyterian Church and president of the association of Protestant pastors in Passaic, organized a meeting of clergy with Weisbord and then the mill owners. On March 12 the clergymen met with Weisbord at UFC headquarters. Talbott was hostile to Weisbord, grilling him on his religious and political views. Talbott and several other Protestant ministers stormed out of the meeting after Weisbord objected to the presence of a stenographer and four newspaper reporters, whom Talbott had invited. Talbott refused "to be present at any meeting with a man who desires to conceal either his religious or political beliefs" and claimed that "the leadership of this strike is tainted." The remaining clergymen in attendance continued the meeting, led by a Roman Catholic priest, Edward F. Schulte, a priest from the Polish National Catholic Church, John Wroblewski, and an Episcopalian priest, Theodore Andrews.[25] The other nine clergymen were from assorted Catholic, Orthodox, and Episcopalian parishes, with the exception of a representative of the African Methodist Episcopalian (AME) Zion Church.[26]

The strike split the local religious community. "The Protestants are against us, and the Catholics for," Weisbord reported to the CP's textile committee.[27] The mill owners and many of the white-collar staff in the wool industry were Protestant. Those Protestants who supported the strikers came from outside of Passaic, including Norman Thomas, the Church League for Industrial Democracy, and the Methodist Federation for Social Action.[28]

Many of the strikers belonged to one of several ethnic Catholic or Orthodox parishes. Given Weisbord's experience in the Hillcrest strike, we can assume that he had no illusions about the Catholic church, but desired to not antagonize the clergy. While the upper levels of the Catholic hierarchy opposed the strike, local priests supported their parishioners. Joseph Magliacano, an Italian-born Communist organizer in Lodi, recalled decades later that the chairman of the local strike committee complained that the priest had attacked the strike as a Bolshevik conspiracy. He organized strikers to meet near the church. Magliacano recalled that he "came to the meeting with a Bible of the old and new testament," and quoted the Ten Commandments and the Sermon on the Mount. "I told the people that if we win the strike, the church would also benefit. The people will win with an increase of wages; then when the go to church, they would be able to contribute more to the church." He advised the strikers to "elect a committee to meet with the priest and discuss his statement." When the committee met with the priest, "over 5,000 people marched in front of the church." At next week's mass the priest spoke in favor of the strike.[29]

The presence of the Reverend Andrews, from the Episcopalian church, reflected the liberal tradition of his church and indicated that the Episcopalian bishop of Newark, Edwin Lines, sympathized with Rabbi Wise's efforts to resolve the strike.[30] In the Episcopalian church there was a tradition of supporting labor reform, going back to the Social Gospel movement during the Industrial Revolution.[31] The Reverend John Howard Melish, of Brooklyn (part of the Long Island Diocese), worked with Rabbi Wise to mediate the strike. Although Bishop Lines of Newark pulled out of Wise's effort at the last minute, he was known for his support of the less fortunate and underprivileged.[32] In his address to the annual Newark Diocese's convention in 1926, Lines referred to the "deplorable industrial conflict" in Passaic and highlighted the role of immigrants in the strike: "Our Churches and our communities will in the future depend largely upon the children of the foreign born growing up among us, and it is the time to win their friendship and good will by making an end of unworthy prejudices which linger among us."[33]

The support of Reverend S. A. Donnell, of the AME Zion Church, might appear strange, since almost all of the woolworkers were white. Black workers were excluded from Paterson's silk mills, but several hundred Black men labored under horrible conditions in the silk-dyeing plants in Lodi, and the UFC made special efforts to include them in the strike, reflecting the Communist

Party's dedication to racial equality. Cyril Briggs, a leading Black Communist, helped edit the strike bulletin, and William Pickens, a leader in the NAACP, was a prominent supporter of the strike. Black newspapers covered the strike sympathetically.[34]

No rabbis were involved in the meeting in Passaic. Jews were on both sides of the strike: Abram Preiskel, Passaic commissioner of public safety and responsible for much of the police violence, was a leading member of the local Jewish community, while Rabbi Wise was a prominent supporter of the strike; Weisbord was also Jewish, although not religious. Nearby Paterson had a substantial Jewish population, including Communists and others active in the labor movement.[35] These divisions, and the propensity of some politicians, like Senator Edwards, to Jew-bait, may have militated against the Jewish community taking an active role.

A "Committee of Three," led by Wroblewski, Schulte, and Andrews convened another meeting for Monday, March 15. In the face of the employers' refusal to meet, the clergymen were unable to mediate the strike. The Catholic hierarchy became increasingly anti-strike. During mass on March 21, the Right Reverend Monsignor Thomas J. Kernan, rector of the English-speaking St. Nicholas Roman Catholic Church, supported Secretary Davis's plan to end the strike and denounced the strike leaders as Communists.[36]

The next week, the local Knights of Columbus organized a breakfast that featured mayor McGuire; the head of the Passaic Chamber of Commerce; the acting corporation counsel of New York City, Arthur J. W. Hilley; and Reverend Kernan. Hilley blamed the Passaic strike on a "false philosophy" that brought in its wake easy divorce, immortality, atheism, and other supposed social ills. Father Kernan urged the Knights of Columbus to name a committee to study the strike. The Grand Knight ran the menswear department at Botany Worsted, so any such committee would not be neutral.[37]

Throughout April, arrests and police violence increased in the strike zone; Weisbord was arrested and given tens of thousands of dollars of bail. This shook up liberals who supported the strike. "There is no need to tell you about what I think of what is happening in Passaic," Wise wrote to his daughter on April 13. "It is the renunciation of all that democracy prizes." Wise added: "My plan is that we offer the strikers, in the absence of Weisbord, who I think should be left in jail for a few days, that we take over the leadership of the strike." Liberals feared that the police violence would discredit (in the words of Paul Kellogg's *Survey*) "the measure of American democracy in the eyes of the world."[38]

The Hague Machine and the Passaic Strike

Rabbi Wise, in a letter to his daughter, noted his efforts "to get hold of Governor Moore's boss, Frank Hague, the mayor of Jersey City and democratic

Warwick of New Jersey."[39] Wise was not alone in his belief that if anybody could resolve the strike, it was Hague, a kingmaker in state politics at the height of power. Both the current governor, A. Harry Moore, and his predecessor (and current senator) Edward Edwards, were integral to Frank Hague's Democratic Party machine. The state's other senator, Walter Edge, although a Republican, was also in debt to Hague for his support in the 1916 gubernatorial election.[40]

In the 1930s, Hague became infamous for the brutal repression his police meted out against union activists from the Congress of Industrial Organizations who tried to organize what was known as "scab city."[41] But in the 1910s and 1920s he had a warm relationship with the American Federation of Labor. In 1916 the AFL invited Hague, then the director of public safety in Jersey City, to speak at its annual convention in Baltimore. Samuel Gompers introduced Hague as "a man of uncommon attainment and character." At the convention, Hague stated that "an employer does not have the right to import into our city armed thugs and to shoot down the innocent working men who may have controversies with their employers."[42] In 1919, Jersey City police prevented fifty scab longshoremen from unloading a steamship. The Hudson County Central Labor Union endorsed Hague for mayor in each election till 1929. Hague's "friendship" with labor was based on his ability to work with the conservative leadership of the AFL unions, most notably in the building trades and longshore unions, in keeping labor peace in Hudson County.

On April 15 Hague declined to mediate the strike. Hague may have been relishing such chaos in Passaic, a Republican town; his reticence also reflected the realpolitik of New Jersey, often described as "home rule," in which each city (or its local machine) ran its own affairs without outside interference. Moore, like his mentor, respected "home rule," but soon found himself being called upon to intervene in Passaic. Local businessmen looked to him to restore calm, and many workers took him at his word as a supporter of organized labor. Since early March the Passaic Chamber of Commerce sought to get Governor Moore to mediate the strike.[43]

Because Moore was known as the "kiddies' friend" due to his support for education, the strike leaders emphasized how the strike affected mothers and children. The same day that Hague refused to become involved, the UFC organized a demonstration of thirty children and their mothers at the State House in Trenton to protest police violence against strikers. Protesters demanded Moore visit Passaic to see the violence against strikers with his own eyes.[44]

The same day, April 15, a delegation of Passaic strikers, including women and children, picketed the White House. Like Governor Moore, Coolidge claimed to be too ill to meet with the strikers. The picket lasted ten minutes until police warned the picketers that the participation of children violated Washington's child labor laws! The picket exacerbated tensions between

Weisbord and the strike's liberal supporters. According to Wise, Walsh had telephoned him at 11 P.M. the day before, "begging me to hold off the strikers who were leaving for Washington to picket the White House," since, in their view, "it would merely irritate the country and serve no purpose."[45]

The various attempts to reach a political conclusion stalled during this period. The Labor Department's chief of mediation told reporters: "If Weisbord really wants this strike settled now is the time for him to retire and let a committee of the textile workers go to the mill owners with their own terms."[46] This shifted the blame for the lack of a settlement to the strikers while masking the mill owners' refusal to negotiate. But it outlined the hope of settlement forged on the removal of Weisbord and the decapitation of the strike leadership.

In early April the Communist Party's Trade-Union Committee passed a motion "that we must not insist on Weisbord being a member of the Public Official Strike Settlement Committee, that is, that this must not be a breaking point in the negotiations for the settlement." The motion added: "If the company refuses to deal with the committee because of Weisbord's presence, that Weisbord then issue a statement on the situation and withdraw from the committee. But this policy shall appear as being on the initiative of Weisbord."[47]

On April 17, Judge John Bentley of Jersey City issued a sweeping injunction against the strikers. The next day Weisbord was released from jail on $25,000 bail; he was arrested again five minutes later. As soon as he was released again, on $5,000 bail, six detectives presented him with the injunction.[48] The headlines of a *New York Times* article summarized the situation on April 18: "Passaic Mill Tie-Up Enters 13th Week—10,000 Workers Idle 3 Months as Dozens of Attempts Fail to End Textile Strike—Their Leaders Are in Jail—Bitter Clashes with Police Mark Struggle of Employees to Better Working Conditions and Pay."[49]

Moore offered to mediate the strike, and issued a statement that he was "glad to cooperate in every way within my power to bring about settlement of the strike." He added: "But I will not be coerced or cajoled into sending the armed forces of the State into the strike zone except as a last resort, and only when I am convinced that such action is necessary to protect law and order."[50] By this time, the National Guard's strike-breaking reputation was secure, and there is no reason to believe it would have done anything else if Moore sent troops to Passaic.[51] Moore's threat to use the National Guard to "protect law and order" as "a last resort" underlined that the National Guard was not neutral. When the four large Passaic mills tried to reopen using scab labor on April 20, Moore made his threat to break the strike more explicit: "The Governor has power to do just one thing and that is invade the strike zone with the armed forces of the State and, obviously, this should only be done where the disorder amounts to rioting and bloodshed and the local authorities are unable to maintain law and order. Such action would, of course, mean the end of the strike, and as far as the strikers are concerned, the loss of their cause."⁵² This was the stick. The carrot was Moore's announcement of a committee to mediate the strike. This committee was composed of the governor himself, Adjutant-General Frederick W. Gilkerson, Brigadier General Bird S. Spencer of the New Jersey National Guard, and Henry Hilfers of the New Jersey Federation of Labor.

Moore's plan was that "the leadership of the strike should now be taken over by the American Federation of Labor." Moore and the AFL shared a similar position: they claimed to sympathize with the strikers, but opposed the leadership of the strike. Moore made clear that his committee would not negotiate with Weisbord. Both William Green and Henry Hilfers supported Moore's plan. Supporters of the strike were wary of Moore's and the AFL's sudden interest in the strike. Samuel Untermyer pointed out that the strikers "might as well accept terms of settlement directly from the owners as from anybody acting on behalf of Gov. Moore." He warned strikers "to have nothing to do with Gov. Moore or his committee," and pointed out that the AFL and the UFC could talk with the mill owners without Moore's help.⁵³

Moore's plan seemed to be to break the strike, effect an agreement between the AFL and the mill owners, outflank Weisbord, and making everybody happy—except the workers. Hilfers gloated that with Weisbord forced out of the picture, "The mills will finally have to accept unionization."⁵⁴ The UFC did not play along. Weisbord responded to governor's plans: "We have won this strike on the picket line. We are not going to lose it over the conference table. The Governor's offer is vicious and asinine. His committee is an iron-heeled one. General Spencer, for example, is an open foe of labor. Nevertheless, if an offer is made to our attorney, Henry T. Hunt, we will meet the mill owners before the committee on Friday morning. But I do not think the Governor means business. I am inclined to believe he designs to break the strike by premature action."⁵⁵ The UFC hired Henry T. Hunt, a New York lawyer, to represent them in Moore's mediation efforts. Before moving to New York less than four years earlier, Hunt was a progressive politician, serving as a reform Democratic mayor of Cincinnati (1912–1913) and a member of the national Railroad Labor Board. Weisbord did not insist on attending the negotiations; he claimed poor health, without ceding his right to play a role in the strike. The UFC elected eight strikers to represent the workers in negotiations.⁵⁶

All of the mill owners, except for Forstmann and Huffmann, accepted the governor's invitation to meet with the committee. When Hilfers complained that there were "too many generals on the mediation committee," Moore dropped Spencer and Gilkerson, replacing them with Dr. Andrew McBride, the state commissioner of labor. (McBride had been the mayor of Paterson during the 1913 silk strike.) But when the UFC insisted that Weisbord be part of any mediation meeting, Moore postponed the meeting until, in the words of the *New York Daily Mirror*, "further efforts could be made to eliminate Weisbord."

On April 26, 1926, the United Front Committee organized a mass rally in Wallington when the government and the textile companies were trying to remove Weisbord from strike leadership. Ten thousand strikers raise their union cards in a vote of confidence in Weisbord. American Labor Museum/Botto House National Landmark.

On April 26 (the same day Justice Bentley in Jersey City was presiding over a hearing on an injunction against the union), the UFC organized a mass meeting in Wallington, a small neighboring town. On an empty lot owned by the city's mayor, Elizabeth Gurley Flynn put the question of whether the strikers still had confidence in Weisbord. Ten thousand strikers unanimously voted to keep Weisbord as their leader. After the vote Weisbord announced he would not insist on attending the mediation meeting. The next day Weisbord demanded that Hilfers and McBride be removed from the committee, and that the strikers and the companies negotiate only with the governor. Both Hilfers and McBride agreed to withdraw, but Moore refused to participate in tripartite negotiations.[57]

On April 29 the frustrated governor announced that he was taking a ten-day vacation in Atlantic City. He gave Hilfers and McBride (the two representatives Weisbord demanded not participate) "full authority to take any action that may appear advisable or necessary" to settle the strike.[58] On May 4, Senator Wheeler telegraphed Moore urging him to settle the strike, and indicated that the Senate would investigate if the strike continued. The same day, Senator Borah announced that he was considering speaking in Passaic. Both Wheeler and Borah violated "senatorial courtesy," the tradition that senators should not interfere in the affairs of their colleagues' home states. Edwards—and many other senators—would have seen this as an affront.[59]

The progressives sought to pressure the AFL to become active—or the government to intervene. Norman Thomas and Stephen Wise wrote to Borah after Moore's efforts had collapsed that the "best possible drive at situation would be through federal investigation," which they predicted might force the mill owners to budge, especially given high protective tariffs on wool.[60] On May 4, W. Jett Lauck wrote to Walsh that while it was important to get the Senate to take up the strike, "My opinion is that what is vitally and acutely needed is for you to take charge of the settlement of the strike there through the Governor's Mediation Commission or some other venue. I believe the time is ripe for settlement and properly handled the support of the A.F. of L. can be secured. The demonstration in the Senate here should then be staged to make the operators feel that it would be expedient to settle. What is needed above everything else though, is some centralizing control in Passaic and the emphasis being placed upon settlement."[61]

So far, attempts to get Congress to pressure the mill owners through an investigation; to get President Coolidge or his secretary of labor to end the strike; or to get Governor Moore to mediate the strike had come to naught. Weisbord and the UFC were willing to negotiate, but were adamant that they would not reach a settlement without the support of the strikers themselves. For them, the resolution of the strike would come through workers' power on the picket line, not the goodwill of capitalist politicians. The mill owners did not want any union, especially one led by Communists. Moore would have been happy to have the AFL take over the strike from Weisbord and settle it, but the strikers were solid in their determination that Weisbord be their leader.

The Slavic Committee

The Associated Societies and Parishes of Passaic and Vicinity (known as the "Slavic Committee" or the "Slovak Societies") was a pro-strike organization of more than forty benevolent, social, religious, and political societies and churches. In mid-April, fifteen clergymen and twenty-seven laymen in Passaic appointed a "conciliation board" headed by District Court judge W. Carrington Cabell to try to settle the strike. Cabell's committee telephoned Weisbord on April 26, telling the strike leader that "the committee was prepared to meet with any committee that [Weisbord] would select." After meeting with the committee, Weisbord reported that "the Cabel[l] committee was very friendly," but wanted to negotiate individual contracts with each mill, to exploit the differences between the owners. The Communists' Textile Committee approved this approach, and sought to get in touch with Reverend Wroblewski to obtain information about the mills' attitude.[62]

On May 5, the 101st day of the strike, the Slavic Committee appointed a seven-person committee headed by Judge Cabell to mediate the strike. Botany Mills, Gera Mills, and Passaic Worsted and Spinning agreed to meet with the committee if Weisbord did not play a direct role. The UFC agreed to this condition, and indicated that Hunt would represent them.[63]

The next day, however, the three mills backed out of meeting the UFC representatives at a conference organized by the Slavic Committee. They refused to accept the condition that any agreement would need approval by the UFC (which presumably meant Weisbord). The mills issued a statement that they would only deal directly with their workers and not with the UFC.[64]

For a week the Slavic Committee continued to try to get the mill owners and workers to negotiate. On May 15 the Slavic Committee announced that in the face of the mills' recalcitrance, it was abandoning a neutral stance and came out in support of the strikers. On May 23 the Slavic Committee organized a 20,000-strong parade in support of the strikers. "One by one the priests of the different parishes spoke—each in a different language," Esther Lowell reported. The six largest mills issued a joint statement reiterating their refusal to meet with the UFC and denouncing "the flood of civic and moral poison that has been poured into this community from strike headquarters."[65]

In late May the strike entered its seventeenth week. Rabbi Wise feverishly met or corresponded with Senators Borah and La Follette, labor leaders such as Hillman, and representatives of the wool companies. His vision seemed to be that Weisbord and other Communists would step aside, an established union such as Hillman's Amalgamated Clothing Workers would take over the strike, and Congress would pressure the textile companies to settle. Hillman believed that it was in the interest of the clothing workers' union to support the textile workers. Hillman spoke in Passaic, and the Amalgamated's general convention in May unanimously pledged support to the Passaic strike. Nonetheless, the wool companies, despite divisions among themselves, refused to negotiate.[66]

On May 18 the Garfield City Council unanimously approved a resolution for a Senate investigation.[67] A delegation of twenty clergymen, publishers, lawyers, and other representatives of the Slavic Committee traveled to Washington to lobby for a Senate inquiry. Weisbord referred to the committee as representing "thirty thousand citizens of the best element in Passaic." The delegation was led by William R. Vanacek, a lawyer, and the Reverends Michael Sotak (from the Saints Peter and Paul Russian Orthodox Church) and Wroblewski. Along with Walsh, they met with Borah, La Follette, and Wheeler, who promised to bring up the strike on the Senate floor if the Committee on Manufacturers refused to authorize an investigation.[68]

On May 26 the Senate Committee on Education and Labor held a hearing on protective tariffs and labor conditions in the textile industry. Deak, Hunt, and Lauck testified "without any casualties," according to Lauck. The head of the UTW, Thomas McMahon, also testified. Lauck wrote to Walsh,

I had quite a talk with McMahon after the hearing, and I believe that if you and I would get together with him, we could probably settle this Passaic strike.

He says that his only fear is that if the A.F. of L. would take it over he would not be protected from discrimination against the strikers after the strike, and would have all the stigma of having lost it by the breaking up of the organization, and he seems to think that you especially would be qualified to arrange terms under which there would be no discrimination against striking employees.

Lauck indicated that when he next visited New York, he and Walsh would go see McMahon.[69]

A week later, on May 29, the Slavic Committee organized a two-hour pro-strike demonstration of 20,000 people. They marched through the "nice" part of Passaic, passing the houses of Julius Forstmann, Abram Preiskel, and Colonel Charles F. H. Johnson. According to the Socialist Party's *New Leader*, "Strikers had never been up in this part before. 'Not for workers,' said one marcher to another as they passed a grand new house in construction." Local priests addressed the march, "each in a different language. But all spoke to the same effect: that the workers must stick together and they would win and win their union."[70]

In early June, Wise and Hillman seemed to reach an agreement with the Botany Mill:

> The workers are to return organized as the Passaic Workers Union,— unaffiliated either with the United Front Committee, the American Federation of Labor, or the Amalgamated Clothing Workers of America, but free to determine their own affiliations in the future, as the Passaic Workers Union. All questions are to be arbitrated by a board of three, with arrangements for permanent arbitration machinery, the only question at issue being the restoration of the wage cut, the strikers insisting upon that restoration as part of the terms of the strike-ending agreement and the Botany Worsted Mills probably insisting that it cannot grant the restoration. The difficulty is heightened by the circumstance that the Botany Worsted Mills for some time cannot give full-time to its workers.[71]

Wise even drew up a draft statement announcing that "following conference with the Hon. Wm. E. Borah, United States Senator from Idaho, Colonel Johnson, General Manager of the Botany Worsted Mills, announced today that the workers in the textile mills of Passaic had been invited to res[u]me their places in the various mills, which invitation they had accepted."[72]

At the last minute, Wise wrote to Borah, "after having written the above . . . the representative of the Mills has just telephoned that they will under no circumstance deal with Weisbord, that all other questions at dispute might be adjusted, but they will have no traffic with a man who is a Communist." He added: "I do not know how we are going to get around this difficulty. I may make an effort to get Weisbord to eliminate himself, but, inasmuch as half the workers would still be on strike, even if the settlement with the Botany Worsted Mills were made, I cannot ask him to withdraw from the leadership. What is more, I feel the workers would not consent."[73]

Wise reported to Hillman that his contact at Botany "sounded quite sepulchral over the telephone," and underlined, "We cannot deal with Weisbord. He is a Communist and I could not get the directors even to consider the thing as long as the workers are under his rule." Wise added: "I should have to send for Weisbord and tell him that he stands in the way of a settlement of the strike. He has got to face that fact and some way must found of having him go off for a week to another field, Lawrence or elsewhere, with power granted to others to negotiate." On June 8, Wise and Hillman met with Weisbord.[74]

Wise wrote to Borah on June 11: "We have reached a point where the strikers feel they can go on indefinitely, and on the other hand, the mill-owners are in an utterly irreconcilable mood. Sidney Hillman and I felt that we must wait for the present and that the situation may change." He urged the senator to "send for Colonel Johnson, the head of the Botany Worsted Mills, and learn from him just what would be the terms upon which the strike could be ended, as far as the Botany is concerned."

6

Repression and Class-Struggle Defense

"Labor agitators will not be tolerated in Passaic," Passaic police court judge William B. Davidson admonished several organizers from the Amalgamated Clothing Workers whom police had arrested outside a local company on January 15. Davidson jailed one organizer for six months and fined the others $25. This anti-labor repression was normal in Passaic and would not be worth noting except that these organizers were arrested ten days before workers at the Botany Mill walked out.[1]

Workers throughout the United States in the 1920s had no recognized right to form unions, bargain collectively, or strike, and judges frequently issued anti-labor injunctions.[2] Workers in the Garden State most likely faced less repression than workers in the South or the West. What distinguished New Jersey was a tradition of corruption combined with the large number of municipal and county governments (eighty-nine in Passaic and Bergen Counties alone), each with its own police force and court system. During Prohibition, Passaic was known as a wide-open town in a state full of illegal gambling, prostitution, and alcohol. Both Chief of Police Richard O. Zober and Commissioner of Public Safety Preiskel were later convicted on corruption charges.[3]

During the 1926 strike, the police and courts worked together to attack, repress, and harass workers and their supporters; they even framed several strikers for bombing strikebreakers' homes. The Communist Party and the International Labor Defense (ILD) forged a successful united front with the American Civil Liberties Union (ACLU) and other radicals and liberals that allowed the strikers to continue to struggle. The ACLU took charge of cases dealing with civil liberties and free speech, and the ILD defended arrested strikers, union organizers, and pickets, and spearheaded fundraising. This united front provided the Communists with an opportunity to put forward their political understanding of the police and court system as the repressive apparatus of the capitalist class, exposing the violence at the core of the capitalist state.[4]

Instead of relying on the courts to bring justice to the workers, the Communists stressed the mobilization of the workers themselves. As the strike wound down, the links forged during the strike between the ILD and the Communists would be useful as the Sacco and Vanzetti campaign gained momentum and mobilized tens of thousands of workers and intellectuals. At the same time, the Sacco and Vanzetti campaign underlined the differences between Communists and the ILD, on the one hand, and the ACLU and other liberals, on the other.

In April the ACLU compiled 197 affidavits "charging the police of Passaic, Garfield and Clifton with unnecessary violence, unprovoked assault, brutality, drunkenness, illegal interference, and other similar activities" from the start of the strike to the end of March. These included "assaults on men," "unwarranted arrest," "tear gas bombs," "clubbing by mounted police," "abusive and profane language," and "assaults on women and children." The ACLU later collected *another* 131 affidavits "made by witnesses to the violence of the police of Passaic and Clifton against the strikers and by-standers."[5]

Police arrested almost 900 people between February 1926 and February 1927, more than 700 of these between March and the end of September 1926. More than half the arrests were on charges of disorderly conduct. Bail totaled more than $600,000—the equivalent of more than $8.5 million dollars today. Fines, ranging from $2 to $52, came to more than $4,000—almost $57,500 today.[6]

By May 1927, after the strike was over, ninety-eight strikers had been sentenced to six months to one year in jail.[7] The police targeted strike leaders such as Albert Weisbord, Jack Rubenstein, Nancy Sandosky, and Lena Chernenko for multiple arrests and high bail. Prominent outside supporters, such as Norman Thomas, were also special targets.

This repression reflected decades of practice in Passaic County, most famously in the 1913 Paterson silk strike led by the Industrial Workers of the World (IWW). An article in the December 1919 *National Police Journal*, "How the Passaic (N.J.) Police Force Handle Labor Problems," outlined "the Passaic Plan" in which labor organizers "were met at the railroad station upon their arrival and calmly informed by the police that their activities would not be tolerated in Passaic and that the only safe course open to them was to take the next train out of town." As a result, the article claimed, "Passaic has become as unprofitable a field for the out-of-town agitator as can be found in this country."[8]

Commissioner of Public Safety Abram Preiskel required all meetings in the city to obtain a permit, with "the agreement that speakers shall confine

Police arrest woman striker. Almost 900 strikers and supporters were arrested between February 1926 and February 1927. American Labor Museum/Botto House National Landmark.

their remarks to the English language" and "that no meetings are [to be] held without some representative of the police department being present." In early April 1920 the Board of Commissioners (which included Preiskel) forbade "street parades, processions, street assemblies and public meetings" if organizers did not submit to the police "notice of the object, time, place or route of said meeting... and the character, purpose and names of officers or persons... in charge" at least twenty-four hours in advance. When the Amalgamated Textile Workers of America and the ACLU tested this requirement, the police ordered the mill workers at the meeting to leave, and forced the remaining civil libertarians to meet in the dark. When the silk workers struck again in 1924, they and their supporters—including of Roger N. Baldwin, the head of the ACLU—faced court injunctions and arrests.[9]

Anti-Worker Repression in the 1920s

State repression during the strike was not unique, but it was unique that the strikers and their leadership refused to back down. Instead, in the face of such violence, Weisbord and other Communists built massive picket lines to shut down struck mills and extend the strike. These picket lines, along with regular mass meetings, built workers' confidence and sense of power. The leadership's Communist politics made them less susceptible to illusions about the neutrality of the capitalist state and government. As the *Daily Worker* argued in April, "Marx, Engels, Lenin and other theoretical leaders of the revolutionary movement have written in detail about the ramifications of the capitalist state power and exposed it as the dictatorship of the ruling class minority imposed by force against the majority of the population, but nothing ever written has done more to convince the working class of the nature of the judicial branch of the capitalist state than this arbitrary nature of this puppet judge."[10]

The police mobilized against the strike from the start: on January 25, Chief Zober sent twenty-five officers to protect strikebreakers. At first there was no overt violence as hundreds of workers picketed the mills each morning before dawn and then held mass rallies later in the day. On Saturday, February 6, workers prevented strikebreakers from entering several mills at the 2:30 afternoon shift change. The *Passaic Daily News* reported that "the police were not strong enough to fully protect all the workers" who wanted to cross the picket line. One company official complained, "The situation has become serious when outsiders can come here, threaten our people and force them to stay out of work, and work against the workers."[11]

That day more than 20,000 workers, including members of the Amalgamated Clothing Workers, marched in more than a mile-long procession to support the strike. By now, five plants were affected: the Botany Mill and the Garfield Mill, which were shut down; Passaic Worsted, with 400 of 600 workers on strike; the Gera Mill, where the company was trying to keep production even though 900 of 1,200 workers were on strike; and the New Jersey Spinning Works, where "only a few" of the 1,200 workers were on strike.[12]

On Monday, February 8, the police chiefs of Passaic, Garfield, and Clifton announced that they were swearing in officers from all three cities for special duty throughout the strike zone. Clifton chief of police William J. Coughlan threatened strikers: "Get back to Passaic. Get out of Clifton." In Garfield, police arrested two workers: Josephine Zempura in front of the New Jersey Worsted Mill for "being a disorderly person" for using "indecent language" and taking too long to move when ordered by a policemen; and UFC leader Felix Penarisi for "disorderly conduct." Recorder Richard J. Baker of the Garfield Police Court fined Zempura $27.50 and sentenced Penarisi to thirty days in jail but released him on $200 bail pending appeal.[13] The next day, February 9, Clifton police attacked 1,500 strikers—half of them women—while they marched from Garfield to the Forstmann and Huffmann mill in Clifton. This "Battle of Ackerman Bridge" came to symbolize

Police club Passaic strikers. Police regularly attacked and arrested strikers and supporters. American Labor Museum/Botto House National Landmark.

police brutality during the strike, especially after the New York City tabloids covered it extensively.

The ILD, the ACLU, and the United Front in Passaic

Communist organizers and supporters forged a united-front defense to keep the strike from being crushed. As elaborated by the Comintern in 1921, the united front was a tactic for united action (in this case, defense work) between Communists and non-Communists, without downplaying political differences. The ILD and ACLU, supported by the American Fund for Public Service (AFPS, known as the Garland Fund), spearheaded the defense efforts. In April, along with the League for Industrial Democracy and the Federated Press, the ILD and ACLU formed a joint defense committee that provided attorneys to arrested strikers, raised money for bail, fought for the strikers' right to picket and protest, and publicized attacks on the strikers to build public support. The ACLU saw defending workers' rights as central to expanding civil liberties. In contrast, the ILD leadership saw defending strikers as part of the struggle to bring the working class the consciousness it needed to struggle for workers' revolution. James P. Cannon, the ILD's founder, stressed that the ILD was not "merely 'defense workers' collecting money for lawyers." Instead, they were "organizing workers on issues that are directly related to the class struggle." The ILD's goal was that "workers who take part in the work of the I.L.D. are drawn, step by step, into the main stream of the class struggle" and "begin to learn the A.B.C. of the labor struggle."[14]

The Garland Fund was founded by Charles Garland, the son of a wealthy stockbroker. Garland used his inheritance to distribute grants to liberal and leftist causes. The ACLU was founded in 1920 by Baldwin, a sociology professor and reformer sentenced to a year in prison for refusing to be drafted in the First World War. In 1919 he joined the IWW, and worked—as a spy for the union—with William Z. Foster in the steel strike. As director of the ACLU and a leader of the AFPS, Baldwin was well connected to liberals, radicals, and Communists active in the strike.[15]

The ILD was founded in 1925 by Cannon, a former IWW organizer and founding leader of the Communist Party. The ILD combined the IWW's tradition of class-struggle defense with the Comintern's struggle against anti-Communist repression. By January 1926 the ILD had grown to 120 branches and published a monthly journal, *Labor Defender*. The ILD was openly aligned to the Communist Party, and its national committee included leading Communists, along with non-Communist leftists, such as Eugene Debs and Upton Sinclair. The ILD sought to build "a broad mass of dues-paying members into one solid organization, which will stand as a bulwark against capitalist persecution." It appealed to "every worker, every working women [sic], every person interested in labor's cause" to join. By its second convention in the fall of 1926, the ILD claimed to have "20,000 individual members and a collective, affiliated membership of 75,000 workers" in "156 branches throughout the country." By September 1926, according to internal party documents, the ILD had 700 members in Passaic, divided into several language branches.[16]

The first issue of the *Labor Defender*, published in January 1926, gives a sense of the group's focus: there were articles on Sacco and Vanzetti; repression against workers in Pittsburgh; defense of twenty miners in Zeigler, Illinois; defense of imprisoned Communist leader Mátyás Rákosi in Hungary; the jailing of Communist leaders in California and New York; among other cases. The ILD emphasized defending the "105 class-war prisoners in the United States," and sent each one a monthly $5 stipend, and ran a regular "Voices from Prison" column featuring letters from prisoners. The journal was designed to be lively and appeal to workers, with many illustrations and concise articles, instead of dense, jargon-filled articles that proliferated in the early Communist movement.[17]

The Passaic strike was the ILD's first major campaign. Joseph R. Brodsky, a Communist lawyer, oversaw the legal work, and the ILD contracted with two local attorneys, Sigmund Unger and Joseph Feder, to defend the strikers. The ILD saw to it that every arrested striker was represented by an attorney, every conviction was appealed, and few of those arrested stayed in jail for more than a few days.[18]

In 1926 the Garland Fund, the Communists, and the ACLU had overlapping membership, drawn from similar social milieus. Communists or future Communists William Z. Foster, Benjamin Gitlow, Elizabeth Gurley Flynn, and Mary Heaton Vorse were active in the Garland Fund, which provided thousands of dollars to Communist projects, including the ILD and the *Daily Worker*. Much of the early work of the ACLU was defending victimized Communists. ACLU founding members (and future Communists) Flynn and Robert W. Dunn frequently spoke in Passaic and the Garland Fund helped pay for the strike's expenses, including Vorse's salary.[19]

There were fundamental differences between the ACLU's civil libertarianism and the politics of the CP and ILD, although the differences had not been solidified. The ACLU emphasized defending the workers' rights through the court system and lobbying Congress for an investigation into abuses in Passaic.[20] In contrast, the ILD did not believe that workers could find justice in the capitalist courts. As Marxists, the ILD leaders believed that the capitalist state, including the police and court system, maintained the capitalists in power and repressed the working class; only smashing the capitalist state and replacing it with workers' rule could bring justice to workers and the oppressed. The ILD aimed to instill in the working class a Marxist understanding of class society and a sense of its own power. The *Labor Defender*'s first article on the Passaic strike, in April 1926, emphasized, "The International Labor Defense is doing more than fighting to keep these strikers out of jail. It is giving security and encouragement to the strikers and making them feel they are not alone in the fierce fight against the brutal attack by the entire force of the tyrannical ruling class."[21]

The differences were most obvious in the groups' views of the Soviet Union. The ILD saw Soviet Russia as a workers state that had overthrown capitalism through workers revolution and should be defended against opponents and attackers.[22] Baldwin, while initially sympathetic to the Bolsheviks, opposed what he saw as the Soviet government's violation of civil liberties and did not focus on the class nature of the Soviet state. In 1925, relations between the ACLU and the Communists reached a low point when Communists heckled the U.S. tour of Raphael Abramovitch, an anti-Soviet Menshevik, which the ACLU considered an attack on free speech.[23]

During the Passaic strike the groups' differing focuses allowed them to reach a division of labor. As Baldwin wrote to Cannon during the strike, in reference to the relations between the ILD and the ACLU in general: "I am not troubled, as you say, about any issues of theory or principles. Forget that. I want the same results as you do, and I have one crowd to reach and you another,—both of whom should be pulling together in their respective best ways." Two months later, on the eve of the ILD's second national conference, Baldwin wrote to Cannon, denying "any competition between the Civil Liberties Union and the International Labor Defense." "Our joint efforts have demonstrated that we both understand what practical cooperation means." Soon after the Passaic strike, these two trends split apart. During the Sacco and Vanzetti campaign in 1927, the ACLU and ILD worked at cross purposes, highlighting the political differences between those who, in Cannon's words, advocated the "policy of the class struggle" and those who embraced "the policy of 'respectability,' of the 'soft pedal,' and of ridiculous illusions about 'justice' from the courts of the enemy."[24]

Police Harassment of Strikers

The *Labor Defender* observed that "almost every day men and women were arrested" for defending the strike. From the start of the strike until the end of April, there were at least 264 arrests. Several workers were arrested more than once, and Communist militants were frequently police targets. On May 16 the *New York Daily News* noted that Rubenstein had just been arrested for the *seventh* time in four months, and after the strike Rubenstein later claimed to have been arrested *thirty* times. By early October, 776 people had been arrested.[25]

The municipal courts (called police courts) worked hand-in-glove with the police. On February 12, Justices William B. Davidson of Passaic, Richard J. Baker of Garfield, and John C. Barbour of Clifton, met with Chief Zober in Passaic for more than an hour—they denied the meeting had anything to do with the strike, but refused to explain what they were discussing.[26]

One common charge was insulting strikebreakers or police. On February 15 the police arrested J. O. Bentall, a writer for the *Daily Worker*, for "verbal attacks" on the Garfield Police Department at a public meeting. Police repeatedly arrested strikers for calling strikebreakers "scabs," or police "rats" and "cossacks."[27]

On February 20 the police closed Neubauer's Hall in Passaic, the UFC's headquarters. Police claimed that Julia Gulich, a forty-eight-year-old striker, had thrown hot pepper in the face of a strikebreaker and then ran into the hall. Two days later the police allowed the hall to reopen, but Gulich was arraigned and held on $600 bail. In an editorial titled "With Violence Comes Suppression," the *Passaic Daily News* warned: "The strike-breaker is protected by the law more than the striker, for the strike-breaker—if one chooses to call him that—is working and the striker is not."[28]

Almost on cue, the next day Forstmann and Huffmann announced that its two plants would shut down because of a "reign of terror" of supposed striker violence. Preiskel forbade workers to gather in groups outside the struck mills. Rather than retreat, Weisbord promised "firmer and stronger" picket lines and to "not be provoked into violence by police clubs."[29]

On the first day of March, 3,000 people, including strikers and spectators, came out to a march down Dayton Avenue led by Gustav Deak. The police briefly arrested four strikers.[30] The next day the police were more violent. The *Passaic Daily News* reported, "Tear gas bombs and powerful streams of water were brought into play shortly before 5 o'clock ... when 3,000 strikers most of whom came from the mass meeting in Neubauer's Hall, refused to disperse upon the orders given by twelve mounted officers and fifteen on foot." Zober ordered three tear gas bomb attacks on the strikers, then called the fire department, who unleashed high-pressure water. The paper reported: "The strikers ran helter-skelter, in all directions . . . in an effort to get out of the way of the water. Hundreds, however, failed to escape the streams and they were blocked in their attempt by the hundreds who clogged the streets."[31] In response to this attack, Weisbord indicated that he was working with the ACLU to have Preiskel and Zober arrested on assault charges.[32]

At the March 3 meeting of the CEC's textile committee, Weisbord proposed that the Workers Party lead a petition campaign to remove Preiskel and Zober from their posts and pursue a court injunction against them; the textile committee defeated these motions, with the minutes recording that "all these proposals be dropped, that we are opposed to them, and that we cannot as Communists accept such tactics." The minutes did not spell out the reason behind this opposition, but a letter by Ruthenberg in September against another attempt to obtain an injunction warned that "the effort to secure an injunction . . . might lead the workers to rely upon the injunction in place of their activities against the scabs, and if the injunction were not secured it would result in demoralization."[33]

The futility of calling on the court system in Passaic to reform itself was shown on March 6, when Passaic justice of the peace Julius Katz issued warrants to arrest Zober and two patrolmen for assault and battery. Passaic police refused to serve the warrant on their chief, who was home sick. Katz drove to West Paterson to find a policeman willing to serve the warrant. The next day, justice Katz reported having received a death threat.[34]

Unrestrained police violence, especially against reporters and photographers, drove the New York City and national press to sympathize with the strikers. At one point, newspaper reporters appeared in armored cars and airplanes while pickets donned helmets and gas masks.[35] On March 8, Passaic mayor John H. McGuire, the Passaic Chamber of Commerce, and other business and political leaders organized a campaign against what they called "the outrageous attacks upon it by misleading and untruthful statements of the press." At Preiskel's instigation, the mayor appointed twenty-five merchants, doctors, lawyers, and Rotarians to a Committee on Public Information and Accuracy. Such men likely agreed with the *Passaic Daily News* that "mass picketing, as the very term indicates, implies intimidation; intimidation is violence, and violence is unlawful." The Committee soon claimed only 19 people had been arrested, 250 fewer than strike supporters estimated.[36]

Many middle-class groups opposed the strikers. Elks Lodge No. 337 in Passaic passed a resolution supporting police for "enforcing law and order and in their endeavors to preserve these communities from the red flag and its consequences." The Elks announced that delegates from the local Police Benevolent Association (PBA) along with Preiskel would be at an upcoming dinner to discuss the strike; they also invited the mayor and the entire Board of Commissioners.[37] Not surprisingly, the New Jersey PBA backed the local police.[38]

On March 10 Weisbord received a letter, typed in red ink and postmarked the day before, signed by the "Avenging Committee K.K.K." The letter demanded that Weisbord "leave this city at once or drastic action will take place at once." This was no idle threat: in the 1920s the Klan was a mass organization with millions of members. There were 60,000 Klansmen in New Jersey during the 1920s; Passaic, Hudson, and Essex Counties were centers of Klan recruitment. In August 1924 more than 12,000 Klansmen in 3,500 automobiles rode through Bergen County and staged a cross burning. The Passaic strikers symbolized much of what the Klan despised: immigrant and Catholic workers led by a Jewish Communist.[39]

Martial Law in Bergen County

On March 10, four thousand strikers marched from Garfield to the United Piece Dye Workers plant in Lodi where between 500 and 800 workers were on strike. Lodi, like Garfield, is in Bergen County, and the county government was determined to prevent the strike from spreading. County prosecutor Archibald Hart, a Democrat and former U.S. congressman, sent special detectives to Lodi with orders "to arrest every person who creates disorder or attempts a crime, and not to be too technical about it." When Felix Penarisi tried to attend a meeting of United Piece Dye workers, Lodi police chief Henry Witte barred him from entering, although Witte relented when the workers demanded to hear Penarisi.[40]

Soon Bergen County sheriff George P. Nimmo enlisted one hundred special deputies and distributed to them thirty cars and twelve motorcycles, along with riot guns, revolvers, and clubs. Weisbord announced that he would organize 5,000 workers to march to the National Silk Dye Works in East Paterson, Bergen County. Nimmo warned, "We are ready to preserve peace and order in East Paterson. . . . If Weisbord carries out his threat to have his 5,000 there in massed formation, we will bust 'em up with a bang." Nimmo threatened that "singing, shouting and jeering the men at work in the mills" would "be interpreted as disorderly conduct and cause for arrest."[41]

The next day, March 16, Rubenstein led 3,000 strikers in East Paterson. Sheriff Nimmo threatened to read the New Jersey Riot Act and call out the militia "at the slightest sign of disturbance." Nimmo arrested Rubenstein and six strikers. "I'll carry on. Don't worry, Mr. Rubenstein," Nancy Sandosky, a nineteen-year-old Botany striker, declared as she took lead of the march: "Come on, I'll lead you through the police lines." Rubenstein was sentenced to ninety days in jail for disorderly conduct, and the six other strikers were sentenced to thirty days in jail.[42]

Throughout this period, the U.S. Department of Labor tried to convince the strikers to return to the mills without a contract. When this effort failed, the Passaic police stepped up repression. On March 19 the *Passaic Daily News* ran the headline "Police Disperse 1,500 Strikers; Use Clubs, Horse and Motorcycles to Clear Sidewalks." Writing of the "wildest kind of excitement," the paper reported that "during the melee the police used their clubs freely in dispersing the crowds." Police arrested fourteen strikers, five of them women. During their attack, the police smashed a camera belonging to a reporter from the *New York Daily News*, guaranteeing hostile coverage in the New York tabloids. Judge Davidson sentenced six strikers to ten days' jail, fined another $10 plus court costs, and released two on bail. From the bench Davidson stated, "These people must learn one thing, that is, they must be taught to obey officers. The quicker they know that the better it will be for them."[43]

The mill owners and their supporters tried to make Communism, and not mill conditions or police violence, the central issue of the strike.[44] The *Passaic Daily News* reprinted with alarm sections of a Communist Party leaflet: "The police, courts, mayors, and cabinet ministers now in control of the City and National Governments are the agents of the bosses. . . . The workers need a Labor Party, a party of the workers which will oust the politicians of the mill owners, and will put Labor representatives in control of the Government."[45] The police of Passaic and Garfield banned Communist Party meetings in late March. The Klan sent another threat to Weisbord and his "radical friends."[46]

Weisbord and the strike leadership redoubled their efforts to win the strike. At a Garfield demonstration, Weisbord stressed: "The Democracy in this country is a fake democracy. It is a lot of hocus pocus and a lot of sham. The Democracy here is czarism of the bosses."[47]

The police continued their campaign of repression: East Paterson police arrested Sandosky and five male workers at the head of 2,000 strikers. The Garfield police claimed strikers had thrown rocks at the house of two strikebreakers late at night. The next day a fight broke out between thirteen strikebreakers returning from the mills and several strikers. At least nine strikers were arrested. The next day police in Clifton, Garfield, and Passaic arrested thirteen strikers at different picket lines. On Friday, March 26, police attacked a meeting of 2,000 strikers, clubbing and arresting workers. Bail ranged from $350 to $1,000. When representatives of the bakers' union in New York City delivered several truckloads of donated bread, the Clifton police chased them to Garfield, and then arrested the three drivers for speeding and reckless driving. They were released with fines between $47 and $52.[48]

On Monday, March 29, mill owners complained to Passaic mayor McGuire and Commissioner Preiskel that the police were not providing enough protection to strikebreakers. In response, McGuire and Preiskel promised "ample protection" to anybody who wanted to work in the struck mills. That same day, the police attacked 800 strikers and arrested four women strikers, including Sandosky, and four men strikers.[49]

Photo of Albert Weisbord behind bars, from the July 1926 *Labor Defender*. Weisbord was arrested repeatedly. In April 1926 he was held in jail for almost a week on $30,000 bail. (Courtesy Communist Party U.S.A.)

After the attack, the ACLU renewed the push to arrest Zober and other Passaic police officers. Justice Davidson refused to issue warrants, telling an ACLU attorney: "I'll not permit complaints to be taken against any member of the police department for what they do in the line of duty." Instead he argued that the strike's leaders "should have been locked up long ago." He then sentenced four people arrested, some for months in jail.[50]

On April 10—about two and a half months into the strike—the United Front Committee organized a march of 20,000 children and youth. When Passaic police prevented the children from marching, they marched in Garfield instead. Police attacked the children. According to the *New York Sunday News*, the police "cut off four children carrying a 30-foot American flag, and with clubs at their side, charged the other paraders. The children scattered and fled." The police arrested 15 people.[51]

That same day attorneys for Forstmann and Huffmann served notice on the officials of Passaic and Garfield that they would hold the city governments responsible for any losses due to the failure of the police to maintain law and order. In response, the city governments renewed their commitment to protecting strikebreakers. Garfield mayor Burke and Chief of Police John A. Forss formally applied for assistance from Bergen County.[52]

Also on April 10, the Passaic police raided the UFC office, looking for proof of a connection between the strike and the Communist Party. They arrested Weisbord, who was held on $30,000 bail and remained in jail for almost a week. On April 12 sheriff Nimmo read the New Jersey Riot Act to 5,000 strikers outside the entrance to the Forstmann and Huffmann mill in Garfield. The ACLU collected twenty-seven affidavits from witnesses to what happened next. Though the Riot Act stated that those assembled should have at least an hour to disperse, the ACLU summarized, "the sheriff's deputies rushed in, on orders from the sheriff himself, and forcibly dispersed them with butts of guns without allowing them any time to disperse quietly and of their own accord." The police clubbed strikers "without regard to age or sex." One witness described the police clubbing an eight-months-pregnant woman on her own property. Police arrested thirteen people and held them on bail as high as $10,000. "Virtually all of the important strike leaders are now in jail," the New York *Sun* observed.[53]

Bergen County sheriff Nimmo and Passaic County sheriff Charles "Two Gun Charlie" Morgan coordinated efforts to declare "martial law" throughout the strike zone—something that they had no legal power to do.[54] The *New York Graphic* wrote that Sheriff Morgan had "plans to post 150 deputies armed with sawed-off shotguns in Passaic to reinforce the police ranks and suppress any demonstrations that may arise as a result of the edict." At Preiskel's request, Morgan took control of the police efforts in Passaic and announced that he would read the Riot Act there if necessary.[55]

On April 14, strikers held a "free speech" meeting in a hall in Belmont Park in Garfield. When Norman Thomas addressed 200 strikers on private property, the police arrested him after eight minutes for violating the Riot Act. Police held Thomas overnight in Hackensack Jail when he could not pay $10,000 bail, then prevented him from consulting attorneys or talking with the press.[56] The same day, the national media reported on a "race riot" between Italian strikers and Black strikebreakers in Lodi, which resulted in the police arrested eight strikers.[57]

The Death of Franciszek Dyda

On April 14, forty-four-year-old Garfield Worsted Mills striker Franciszek Dyda died, leaving behind a wife and six children, five of them young.[58] According to the UFC, Dyda died after Bergen County sheriff deputies beat him, breaking several ribs, during the attack at Belmont Park. A local doctor sympathetic to the strike who had attended Dyda and the county medical examiner cited heart disease as the cause of death, although news accounts also blamed acute pancreatitis and gall stones. Given these conflicting reports and police animosity toward strikers, many workers referred to his death as murder.[59]

On April 17 more than a thousand mourners overflowed St. Stanislaus's Kostka Roman Catholic Church, down the street from Dyda's home. Thomas De Fazio, a UFC organizer, spoke at St. Nicholas Cemetery: "On this grave of this hero who died in the cause of labor I ask you never to go back to the mills without securing the victory for which he died." The *Textile Strike Bulletin* called Dyda "a martyr to the cause of the workers," and stated: "How much he was clubbed the afternoon before his death and how much that contributed to his untimely death is still to be determined."[60]

Defense and Liberal Popular Opinion

Liberals rallied to defend the strikers. Thomas (now out on bail), the ACLU, and the League for Industrial Democracy organized an emergency committee to raise one million dollars for strikers and strike leaders. Within two weeks they raised $287,000 from forty supporters. Contributors included liberals such as Roger Baldwin ($10,000); New York City attorney and daughter of the Supreme Court justice, Susan Brandeis ($10,000); ACLU attorney Arthur Garfield Hays and his wife ($12,000); New York City housing reformer Ira S. Robbins ($250); the Reverend Nevin Sayre ($10,000); writer Rex Stout ($5,000); Irving S. Ottenberg ($5,000); and *Nation* editor Oswald Garrison Villard ($20,000).[61]

Despite this support, many surety companies did not want to underwrite bail bonds for the prisoners because of pressure from local authorities. Several companies refused to write bail bonds for Thomas, and no company would write a bond for Weisbord except for full collateral. Eventual public pressure forced the surety companies to issue bonds for Thomas and the strikers for the same security as the companies' common criminal customers. Weisbord's bonds were written on collateral of thirty shares of First National Bank stock lent to the defense committee.[62]

Morgan announced that he was moving 350 deputies to Passaic in anticipation of mass picketing.[63] This repression embarrassed many New Jersey politicians. In early March, New Jersey senator Alexander Simpson, a Democrat from Jersey City, introduced a law to allow "peaceful picketing" in labor disputes. With the support of the New Jersey Federation of Labor, the bill passed both houses of the state legislature and was signed by Governor Moore in late March. It is clear that the bill was finally passed, after nineteen years of lobbying by the AFL, because of the strike. Equally clear was that the law would not help the Passaic strikers, thanks to an amendment by Senator Henry Williams from Paterson, that banned "mass picketing." In August a judge ruled that even peaceful picketing "is just as potent as a threat of physical violence," in granting an injunction against a Communist-led campaign to organize waiters in Newark.[64]

Fighting the Court Injunction

By early February, according to the *Passaic Daily News*, judges had issued injunctions against more than a hundred strikers and organizers. In mid-April, Forstmann and Huffmann asked the courts for a broad injunction against the United Front Committee and the strikers. The complaint blamed "one Albert Weisbord, an agitator," for "a campaign of intimidation and threats not only against the workmen who remained at work" in the mills first targeted by the strike, but also the Forstmann and Huffmann mills. "Acting under orders of Weisbord and his lieutenants, large gangs of men and women paraded the streets, blocked the mill gates and all points of ingress and egress, and accosted the operatives going to or from the mills of the complainant, calling them vile names, endeavored by threats and intimidation to dissuade them from working, and produced a state of fear and fright on their part to such an extent that after this had continued for about four weeks many of them became completely demoralized." The complaint alleged "a campaign of organized terrorism" against strikebreakers.[65]

The complaint sought an injunction against the UFC leadership and dozens of named workers from trying to "induce the employees of the complainant to cease their employment to injure the business of complainant," from "advising or consulting with, or encouraging any striking employee of complainant and from contributing money or advice to the said strikers, or toward the success of said strike." The complaint sought to prevent the UFC from organizing or participating in pickets, demonstrations against the mill, talking with workers, or trying to prevent workers from going to work through "intimidation or annoying such employees by annoying language, acts or conduct." Attached to the complaint were several affidavits by strikebreakers claiming harassment by strikers. On April 16, Judge John Bentley of Jersey City granted the company an injunction against some eighty people linked to the UFC, including Weisbord, Rubenstein, Deak, Flynn, Vorse, Sandosky, Chernenko, Penarisi, and lesser-known strike militants. Margaret Larkin, the UFC's director of publicity, who was named in the injunction, quipped, "Under the court's ruling I am enjoined from doing anything at all except perhaps eating my breakfast."[66]

The same day Justice Bentley issued his injunction, Bainbridge Colby, Woodrow Wilson's secretary of state and a New York City lawyer, announced he would argue the ACLU's case that Weisbord should be granted habeas corpus in front of the New Jersey State Supreme Court.[67] The next day the court released Weisbord on $25,000 bail. Five minutes after he was released, Weisbord was arrested on an indictment in Garfield, issued the day before, for inciting a riot and held in Hackensack on another $25,000 bail. Eventually the new bail was reduced to $5,000 and Weisbord was released for the second time the same day, but not until Sheriff Nimmo tried to sneak out the jail's back door to avoid having to take Weisbord's bond. As Weisbord left the Hackensack jail, six detectives served him a copy of Bentley's injunction. Weisbord scoffed at the injunction, calling it a piece of paper designed to break the strike. Sheriff Morgan claimed that this violated the injunction and threatened to arrest Weisbord a third time.[68]

This violence inflamed liberal opinion. The ILD mobilized to turn such outrage into pressure "for the uniting of all Labor and progressive organizations [throughout] the country for [a] unified drive of protest and the provision of adequate defense for those arrested." Cannon declared: "The greatest need of the hour is the immediate organization of a gigantic, united, nation-wide campaign of agitation and protest to wake up the labor movement and throw it into action."[69]

Victor Berger, Socialist Party Congressmen from Wisconsin, introduced a bill to protect First Amendment rights, citing the arrests in Passaic. He sent a telegram to Cannon and the ILD: "The Passaic strike is only one of the many systems of the Mussolinizing of America." Telegrams of support came from other radicals, including Max S. Hays, a labor leader from Cleveland, and Oswald Villard. Upton Sinclair, Daniel W. Hoan, Socialist mayor of Bridgeport, and Reverend David Rhys Williams expressed support to the strikers.[70]

Moore claimed there was nothing he could do to rein in local authorities and warned that if there were "rioting and bloodshed and the local authorities are unable to maintain law and order," he would "invade the strike zone with the armed forces of the State." Moore emphasized that this would "of course, mean the end of the strike, and as far as the strikers are concerned the loss of their cause."[71]

The Defense Committee

In New York City on April 22, the UFC, the ILD, the ACLU, the League for Industrial Democracy, the Federated Press, and strike relief groups organized

Cover of May 1927 *Labor Defender*. The class-struggle defense efforts of the International Labor Defense emphasized class solidarity and connected the Passaic strike to the broader working-class fight for emancipation. (Courtesy Communist Party U.S.A.)

a Joint Committee for Passaic Defense, with Elizabeth Gurley Flynn as secretary.[72]

Sheriff Nimmo insisted that all meetings were illegal so long as Garfield remained under "martial law." Samuel Nelkin, Republican mayor of Wallington, a square-mile borough in Bergen County, offered strikers use of vacant land in his city to meet and vote whether Weisbord should continue to be their leader. As many as 10,000 strikers came out to support Weisbord on April 26.[73]

That same day in Jersey City, the ACLU and Forstmann and Huffmann faced either other in court as Justice Bentley, the former commissioner of public safety in Frank Hague's Jersey City, heard an appeal to his injunction. The hearing attracted the attention of distinguished jurists from New Jersey and the country as a whole. Former New Jersey Republican attorney general and leading corporate lawyer Robert H. McCarter, assisted by his son George, presented Forstmann and Huffmann's case for an injunction. Passaic lawyers Unger and Feder represented the United Front Committee. They were aided by Arthur T. Vanderbilt, a leading Republican jurist who had worked with the ACLU in defending Baldwin and the silk strikers in Paterson in 1924, and future chief justice of the New Jersey Supreme Court; Henry T. Hunt, former Democratic mayor of Cincinnati and current New York attorney; and Alexander Simpson, Democratic New Jersey state senator from Hudson County and Hague ally. Harvard Law professor and future Supreme Court justice Felix Frankfurter submitted a brief against the injunction.[74]

A few days later, on April 30, in defiance of Nimmo the ACLU organized another meeting in Belmont Park in Garfield, featuring Norman Thomas and John Haynes Holmes. For three and a half hours, sixty shotgun-toting police and sheriff deputies blocked 2,000 strikers and sympathizers from entering the park, until at 5:30 P.M. attorneys presented the police with an injunction (signed by Justice Bentley) allowing the meeting to proceed. Weisbord declared the successful meeting "the end of the reign of terror in Garfield."[75]

This points to cracks in the support to police repression. Hart, the Bergen County prosecutor, reportedly opposed Sheriff Nimmo's imposition of "martial law." The director of the Bergen County Board of Freeholders wanted Forstmann and Huffmann to pay the sheriff's costs in Garfield and the National Silk Dyeing Company to pay the costs in East Paterson, underlining the role of the police as agents of the companies.[76]

On May 6 Bentley modified his injunction, relaxing its most draconian aspects but keeping the ban on mass picketing. Even while recognizing that "this strike has been singularly free from acts of violence by the defendants [the strikers] and their sympathizers," he ruled that mass picketing violated the "right" of mill owners to run their plants with scab labor. That this changed little was shown the next day, May 7, when police prevented a small group of strikers from picketing the Forstmann and Huffmann mill in Clifton. In response the UFC announced that it would send a larger picket team to the plant later in the day to test the "arbitrary enforcement of Police Chief Coughlan's interpretation of the law." The UFC statement continued that the union was "sick and tired of having some petty official arbitrarily dictate to us what shall be our American rights." It promised "to have picket lines at the Forstmann and Huffmann mills at any cost."[77]

On May 11 Bentley again modified the injunction, limiting pickets to eight strikers per mill gate, but allowing strikers to talk to anybody willing to listen.

On May 14, after reading from the injunction, police attacked 1,300 picketers outside the Forstmann and Huffmann mill in Clifton. Five strikers were injured in the police charge.[78]

On May 23, fifteen thousand strikers and sympathizers marched through Passaic. The *New York Daily News* reported: "Youths of both sexes marched in their Sunday clothes, with inspired smiles on their faces. Children of all ages followed. Many babies in carriages gurgled happily. Poles, Russians, Hungarians, Italians, Slovaks, marched under the banners of their new country, and the many flags of their old, with the bunting of many churches. They were led by priests of many denominations." The march started in the East Side of Passaic, where most of the strikers lived, and went through the wealthier West Side. They booed Julius Forstmann's house and Preiskel's $50,000 mansion.[79]

On June 1, Bentley dismissed the injunction entirely, but clashes between the police and strikers continued. On June 2, seven strikers were arrested in Lodi outside the United Piece Dye Works. On June 3, Garfield police harassed Jack Moro, a member of the city council and head of the city's police committee, for not moving quickly enough when ordered by the police when he was with picketers outside the Forstmann and Huffmann plant.[80]

On July 7, three hundred businessmen, religious leaders, lawyers, and other prominent men of Passaic, Clifton, Garfield, Lodi, and Wallington met in the district courthouse in Passaic to organize an anti-strike Citizens' Committee to combat "the imported Communistic agitators who are deluding working men with false promises." On July 8, thousands of strikers met in Belmont Park in Garfield to support Weisbord and the UFC and reject the Citizens' Committee.[81]

By this time the police and courts were going all-out to break the strike, including hiring spies and provocateurs. On July 13, police in Lodi police beat Black striker Sam Elan and arrested him for "using indecent language," causing 300 strikers to rally and demand his freedom. On July 17, Garfield Police Court judge Richard J. Baker fined a striker $25 for thumbing his nose at a cop. The justice fumed: "You strikers have declared an open war on the police and law abiding residents of this city and it has become necessary to fight back. . . . You people have been trying to make fools of the police officers and we will stand for it no longer." On July 22, police arrested Gustav Deak at UFC headquarters for supposedly attacking a strikebreaker at home, and charged him with "atrocious assault" and carrying a concealed weapon after they claimed to find a pistol on him. On July 26, police arrested another organizer at UFC headquarters, this time for supposedly firing a revolver at a strikebreaker boarding a bus at 6:30 A.M.[82]

Two days later, Passaic police arrested Weisbord and Rubenstein in an automobile outside of strike headquarters and charged them with possession of a concealed weapon, a large knife. Weisbord denied ever having seen the knife before: "It seems that I am to be visited with every frame-up that the police officers of Passaic can imagine."[83] In early July an unknown "Miss Rosalind Lapnore" filed a $50,000 breach of promise to marry suit against (the married) Weisbord in New York; the case was dismissed three weeks later when the complainant could not be located. Her attorney admitted "Miss Lapnore" had been accompanied to his office by Jacob Nosovitsky, an *agent provocateur* and former informant for the Department of Justice.[84]

Through August the UFC and the AFL negotiated for the United Textile Workers (UTW) to take over the strike. When Weisbord agreed to step aside from the strike and let the UTW take over, the police did not stop their repression, although the number of arrests did not reach their peaks from June and July. On August 23 Chief Zober ordered police to attack pickets outside the Botany mill, claiming that the union's plan to picket each of the plant's nine gates with twelve strikers would have resulted in mass picket lines.[85]

The "Bombing" Campaign

On April 19 a bomb exploded on the porch of the Garfield home of a Forstmann and Huffmann foreman and blew out several windows. There were three other alleged bombings in May at the homes of strikebreakers in Garfield and Passaic. In one the strikebreaker claimed to have exchanged gunfire with his attackers. In May, Weisbord speculated that the police had planted the bombs themselves. The papers reported more bombings of strikebreakers' homes in Clifton and Garfield during June. Although the explosions had not injured anybody, the police warned of a gang of strikers raining terror on strikebreakers. By June 19, after seven homes (mainly in Garfield) had allegedly been bombed, the mills owners offered a $1,000 reward for the bombers. In late August the Clifton police blamed strikers for supposed attacks on the homes of two strikebreakers. Nobody was injured in either attack.[86]

By late September there had been at least twenty alleged bombings, and the governor's office warned that it was considering instituting martial law. On September 22, Clifton policeman (and future chief) Tunis Holster claimed to have seen a group of five men light a bomb outside the house of two strikebreakers. Three of the bombers escaped by car, but Holster arrested two. The same day, police arrested seven men accused of being involved in the bombings: Alex Kostamacha, Paul Ozanak, Tony Pochna, Joseph Bellene, Charles Current, Thomas Regan, and Thomas Winick. Police arrested five more men on September 24: Joseph Toth, Paul Kovacs, William Sikora, Adolf Wisnewski, and Nicholas Schellacci. The accused were held on bail ranging from $25,000 to $100,000, for a total of $350,000.[87]

The mill owners, police, and local papers whipped up a hysteria to vilify the strikers and justify repression. Governor Moore sent the head of the state National Guard to interrogate the prisoners. Garfield mayor Burke cited the bombings in late June to call on Sheriff Nimmo to resume control of the area (although Nimmo refused to do so). The police claimed that some of those arrested had confessed "to the possibility of trying to assassinate President Coolidge and Gov. Moore, because these officials last April refused to deal with delegations representing the strikers," according to the *New York World*.[88]

Some of the men arrested were prominent strikers. Bellene was a member of the union's executive committee and independent candidate for city council. The police had long targeted Thomas Regan; in March he was sentenced to thirty days in jail; in April he was arrested again and sentenced to sixty days; he was arrested in late June and held on $200 bail. Others were just unlucky and were swept up in the dragnet.[89]

The union denied any involvement in the bombings, and there is no reason to believe the police. The Communist Party and the ILD denounced the frame-up of the arrested workers, underlining that the Passaic police were infamous for beating confessions out of suspects and planting evidence. They pointed out that similar police tactics were common in other strikes such as the IWW textile strike in Lawrence in 1912. Robert Dunn highlighted the presence of private detectives in Passaic and suggested that these spies were provocateurs. A union-affiliated doctor reported that the police had broken several ribs of prisoner Paul Kovak, and knocked one of Tom Regan's teeth. Weisbord warned: "In their sheer desperation the mill owners are resorting ever more openly to violence and provocative tactics."[90]

In early October the Communist Party leadership decided that the ILD "should take up the case and start a nation-wide campaign in defense of the workers involved." Ruthenberg suggested that the ILD "revise the united front which was organized at the time of Weisbord's arrest for the defense of the newly arrested strikers." A subsequent issue of the *Labor Defender* denounced the arrests as "another big offensive campaign of the police and courts of the textile district against the strikers." Pointing out that "the facts of the case are few," the *Labor Defender* asserted that the "bombs" were "certain fire-crackers, often used in the district at Italian festivals," and underlined that "not a soul was ever hurt at any time." The ILD argued that the police used the explosions as a pretext to round up and jail at least twenty militants. Then the police beat up the jailed workers to get them to confess.[91]

The prosecution depended on police testimony and confessions— both dubious, given the months-long campaign of police violence. Ozanak described how these confessions were obtained: "The detectives jumped on me, kicked me any place they could, punched, blackjacked me and pummeled me until I was weak and dizzy. Then they gave me a paper to sign. They told me if I would not sign it they would beat me up worse. I cannot read or write English, so I do not know what I signed."[92] According to the defense committee, the police broke three of Toth's ribs, causing so much pain that he "went out of his mind." McMahon, head of the UTW and no friend of the Communists, denounced it as a frame-up. The bombings were convenient for the mill owners; Botany Mills and Forstmann and Huffmann seized upon the bombings as a reason to refuse to settle with the UTW.[93]

In November 1926 ACLU attorney Arthur Garfield Hays defended several of the accused. In early 1927 a Paterson court convicted Bellene, Kostamacha, Ozanak, Pochna, and Sikora and sentenced them to three years in state prison in Trenton. Current, the only nonstriker among the accused, turned state's evidence after claiming to have been beaten by the police; he was sentenced to a year in prison. Adolf Wisnewski was convicted at another trial in early April and sentenced to five to twenty years in state prison, while more than a dozen other strikers were fined from $25 to $100 for involvement in the alleged plot. Police dropped charges against Toth; Schillaci pled guilty to a lesser charger. On March 10 a jury acquitted Regan.[94]

The ILD demanded freedom for the prisoners, and made them part of their monthly stipend program. As the *Labor Defender* put it in May 1927, "The Passaic strike is over, but the struggle to protect the strike prisoners must still be waged to a successful conclusion." In May 1928, Bellene, Pochna, Ozanak, Kostamacha, and Sikora were released from prison after having served sixteen months.[95]

After the Strike

Even after the strike, several strikers and supporters faced legal danger, especially in Sheriff Nimmo's Bergen County. Through 1927 the ACLU and the ILD devoted considerable effort to dealing with bail bonds for those arrested.[96] In April 1927 Rubenstein was jailed for a charge of assault and battery stemming from an attack against him in the Bergen County jail during the strike, and held on $5,000 bail. Rubenstein was convicted in April 1928, sentenced to six months in jail, and fined $500. After the New Jersey State Supreme Court reversed the conviction in March 1928, he was acquitted in a retrial in October 1928; the jury deliberated ten minutes.[97]

In December 1926, as most of the wool workers returned to work, Norman Thomas and the ACLU filed a suit against several Bergen County officials, including Sheriff Nimmo, for his arrest and mistreatment. Nimmo died in May 1927, which removed one of the main obstacles to resolving the Passaic cases in Bergen County. In February 1928 Thomas dropped his suit for false arrest. On July 16, 1928, the ILD and the ACLU succeeded in having charges against 150 strikers dropped, but the authorities refused to drop charges against Weisbord, who remained on $3,000 bail. "We understand the authorities are retaining this one case, not because they intend to try it," Roger Baldwin argued, "but because of pressure on them not to release completely the leader of the strike." Not until January 1930—almost four years after the strike began—did Bergen County drop charges against Weisbord.[98]

7

Building Relief and Solidarity

The Communist Party built solidarity networks throughout the country and organized relief efforts for the strikers and their families during the year-long strike. The *Daily Worker* and foreign-language Communist papers carried articles about the strike in most issues.[1] International Workers' Aid published a pictorial magazine and produced a film, raising awareness (including internationally) and money for the strikers. These efforts aimed to supplement, not substitute for, strong workers' picket lines to shut down production. This chapter examines this relief and solidarity work, and its connections to the Communists' broader politics.

Alfred Wagenknecht, International Workers' Aid, and the Passaic Strike

On February 3, 1926, the Trade-Union Committee (TUC) of the Communist Party's Central Executive Committee (CEC) passed a motion that instructed "the United Front Committee [to] immediately start a wide campaign throughout the textile industry for relief and for the broadening out of the strike." The Communist leadership conceived of relief work as part of an effort to spread the strike to other textile workers and build working-class solidarity. On February 5, William Weinstone, head of the New York district, asked Alfred Wagenknecht to organize relief work. The next week, the CEC Textile Committee passed one motion to establish a strike bulletin edited by Mary Heaton Vorse, and another that Wagenknecht "be introduced to the

General Strike Committee as the representative of International Workers' Aid and is to get the official approval of the strike committee to handle the relief."[2]

The Internationale Arbeiter-Hilfe—alternatively translated as International Workers' Aid (IWA) or Workers' International Relief—was an initiative by the Communist International in the early 1920s to build support for the Soviet Union's anti-famine efforts.[3] Under the leadership of the German Communist Willi Münzenberg, the IWA became a working-class alternative to the Red Cross that provided aid to strikers and their families as well as working-class victims of natural disasters, and organized exhibits of Soviet art in the West to raise money and solidarity for the Soviet Republic. Prior to the Passaic strike the IWA had a low profile in the United States. In the fall of 1925 the group participated in a solidarity campaign to raise money for Chinese workers and another for Irish workers and farmers facing starvation.[4]

Wagenknecht, then in his forties, was a tested Communist cadre who had withstood repression and was not interested in the spotlight. With C. E. Ruthenberg, Wagenknecht (called "Wag") had been a left-wing leader of the Ohio Socialist Party and was convicted, with Ruthenberg, for opposing the First World War. In 1919 he became a charter member of the Communist Party. By the time of the strike he had found a niche among the ranks of the faction led by William Z. Foster and James P. Cannon, but he was not a central factional figure.[5]

Wagenknecht was a skilled fundraiser who connected relief work to the broader class struggle. In the early 1920s Wagenknecht was secretary of the Friends of Soviet Russia (an earlier incarnation of the IWA) and, according to historian Theodore Draper, "won . . . a lasting reputation as the party's champion money-raiser." Wagenknecht spelled out his view of the role of relief during a miners' strike in 1928: "Relief can lose a strike as well as win it." The key, he stressed, was to link relief to militancy: workers should see collecting relief as part of the struggle to win the strike, not as charity that demobilizes them from the strike. Every day Wagenknecht took the commuter train to Passaic from Manhattan early in the morning and returned at 11 P.M. He played a central role in the strike and served on the ten-person executive committee along with Weisbord and other Communists. Not interested in personal glory, he usually stayed in the strike headquarters, allowing other leaders to become the public face of the strike.[6]

Using donated goods and labor from union workers, especially from New York City, Wagenknecht created a system of "stores" that provided food and clothing to workers. The bakery workers' union in New York donated several truckloads of bread, clothing workers' unions donated 20,000 pounds of sugar, and other unions donated shoes and clothing. Based on the size of their families, workers were allowed a certain amount of "purchases" at the relief store, punched on cards issued by the relief committee. The committee organized a shoe store to repair strikers' shoes worn down by picketing, medical workers to provide free services, and barbers who provided free haircuts on Fridays. The Relief Committee provided coal to families in need. There were five coffee and sandwich stands where strikers could "spend" relief funds after picketing duty.[7]

Along with the United Council of Working-Class Housewives, the IWA set up four kitchens in Passaic that fed thousands of strikers and their families. Communists organized alternative schools for the strikers' children, a playground, "Camp Victory," and several summer camps. By late March, between 2,500 and 3,000 families were receiving relief, costing $10,000 weekly.[8]

The goal of these relief efforts was to enable strikers to remain on strike by providing them and their families with food and other necessities. "No family in need of food has been turned away from the relief committee without aid," the *Textile Strike Bulletin* announced in March. "The bosses shall not starve the workers back," the article declared. "There are 40,000,000 workers in America who will answer the bosses with funds for the strikers."[9]

Like much of the Passaic strike, relief work drew upon the tradition of the IWW in the Lawrence and Paterson textile strikes.[10] Relief appeals stressed the importance of the working class as a whole supporting the Passaic strikers: "Now listen—*Food Will Win This Strike!* Send us money for food *at once* and we will beat the bosses and together we will win one of the biggest and best strikes in labor history! *Act!*"[11] Rank-and-file workers donated money even though the anti-Communist AFL leadership opposed the UFC's relief efforts. The New York City garment workers unions donated tens of thousands of dollars. The Amalgamated Clothing Workers' union urged its membership to donate one day's wage; the International Ladies' Garment Workers, the Fur Workers, and the Cloth, Hat, Cap and Millinery Workers unions all donated money. The American Shoe Workers, the Window Cleaners, and the Bakers' Union Local 100 contributed. The Chicago Typographical Union Local 16 donated $1,000.[12] Supporters organized tag-day sales and bazaars, concerts and collections at street corner demonstrations.

Relief Conferences

Relief committees were organized in more than twenty cities between February and early April, including in industrial centers such as Buffalo, Detroit, Minneapolis, Philadelphia, Pittsburgh, St. Louis, and Youngstown. The General Relief Committee built a "Support the Passaic Strike" conference in Passaic itself on May 29, stressing, "The bitter fight being waged against us by the textile barons is a fight against all of labor, against labor unionism. . . . If we win, you win. If we win, organized labor wins." According to the *Textile Strike Bulletin*, 197 delegates attended a general relief conference in New York City in June, representing organizations with 500,000 members, including unions of clothing workers, photographic workers, marine and transport workers, carpenters, pressmen, food workers, machinists, and fraternal organizations. Later in June, 250 organizations sent delegates to a "Support the Passaic Strike Conference" in New York City.[13]

On July 2, delegates from several unions met in New York City to organize aiding the strike. A similar meeting was held several days later in Pittsburgh, followed by meetings in Buffalo, Chicago, Cleveland, Detroit, Milwaukee, St. Louis, Toledo, and Youngstown. Organizers from the local United Mineworkers of America and the AFL organized two relief conferences in Brownsville, a small town in Western Pennsylvania. Besides raising thousands of dollars, these meetings reinforced the idea that the struggle of the Passaic workers was the struggle of the entire working class.[14]

In early March the American Civil Liberties Union and the League for Industrial Democracy organized the Emergency Strikers Relief Committee, whose board included Norman Thomas (chairman), Roger Baldwin, Lillian Wald, Elizabeth G. Flynn, and Communist Clarina Michelson (secretary). The American Fund for Public Service paid the salaries of Vorse and Flynn, and also donated money for strike publicity and research, as well as for attorneys' fees. The New York *Forward*, a Yiddish paper sympathetic to the Socialist Party, donated $1,500 to the relief effort. Appeals to liberal sympathizers differed in tone from those to workers. "Your help in the past has been a large factor in keeping the strikers encouraged and helping them win in their plucky fight," read one letter to donors in May. "A little more and they will probably win."[15]

Local merchants donated, reflecting sympathy with their customers. An owner of a leather goods store recalled decades after the strike that by helping the strikers, "everybody knew they were cutting their own throat, but everybody also knew what a bum deal the strikers had been given." Thus "we stood by the strikers and extended credit. That was our way of fighting for the human dignity that Johnson refused to give the workers." By early March the Gold Star Merchants Association of Clifton had donated more than $1,000. The *Textile Strike Bulletin* carried advertisements for local businesses until April. For example, the March 22 issue had advertisements for fruits and vegetable sellers, an auto supply store, several clothing stores, and a restaurant.[16]

Although the *Textile Strike Bulletin* printed lists of weekly donations, there is no way to know exactly how much was donated. At the height of the strike, the Relief Committee collected between $10,000 and $15,000 weekly. Communist textile leader J. J. Ballam claimed that more than $700,000 was collected (the equivalent of more than $10 million dollars today), a figure that Morton Siegel determined was believable. The Relief Committee did not make its books public, but they were audited by an outside auditor and nobody at the time claimed that the Relief Committee misappropriated funds.[17]

Building a Cultural Front for Solidarity

In a pamphlet written during the strike, William Z. Foster stressed: "An essential of good strike strategy under present day conditions in the United States is to lend a dramatic character to strikes and organization campaigns, especially those among unorganized workers." In her *New Masses* article, "The Battle of Passaic," Mary Heaton Vorse wrote: "So many extraordinary things happened at Passaic at that time, one could write a play in ten shocks, a thrill in every shock, called *Chief Zober and the Picket Line*." Drama had been central to the strike from the beginning, including the union's mass picket lines and demonstrations. In March, male strikers marched in helmets and gas masks from the war to emphasize police violence, while a woman striker led the march with a baby carriage to underline the importance of mothers in the strike. Sara Fanny Simon described "a dramatic strike" in which "the strikers were acting a living drama." Besides their immediate aims, mass meetings, mass picketing, parades, and demonstrations drew workers and their families deeper into the strike and combated passivity.[18]

As the strike entered its ninth week in late March, the UFC had the difficult task of maintaining momentum and support. Wagenknecht wrote to his family in mid-May: "The textile strike is marking time. Nothing BIG is happening and so the newspapers have shut down on the stories about the strike considerably. I hope it is not lost by a mere petering out. I like things to die dramatically." He noted that the strike leadership was beginning a campaign to raise money and food for the strikers' children to re-energize the strike. He added: "Then, also, we have a movie on tap, are getting out the pictorial, are to issue first million leaflets."[19]

The strike resonated with writers and artists. Louis Zukofsky wrote a poem at the time, "During the Passaic Strike of 1926," that referred to the strike: "For Justice they are shrewdly killing the proletarian,/For Justice they are shrewdly shooting him dead." In March, drama students from the Brookwood Labor College traveled to Passaic and performed *Shades of Passaic: A Dramatic Study in Expressionism*. In July, according to the *Daily Worker*, the strikers' entertainment committee invited the Philadelphia-based Workers' Theater Alliance to perform two plays.[20]

Several artists and intellectuals contributed directly to the workers' cause, including labor journalist Mary Heaton Vorse, who edited the weekly *Textile Strike Bulletin* and wrote sympathetic articles about the strike that appeared in various publications. One was published in the first issue of the *New Masses*, a cultural magazine established by supporters of the Communist Party that spring. The journal's second issue in June carried "A Passaic Symposium: Snapshots of the Textile Strike." The introduction noted that the "symposium printed here consists of snapshots of the Passaic strike by New York liberals and radicals, who were stirred from their usual occupations by the strike, and went out to Passaic to show their solidarity with the workers." It added: "Some of them were arrested, others were a trifle manhandled, and all of them learned a great deal about the kind of justice handed out to workers who strike." Contributors included Robert Dunn, John Dos Passos, Margaret Larkin, Marguerite Tucker, Grace Lumpkin, Arthur Garfield Hays, Esther Lowell, and Norman Thomas.[21]

The mobilization of intellectuals and artists for left-wing and labor causes constituted part of what art historian Andrew Hemingway called "a grand project to form an alternative American culture." This was a precursor to what became in the 1930s, under the popular front, what Michael Denning called a cultural front. The most visible examples of this were a pictorial booklet, *Hell in New Jersey*, and a film about the strike.[22]

In late March, Wagenknecht wrote to his wife that he and Beatrice Carlin, former wife of the Socialist attorney who had defended Eugene Debs in Atlanta, were "at work for getting out a pictorial magazine of pictures of the strike." Eugene Lyons, then sympathetic to Communism, worked on the pamphlet as well.[23.]

The forty-eight-page booklet emphasized photographs over text, reflecting an aesthetic shared by the International Labor Defense's *Labor Defender*. Many of the photos depicted strikers on the picket lines, marching, and otherwise acting collectively. There were several photos of police attacks on workers. There were photos of many of the strike leaders and activists, including Weisbord, Jack Rubenstein, Lena Chernenko, and Nancy Sandosky, but they were usually shown as part of a mass or being arrested.

The booklet's text told the story of the strike from its origins. It stressed the "powerful picket lines—singing and waving banners—young and old—a sea of nationalities represented." The text and photos presented to the reader the poverty of the workers and their poor living conditions. Rather than being portrayed as passive victims, the strikers were shown fighting. "The strike of the textile workers in Passaic and vicinity is one the most significant episodes in the American labor movement," the pamphlet declared. "The spectacle of the Passaic strikers' courage and spirit should hearten all labor."

The booklet was explicit in its purpose. "Take These Pictures of the Textile Strike to Your Shop," one box in the pamphlet commanded. "Spread the lessons and pictures of the textile strike among all workers," it continued. Readers were urged to order bulk copies—bundles of one thousand cost $120—and sell them to workmates. "And as you show these pictures to others, as you interest others in the heroic struggle of these exploited and persecuted textile workers, *remember to collect dollars for relief.*" Another box insisted, "Every Worker Should See 'Hell in New Jersey'." The last page, under the headline, "Not Back to Hell—But on to Victory!", was a sign-up sheet for contributions to the General Relief Committee.

Wagenknecht urged attendees of the Support the Passaic Strike Conference, held in New York City in late June, to "sell *Hell in New Jersey*," noting,

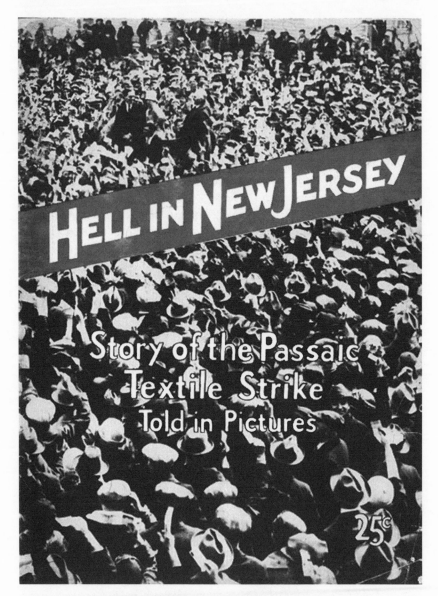

To build solidarity, the General Relief Committee published *Hell in New Jersey*, a 48-page booklet featuring photos from the strike and text written by Eugene Lyons. Strike supporters sold 150,000 copies to workers and sympathetic unions throughout the country. General Relief Committee of Textile Strikers.

"Every time a Pictorial is sold a meal is bought for a strikers' child." "For the first time in the history of labor struggles," declared the Federated Press, "the 16,000 textile strikers have placed before interested workers and others a pictorial review of their situation, during the actual progress of a strike." An advertisement in the *Textile Strike Bulletin* stated that the booklet "should be placed in every workers home" and that "All Unions, Workers' Fraternal Organizations, Sympathizers should order a bundle to sell to their membership." Lyons claimed that 150,000 copies of the pamphlet were sold.[24]

A letter published in the *South Bend Tribune* in July described how labor and fraternal organizations met in the Indiana city "to discuss ways and means of aiding the textile strike." Delegates bought copies of the pamphlet, and decided to sell the pamphlet to raise money and support. In July several supporters made a "short tour of Connecticut in a laundry truck for the Passaic strikers," where they sold more than a hundred copies of the pamphlet. Dozens of copies were sold in Arnold, Pennsylvania, outside of Pittsburgh, at a picnic for the strikers. In August, union members in Detroit bought over 600 copies of the pamphlet in one week.[25]

Enemies of the strike hated the booklet. In Passaic in early July, the Citizens' Committee denounced the "slanderous publication of a vicious pamphlet, filled with lurid photographs, misleading figures and false propaganda." Governor Moore, speaking to the Passaic Rotary Club later that month, pointed to the pamphlet as an example of lying propaganda about the strike.[26]

The Passaic Textile Strike Film

The IWA produced a seven-reel silent film, *The Passaic Textile Strike*.[27] As historian Steven Ross put it, the film "was an important cinematic bridge between the melodramas of earlier worker-made films and social realism that was to dominate radical films of the 1930s."[28] Communists used the film to build solidarity with the strikers by creating a sympathetic narrative of the strike and raising money and support for the strikers among the labor movement. The Communists tapped into radical traditions—such as IWW attempts to use spectacle to build support for strikers in the Paterson Pageant of 1913.[29] The IWA drew upon earlier films that it and its sister organizations had produced to raise awareness about famine in the Soviet Union; they also drew upon a tradition of labor movies in the United States.[30]

Wagenknecht and the IWA hired a professional director and film crew.[31] When these professionals failed to produce the desired film, the relief committee asked a strike sympathizer to take over, "then brought a movie camera and a projector, got together a staff from the strikers and photographed the real happenings."[32]

The film is divided into two parts.[33] The twenty-six-minute "prologue," derivative of Upton Sinclair's *The Jungle* (1906), tells the story of the Breznac family. (Although the Breznacs were a real family, the account in the film appears to be fictionalized.) In the film, Stefan Breznac had migrated from Poland and found a job in a textile mill in Passaic and in 1907 sends for his sweetheart. In 1925, after Stefan's wages are cut, their fourteen-year-old daughter, Vera, goes to work in the mills. Vera catches the eye of the big boss,

Mulius (a composite of Julius Forstmann and Colonel Charles F. H. Johnson), who takes advantage of her and then fires her. This causes Stefan to work sixty-six hours a week to make up the shortfall in family income, and causes him to collapse from overwork. Despite a doctor's orders for two weeks' rest in bed, Stefan returns to work. He becomes a supporter of attempts to organize a union, but within days the overwork kills him. The last part of the prologue is a semi-fictionalized account of Gustav Deak's attempt to organize a union and the start of the strike at Botany.

Much of the remaining section of the film is composed of images of leaders of the UFC speaking, interspersed with footage of mass picketing and strike meetings. The film includes footage of police violence against the strikers—including unique images of the police attacking the strikers, filmed from a rooftop because the police had attacked newspaper reporters and photographers. While denouncing the brutality and violence by the capitalist state, the film celebrates the creativity and determination of the workers. The film asserts: "We will not be clubbed back into the mills, we will not be starved into submission; the American Labor Movement is behind us."[34]

Significant portions of the film focus on children, young workers, and women. The film highlights the relief "stores" and playgrounds that the IWA organized. The film informs the audience that the General Relief Committee distributed more than five million loaves of bread, more than a million pounds of potatoes, along with large amounts of spaghetti, rice, tomatoes, pork and beans, pea beans, sugar, meat, milk, and cheese. The "flood of donations was the loyal answer of the American Labor Movement" to the urgent need for relief. Strikers must collectively take care of one another and workers outside of Passaic must collectively support the strike: "They are all children of the working class whom the working class must support."[35]

Again and again the film emphasizes solidarity: "The Passaic strike of 1926 has demonstrated the splendid solidarity of the American working class. From over the nation the leaders of labor have brought the lessons learned in other struggles, have brought messages of cheer to sustain courage and hard cash to feed those soldiers in labor's battle." As the film is ending, it quotes Ben Gold, a Communist leader in the furriers' union: "Your task is but a part of the greater task of American labor. Millions of unorganized workers in steel and oil and rubber and textiles are looking to you for inspiration. Your victory in Passaic is the beginning of their nation wide triumph." As these quotes indicate, the film alternates between addressing the strikers in Passaic and the working class as a whole. This dissolves the division not only between audience and the drama, but between different sections of the working class.[36]

The production of a film by the strikers was an attempt by the strike leadership to control the strike's story to build solidarity. The *Daily Worker* underlined how the police tried and failed "to prevent this celluloid record of their

The International Workers' Aid ran relief "stores" that provided food to strikers and their families, allowing them to hold out in year-long strike. Unions from throughout the metropolitan area donated money, services, and products in solidarity with the strikers. American Labor Museum/Botto House National Landmark.

atrocious brutality against the girl pickets and even the children of strikers" and how the mill owners would "take no pleasure in these motion picture photographs of their misconduct."[37]

The *Daily Worker* described the film's showing to an audience of strikers in Garfield: "They were packed into Belmont park, the same park that was closed by an officious sheriff months ago, and had to be reopened because even the courts decided this was too raw a violation of the law, and as far as I could see the only reason there weren't sixteen thousand instead of ten was that there wasn't room." As the audience members recognized strike leaders, locations, and their fellow workers, they called out their names. According to a front-page article in the *Passaic Daily News*, when the film opened several days later at a normal cinema in Passaic it was shown twice to a "capacity house," and then continuously from 2 P.M. till 11 P.M. for two days.[38]

The Passaic Strike Film and Solidarity

In August the UTW leadership agreed to accept the Passaic strikers as UTW Local 1603 on the condition that Weisbord and other Communists withdraw from the strike (see chapter 9). The leadership of the UTW demobilized the workers and criticized the militant tactics of the UFC. These developments did not diminish the political importance of the strike or eliminate the need for relief work. "Reports of the settlement negotiations now going on," Wagenknecht declared in early August, "should not be permitted to slow up relief." There was no guarantee the negotiations would be successful, and "even if the settlement negotiations take up less time than is anticipated, the General Relief Committee will be compelled to issue relief cards for several weeks after the workers have returned victorious to the mills." The August issue of the *Textile Striker* declared that "strike relief must be kept up and *intensified*" during negotiations. In September the new UTW local requested that the General Relief Committee "continue to function in the relief field."[39]

Excluded from the strike itself, the Communist Party shifted focus to relief work and building support for the Passaic strikers. Despite their dislike of the Communists and their method of organizing the strike, the UTW leadership could not end the relief work. Sara Conboy, secretary of the UTW, admitted that the relief work in Passaic was "the most splendid piece of organization work I have ever seen" and called Wagenknecht "a financial genius." The Lauck Committee spearheaded by economist W. Jett Lauck in the summer and fall to bring the strikers into the UTW (see chapter 9), hoped to up a relief organization more palpable to the UTW and liberals, but was unable to do so.[40]

In late August, Ruthenberg spoke to a picnic of 2,700 people in Hartford, Connecticut. Among the other speakers were a "Mrs. Smith" (likely Vera Buch) representing the Passaic strikers, and J. O. Bentall from the Passaic Relief Committee. A large concert in late August that the Relief Committee organized in Coney Island, Brooklyn, drew 20,000 people and raised $100,000. After Weisbord left Passaic, Wagenknecht (in the words of the *Daily Worker*) "warned organized labor that the Passaic strike was not yet over, as the mill-barons had so far refused to deal with the United Textile Workers." He urged workers to continue to donate to relief work. Later that month, the *Daily Worker* criticized UTW-head Thomas F. McMahon for seeking friendlier relations with the mill owners. "Relief activities will continue to be carried on by the old Passaic Strikers' relief committee," the Communist paper assured its readers at the end of its article.[41]

The Passaic film was central to this work. The *Daily Worker* announced the film in mid-September: "Nothing will so simply, graphically and vividly bring home the big strike and its lessons to the working class as will this gripping motion picture of strike events as they occurred." Several days later, the paper stressed that the film "should receive the whole-hearted support" from "every intelligent worker, both because of its educational value and its help to Passaic strike relief." The *Daily Worker*'s film column emphasized that "you can do a service to the labor movement by starting the wheels going to have it shown in your city" and urged readers to write to the Passaic strike relief committee in Passaic. A box advertising the film in the *Daily Worker* stressed that the film "should be shown in every locality where groups of the 20,000,000 unorganized workers slave away day after day, at the mercy of the organized employers, without the protection of a labor union." It urged readers to "arrange for a showing in your city—at your organization—in your hall or in any motion picture house available."[42]

The film underlined that the cause of the strike was low pay and poor conditions in the mills, not Communism. At the same time, because many of the leaders whom the film spotlighted were sympathetic to the Communist Party, the film emphasized that Weisbord and the UFC had provided leadership to these workers when nobody else would. (The film never mentioned the Communist Party itself by name.)

In its announcement for the film, the Passaic UTW claimed that the film "represented the biggest thing done by labor in a long time." A press release issued by the union stated that the film "has the endorsement of organized labor throughout the country and of many prominent people in the liberal movement." Notices in the *Daily Worker* and the union's press releases detail the wide distribution and showing of the film in working-class communities throughout the country. The film was shown throughout the United States, often in two cities on the same day. In early November the *Daily Worker* claimed the film would be shown in twenty cities within a month. By January the film had made its way as far as California. Communist textile leader John J. Ballam estimated that by late January 1927, picture showings had raised nearly $30,000—the equivalent of more than $440,000 today.[43]

Typically, local labor unions and a local relief committee co-sponsored the showings; venues included halls of ethnic organizations, large cinemas, and meetinghouses. Local unions bought blocks of tickets, and the local projectionists' and musicians' unions donated the labor of their members at the showings. It was common for the film to be shown for several hours continuously, often with music and dancing. Funds raised were dedicated to relief efforts for strikers and their families. By dissolving the division between the audience and the drama on screen, the film brings the working-class viewers into the class struggle.

Throughout March 1927 the *Daily Worker* ran an announcement by the General Relief Committee that indicated that "although the strike is almost over, [the textile mills] are taking the workers back very slowly, with the result that thousands of families are without means of existence." The committee noted it was "maintaining a few food stores in Passaic," and appealed to supporters who had "taken out milk coupons to send in their money as soon as possible, no matter how much you have collected." On March 10 the *Daily Worker* ran an article under the headline "Relief Is Still Needed in Passaic Region; Most of the Workers Not Yet Returned." In early April the UTW local in Passaic organized a meeting to demand government aid for textile workers who remained unemployed despite the strike settlement.[44]

With the strike over, Communist attention turned elsewhere, particularly to the growing international struggle to free Nicola Sacco and Bartolomeo Vanzetti. Most Communists, including those active in Passaic, threw themselves into the campaign, using connections and the influence they gained from the strike. Even as the Passaic strike faded from memory, and the strike film lay forgotten, the type of publicity and relief efforts developed during the strike became central to future struggles.[45]

8

Women, the Family, and
the Passaic Strike

In late July 1926 the *Daily Worker* reported that the police had just arrested nineteen-year-old Nancy Sandosky for the twentieth time. Leading strikers in the face of police terror, she became a symbol for the strike, causing one paper to call her "the outstanding girl leader of the strike" and others to label her the strikers' Joan of Arc. To the United Front Committee and the Communist Party she represented the bravery and determination of women workers. In the spring of 1926 she toured the Midwest to raise money for the strikers. In Chicago on May Day, she shared a platform with William Z. Foster.[1]

The *New York Times* trivialized her as "Weisbord's girl aid." Even her last name is rendered inconsistently. Born Nancy Shedosky in Passaic, the daughter of Polish immigrants (who also used the name Sidorski), she grew up in Garfield with several siblings. She does not appear to have been a Communist or an activist before the strike. Nor does she appear to have remained politically active after the strike, although she continued working in the mills. She died in 1983, at age seventy-five; her last address was in Garfield. The *Passaic Herald-News* ran a short notice of her death that did not mention the strike.[2]

In the *Passaic Textile Strike*, Mary Heaton Vorse, writing of strike meetings, observed that "The unusual thing about these [strike] meetings is the number of women.... Young women, pretty rosy girls, older women, tired women." Later Vorse described a striker, Anna Breznac, a Czechoslovak immigrant and mother: "A lifetime spent the service of the mills, piling up money for somebody else. At the end of all these years of effort, nothing to show for it except for nine children."[3]

The *Textile Striker Bulletin* listed Breznac and Sandosky as members of the strike committee. Breznac was part of a strikers' delegation to Washington in March. In April, Breznac and four other strikers went to Jersey City to picket the home of U.S. Senator Edward I. Edwards. Like Sandosky, Breznac disappeared from public view after the strike: the 1940 Census indicates that she lived in Passaic, working in a mill making woolen goods. Breznac died in April 1976, fifty years after the strike, seventy-one years old, without an obituary.[4]

Women like Sandosky and Breznac were active in the strike, beaten and arrested by the police alongside their male coworkers. Between February and April 1926, the police made 264 arrests of strikers and activists; 75 (28 percent) were women. When a judge issued an injunction against some 80 strikers and sympathizers in April, more than a third of those listed were women. "Without the women," Albert Weisbord wrote, "the strike would have been lost long ago." Their story underlines the liberating effect of the strike on women workers, from what one journalist called "the shawled women of Passaic," to workers' leaders.[5]

This chapter examines the role of women and children in the strike, and how the strike leadership—especially the Communist Party—addressed what Communists described as the "woman question," or the fight against women's oppression. The strike highlighted the ability of many women Communists and showed the Communists' determination to organize women workers. The strike also provides an opportunity to examine how Communists approached young workers. In Passaic, Communists addressed education, childcare, and family, but only in a semiconscious way, not drawing theoretical conclusions from their activity. The strike depended on women strikers and activists at all levels, but most of the Communist Party and UFC leadership was male. Had the leadership connected the strike to the fight for women's oppression in a concrete way or provided a clearer analysis of women's oppression under capitalism, they might have been able to draw more women into the strike leadership and into the broader Communist movement, just as they attracted many young workers.

The Labor Movement, Women, and the Family

By the 1920s, three out of ten wage-earning women worked in factories.[6] But in 1920 union membership was 92 percent male, and more than 93 percent of women workers were unorganized. Several AFL unions refused to organize women, but in the first fifteen years of the twentieth century, unprecedented numbers of women workers, many of them immigrants—most notably in the garment industry—mobilized in what historian Annelise Orleck called "the most intense period of women's labor militancy in U.S. history."[7]

These strikes politicized a generation of working-class women and expanded the terrain of class struggle to include broader social, gender, and family questions. In the Lawrence, Massachusetts, textile strike in 1912, the Industrial Workers of the World (IWW) organized grocery stores and kitchens for strikers and a "children's exodus" of strikers' children to sympathetic families elsewhere.[8] During a strike by largely women white-goods workers in New York City in 1913, prominent Socialist Rose Pastor Stokes opened five free lunch rooms for strikers.[9]

Unlike some unions, the United Textile Workers (UTW) was not overtly hostile to women workers, and even employed Melinda Scott, a former garment unionist in New York, as an organizer. Still, the UTW's emphasis on skilled workers excluded most women workers. In 1927, of 471,000 women textile workers, only 20,000 were unionized.[10]

Women constituted half of the workforce in Passaic. Women held less-skilled jobs, including wool sorting, scouring, and operating machines. Ninety-five percent of bundlers, menders, and cloth inspectors were women. According to one report, two-thirds of women workers at Botany earned between $14 and $22 per week in 1925, while 47 percent of male Botany workers earned between $24 and $28 per week.[11]

The investigators interviewed women strikers and concluded, "Women go into the mills in order to make the family income sufficient to support the family, and they work on the night shift in order to be at home during the day to take care of the children, cook, clean house, do the washing, etc. Many of them work 9-1/2 to 10 hours with little or no time for lunch or rest." Often both parents would work alternating shifts. Passaic parents had more children to care for than elsewhere: an average of five children per family compared to the America average of three. Passaic was so synonymous with working mothers that the Department of Labor commissioned a study of Passaic, *The Family Status of Breadwinning Women*, published in 1922. This study found that "the woolen and worsted mills employed a much larger proportion of married or once-married women than did the other factories."[12]

The Communist Party and the "Woman Question"

The Passaic strike underlines that the Communist Party was more advanced than most of its contemporaries in the labor movement on the woman question, and at the same time it highlights Communists' limitations. The Bolsheviks, basing themselves on Friedrich Engels' *The Origin of the Family, Private Property, and the State*, argued that women's oppression was the oldest form of social inequality in history, was rooted in private property, and would be ended only through the destruction of class-divided society with the goal of laying the material basis for the creation of a international communist society. Engels saw the family as the social institution that oppressed women. Communists sought to replace the family by collectivizing the raising of children and making marriage (and other family relations) a purely voluntary arrangement that could be ended at will. Although women's liberation (like much else) in Soviet Russia was hindered by poverty and backwardness, the Bolsheviks implemented measures giving women full legal equality. In 1919 the Russian Communist Party established a special department of the Central Committee dedicated to work among women. The Bolshevik leadership sought to make women's liberation central to Communist parties throughout the world. A resolution at the Comintern's Third Congress (1921) instructed all Communist parties to fight for women's liberation, create special party bodies to reach women, and emphasize the unity of male and female workers in the class struggle.[13]

Although the American Communist Party was organized amid a decline in women's activism after the ratification of the Nineteenth Amendment giving women the right to vote in 1920, the early party recruited several women from the Socialist Party—such as Ella Reeve Bloor, Rose Pastor Stokes and Charlotte Anita Whitney—who had been active on women's issues. Communists in the United States maintained the Comintern's focus on women's equality within the working class and the need to organize women workers but downplayed the special nature of women's oppression, including questions of family and sexuality.[14]

In 1922, in response to this Comintern insistence, the Central Committee of the American CP established a women's bureau, which organized the United Council of Working-Class Housewives (UCWCH) as a united front of several women's organizations. By 1924–1925, just before the Passaic strike, women constituted 10 to 15 percent of the party's membership, or 1,700 to 2,500 women comrades.[15]

Some historians have argued that the Communist Party's focus on heavy industry in the 1920s excluded women from the party's vision of the working class. But in fact, the first major Communist-led strikes were in the textile and garment industries, which had many women workers. As Rosalyn Baxandall pointed out, for all its problems on the women question "the CPUSA empowered women" because "for many working-class and immigrant women in North America, the Communist Party opened up new horizons, providing opportunities for activism in both their jobs and communities."[16]

The early Communist Party struggled to find a balance between focusing on the exploitation women workers faced as workers and the oppression they faced as women. In an article written for International Women's Day in 1925, the *Daily Worker* urged women to support the Communist movement and warned: "The proletarian women must know that there is no such thing as a separate 'women's question'." A few months later the paper offered a more nuanced approach, asserting that "Women are on the whole more exploited than men, their economic organization is weaker, they are more limited by family ties." The article continued that the Communists "must have special women's campaigns, as for instance campaigns for organizing women into trade unions, for equal wages for equal work, against high rents, for sanitary conditions in homes and shops, better conditions for the children in the schools, etc."[17] The Passaic strike offered a chance to connect the social oppression of women to their class exploitation—an opportunity that the CP only partially seized.

Communists and the Woman Question in the Passaic Strike

On a rhetorical level the Communists paid special attention to women in the strike. Weisbord, in his pamphlet on the strike, wrote: "From the start of the strike the union had made special efforts to educate and awaken the women."[18] Nonetheless, there were weaknesses in the Communists' approach.

Although the *Young Worker* ran a list of demands specific for young workers, there was no similar list for women.[19] The strike demand for "decent sanitary working conditions" most likely resonated among women workers. An ACLU report based on workers' affidavits concluded: "The toilet facilities are dirty and unsanitary and there is vermin present. There are also intolerable regulations. For instance, in some cases women are obliged to ask permission of a man foreman before going to the toilet, and in some cases the foreman (occasionally the forewoman, but not always) follows them to the toilet to make sure that no time is wasted. One foreman even nailed open the door of the toilet so he could see how many women were in there. Many of the toilets have no seats."[20] Neither the strike leadership nor the Communist Party drew out the relationship between the fight for better sanitary conditions and the struggle against women's oppression.

The demand for subsidized childcare would have addressed a burning need for most women workers. Although capitalist France had a tradition going back to the 1830s of government-sponsored crèches for working women, in the United States childcare was (and still is) looked upon with suspicion as undermining traditional roles of men and women. In Germany, amid a liberalization of attitudes concerning sexuality in the Weimar Republic, a conference of women textile workers in 1926 raised demands for *Stillstuben* (rooms where mothers could nurse babies); protection for pregnant workers; emancipation of women from housework through communal kitchens, cafeterias, and childcare; and legal abortion.[21] Communists in Passaic did not raise any of these, even as long-term goals.

In April the *Textile Strike Bulletin* ran an article on an inside page titled "Why the Dye Workers Went on Strike." The article highlighted the low wages that the mills paid women for night work and concluded: "Now a woman should not work in the mills at all. Her duty is to stay home and take care of the children and housework." As the strike progressed, the *Textile Strike Bulletin* emphasized women workers more. In early May the paper urged women strikers to contribute to "the women's column." This stressed that women "worked in the mill also but besides that . . . had to bring up the children and manage the home."[22] By summer the paper was carrying regular articles about women.

One article, "Women Workers Suffer Most," apparently written by a man, was ambiguous regarding whether the union should welcome or oppose women working. The article urged women workers to join unions, but called women workers "a great menace." The article stressed, "Most mothers are forced to work because the wage their husband earns is too small to provide for his family. Young women and girls are employed because they are a cheap source of labor to be used against the union workers in times of strikes and in normal times."[23] The article did not specify whether the goal was to raise men's pay high enough so women could remain at home, or equality for men and women workers.

Women Activists in the Strike

Even though the Communists and the UFC did not discuss women's oppression in a theoretical way, women were central to the strike. In her book Vorse described the "enthusiasm" at strike headquarters in late February, emphasizing the contribution of women picket captains, strike sympathizers, magazine writers, authors, and secretaries, as well as the strike's publicity director.[24] Vorse herself and Elizabeth Gurley Flynn were the most prominent women involved in the strike.

In the IWW textile strikes in Lawrence and Paterson, Flynn organized women workers and strikers' wives, and built support among liberal and Socialist women. After the strikes Flynn honed her sense that women's liberation was central to the labor movement in discussions of the all-female "Heterodoxy" group in Greenwich Village. In the 1920s Flynn was active in the Garland Fund and the ACLU. Her influence was shown in New York in February 1926 when 300 liberals, radicals, Socialists, Communists, and others celebrated her twentieth anniversary in the labor movement.[25]

Flynn threw herself into the Passaic strike and soon was traveling to Passaic daily from her apartment in Lower Manhattan and giving speeches as often as ten times a day. Her work in Passaic drew her closer to the Communist Party and the International Labor Defense, and she may have joined the party in this period.[26]

Flynn brought to the Passaic strike her understanding of the centrality of women workers; a sense of how outrage against police violence against women and children could generate broad sympathy for the workers' cause; and an appreciation of the importance of defending free speech and arrested strikers. She also convinced the Garland Fund to pay for her friend Mary Heaton Vorse to be in charge of the strike's publicity. Vorse was one of the most famous labor journalists of the day, having written about Lawrence and numerous other strikes.[27]

Elizabeth Gurley Flynn holds up a gas mask to a meeting of strikers, March 4, 1926, shortly after police used gas bombs against strike picketers. Flynn, a former IWW leader in the Paterson and Lawrence strike and a future leader of the Communist Party in the United States, regularly spoke at strike meetings and rallies. American Labor Museum/Botto House National Landmark.

In the early 1920s Vorse apparently became a secret member of the Communist Party. In a letter to C. E. Ruthenberg, Benjamin Gitlow wrote that "Comrade Mary Heaton Vorse is now doing very good work for the Party in the Passaic strike.... She requests that an understanding be had in her case that her membership be kept secret so that she can mingle in those circles where it would be impossible to do so by one who is labelled as a communist. She told me that she had such an understanding before." Before the strike Vorse was the chair of the CP's women's bureau. Vorse directed publicity and propaganda during the strike, shaping the strikers' perception of their own struggle and the public's view of the strike.[28]

Like Flynn, Vorse connected the Passaic battle to earlier IWW strikes. Her experiences informed her appreciation of the determination and dignity of women workers in union battle.[29] In the *Nation* she emphasized "the spectacle of hundreds upon hundreds of women, the most overburdened of all the population, the mothers of large families, forced by their husbands' low wages to work in the mill." In an article for the Federated Press news service, under the headline "Follows Happy Bride to Textile Slavery and Rat-Hole Home," Vorse described the endless toil of a woman mill worker: "Work that went on through the day and began again at night. Life that was a maze of fatigue. Life where the coming of a new child was such a tragedy that she could not speak of it without tears." Another article, "The Battle of Passaic," published in the *New Masses* in May, highlighted how the strike overturned traditional family roles: "Women and children, young girls, old ladies, grandmothers, all shouting and singing together.... The lines of pickets, the constant file of people was an exciting thing. It became contagious. Picketing became Passaic's favorite game. Children played at picketing. They picketed their schools. They picketed their homes. Children came out after school to go on the picket line."[30] This attention to the struggles of working women and their children was informed by her own experience as a single working mother after her first husband died.

Margaret Larkin, a prominent writer and radical, helped with strike publicity, including writing the continuity script for the film about the strike. Esther Lowell, a descendant of the famous Massachusetts family and a lifelong Communist, was a reporter from the Federated Press and served on the defense committee. Another Communist woman who came to Passaic during the strike was Vera Buch. Buch, born in Connecticut in 1895, had been a Socialist before becoming a charter member of the Communist Party in 1919. A teacher in New York City at the start of the strike, she moved to Passaic to teach English to workers. Then she worked in the strike headquarters, helping with relief and work with women workers. She became romantically involved with Weisbord, whom she later married.[31]

Lena Chernenko, a founding member of the U.S. Communist Party, was an activist in the Amalgamated Clothing Workers in New York in her mid-twenties when the strike broke out. She was arrested at least five times during the strike. As a militant, young, female Communist, Chernenko was a subject of fascination and derision for the press. The Camden *Courier-Post* described her as "pretty, pert, petite ... in the red dress that pleasantly sets off her Oriental features." Vera Buch recalled her as "gray-pale and grim-faced now from her regime of the four A.M. alarm clock, never free of bruises from the policemen's clubs, [hanging] on to her harsh assignment with a will of iron." In September 1926, when most Communists left Passaic as part of the agreement with the UTW, she remained. She left only when a doctor diagnosed her with tuberculosis and she went to California to stay with relatives.[32]

Young Workers' League (YWL) members Martha Stone, Sophie Melvin, and Miriam Silverfarb traveled to Passaic to organize children and youth. Stone joined the YWL in Brooklyn when she was fifteen or sixteen years old. In the strike's third month she dropped out of high school and moved to Passaic, where she stayed with a family of strikers and helped organize children.[33]

Melvin was born in Ukraine but grew up in Brownsville, a hotbed of Jewish radicalism in Brooklyn. In Brooklyn she joined the Young Pioneers then the Young Workers' League. A high school dropout, she quit her job in the garment industry and went to Passaic.[34]

Silverfarb dropped out of Hunter College in New York in the early days of the strike and "devoted all her energies toward helping the poverty-stricken families of the textile workers," according to the *Brooklyn Daily Eagle*. Born in Poland in 1906, Silverfarb emigrated to the United States four years later with her parents. She joined the Young Workers' League in 1924 and the party the next year. In June 1926 the leadership of the Young Workers' League voted Silverfarb a member of the committee overseeing the Young Pioneers.[35]

Helen Allison, another young Communist, went to Passaic to assist the relief work headed by her father, Alfred Wagenknecht. "Passaic was the first time I actually felt the strength of labor," she remembered decades later. The strike "helped solidify some of my attitudes and feelings towards the movement of which I was a part but never had the opportunity of quite seeing from this vantage point." Allison worked in the office, walked the picket lines, raised money, and worked with strikers' children.[36]

Although Elle Reeve "Mother" Bloor did not play an active role on the ground in New Jersey, she publicized the strike, first among textile workers in New England, and then, through a national tour that reached California. She often took strikers with her to speak at the meetings she organized.[37]

Unlike women whom the Communist movement mobilized to go to Passaic, Ellen Dawson joined the Communist Party because of the strike. A native of Scotland, she had worked in the British textile industry before emigrating in the 1920s and getting a job as a weaver in the Botany Mill in Passaic, but had never been on strike before. Dawson's biographer, David Lee McMullen, stressed, "Unquestionably the Passaic strike altered Dawson's life. No longer was she an anonymous weaver in a New Jersey textile mill, working long hours in order to simply survive." She became a Communist activist and was elected to the party's central committee.[38]

The strike resonated among non-Communist women university students, perhaps struck by the differences of their lives and those of the strikers, many of whom were their age. The most famous of these was Yale Law student Justine Wise, who had worked among the millworkers in Passaic in 1924 after graduating from Barnard. She spurred her father, Rabbi Stephen Wise, to get involved in supporting the strike, and organized meetings at Yale. Martha Gartenlaub, a graduate of Garfield High School studying at the New Jersey College of Women, worked in the union's playground.[39]

The Communist Party and Women during the Strike

According to Vera Buch, "The organized participation of the women had much to do with the remarkable vitality of this strike." She added, "From the beginning, the left wing leadership made special efforts to draw in the women." These included organizing "their own mass meetings where the issue of the strike and problems of their own lives were explained to them." In an

Strikers (from left to right) Betty Marandi, Laura Douglass, and Emma Polcari. Young women were often in the forefront of efforts to build and defend the strike. American Labor Museum/Botto House National Landmark.

internal report on Communist work among women during the strike, Buch stressed "the newness of the work for our party," and emphasized that "in Passaic we have had to blaze a pioneer trail."[40]

The United Council of Working-Class Housewives was central to this work. Led by Benjamin Gitlow's mother, Kate Gitlow, it was organized into neighborhood councils and by the fall of 1926 counted several branches in New York City (including Brownsville), Passaic, and Newark. At their regular meeting in New York City on February 26, the UCWCH passed a resolution supporting the strike and offered to organize kitchens in Passaic for strikers and their families. On March 9 the UCWCH organized a mass meeting "in the biggest hall in Passaic, the purpose of which was to acquaint the outside working class women with the striking women and so engage them in the relief work." On March 12 they opened the first kitchen which fed 400 children daily. The group also raised funds, mainly in New York. A meeting in Union Square in late April drew more than 200 people. On June 19 the UCWCH held a conference of women's groups in Passaic "to bring women's organizations together to help with the feeding of the strikers' children." This was called the United Women's Conference and met monthly.[41]

Because Buch was staying in Passaic while Kate Gitlow remained in New York, she assumed much of the day-to-day oversight of work among women.

Buch was critical of the lack of attention and resources that the party had given the work. Buch organized women strikers themselves to run the soup kitchen, expanding to Lodi and Wallington. "It looked as though the women had only been waiting for a chance to apply their creative energies; it took just a little push and a minimum of direction to get them started." By September 1926 the *Daily Worker* reported that these soup kitchens were feeding 1,000 children daily.[42]

Buch recalled that these women "carried three jobs: mill worker, houseworker, and mother." Or as she pointed out in her report, "the housewife of today is the worker of tomorrow and vice-versa," since many women worked in the mills intermittently and thus "it is difficult to draw a line between the housewife and the worker." According to Buch, the local Council of Working-Class Housewives tried to educate women strikers, not just cook. At the first educational meeting, Communist Jacob O. Bentall spoke on "Why the Workers Are Poor." At the second, Stanislava Piotrovska spoke on "The Working-Class Mother and Her Children." Buch noted: "Since I wanted the councils to survive after I left, I trained the women to run their own meetings," insisting that each one "had to take her turn as being chairwoman," even if she could only conduct the meeting in Polish or Italian.[43]

Buch and others organized 600 women into eight functioning groups. "Many of the workers have never been as far as New York City," she reported, "though they have lived in Passaic for fifteen or twenty years and New York is a half hour away." The majority were "superstitious, religious, and generally backward" and many were "the slaves of backward husbands who do not allow them to go out at night and resent their being organized."[44]

Besides running the kitchens and raising money for relief, women "sent out committees to visit scabs," "helped to stiffen up picket lines," regularly visited the families of strikers in jail, and organized and spoke at mass meetings. This work raised the political consciousness of women workers in Passaic, and trained women Communists in leadership positions. Yet, Buch argued in her memoirs, the strike's (male) Communist leadership did not encourage women to come forward as leaders beyond working with women and children—traditional women's work. Buch later noted: "The attitude of the party leaders, and of almost all the men in the party, was just what it was in the world outside. . . . If you were a wife, it was assumed you were just an echo of your husband."[45]

Sophie Melvin dismissed Buch's recollections as bitterness that "all emanates from the way she was treated by her own husband," Albert Weisbord.[46] This may be true, but while women played important roles in the strike, not only was the leader of the strike, Weisbord, male, but the Communist Party's textile committee, trade-union committee, and central executive committee were all overwhelmingly male. Furthermore, in her report Buch reported that the Communist Party had recruited only three women by November, and was poised to recruit five more—out of thousands of women workers. Buch warned that during strikes "work among the women should never be regarded as something isolated, and artificially detached from other work." She complained that there was "no party literature for women."[47]

Indicative of this is the saga of getting Kate Gitlow's article on women and the Passaic strike published. In late September, Gitlow sent Jay Lovestone a copy of the nine-page manuscript, proposing that it be printed as a pamphlet and sold for five cents. On behalf of the UCWCH, she offered to pay for the printing. "It would be a help in organizing the women," she stressed. Three weeks later, she wrote to Lovestone again, complaining that she had been told the article was too long and should be reworked. In late November—more than two months after she submitted the draft manuscript—Gitlow wrote to C. E. Ruthenberg, detailing the runaround she had received by leading Communists in trying to publish it. Ruthenberg responded that he would make sure that the article was published since it "should help a great deal to stimulate interest in the work among women on the part of the Party members." In early December the *Daily Worker* finally published the article.[48]

Children, Youth, and the Passaic Strike

In her 1928 Columbia University master's thesis on the strike, Sara Fanny Simon observed: "It was the young worker who led in the Passaic strike and was the most militant." Gustav Deak had begun work at age fourteen in the Botany finishing department, and was twenty-two years old when the strike broke out. Weisbord was only twenty-five at the start of the strike; his history as a leader in the Young People's Socialist League may have attuned him to the importance of young workers. From early in the strike, Weisbord sought to win over young workers, most of whom were children of immigrants.[49]

Mill management claimed that they employed only twenty-eight workers who were sixteen years old, "and then only upon special recommendation from the school authorities." This is not credible. According to the federal Department of Labor, in 1925–1926 there were 652 children employed in Passaic and 426 in Garfield. Rexford G. Tugwell, then a liberal economist at Columbia University, visited Passaic during the strike and concluded that "about 7 per cent. of the mill employees are between the ages of 10 and 18, and Passaic has the largest percentage of any northern textile town of children taking papers at the minimum age"—that is, fourteen years old.[50] This would mean that there were at least a thousand textile workers aged eighteen or younger.

The Communist Party had two youth organizations, the Young Workers' League and the Young Pioneers, for younger children; each had its own paper. Both were active in the strike. The YWL raised "special demands for the young workers." These demands included equal pay for equal work; no night work for workers under twenty-one years old; young workers to be considered minors; breaks and vacations; and "continuation schools" and "recreational facilities in the mills under workers' control." The *Young Worker* justified these demands by arguing, "The young workers felt the effects of the long hours, the wretched unsanitary conditions, and the low wages even more than the older workers."[51]

In late February the *Young Worker* ran a front-page article hailing the "many thousands of young workers between 14 and 20 years of age who are in the forefront of the strike movement." In early March the *Young Worker* claimed that 1,000 people had attended two YWL meetings. Later in the month, the paper claimed that 1,500 youth turned out to hear Jack Rubenstein and other militants. "In the whole strike you can see the young workers always in the forefront," the *Young Worker* bragged. "They are arrested, mutilated, and the police are usually after the young strikers trying to terrorize them." In March the *Young Comrade*, published by the Pioneers, claimed to have organized, together with the YWL, "two big overflow meetings with more than two thousand young workers." Despite these efforts, an internal Communist Party document reported that there were 35 members of the Young Workers' League in Passaic, compared to 60 textile worker members of the Communist Party.[52]

The same report indicated that Young Pioneers had 2,000 members. The efforts of the UFC and the CP among the strikers' children reflected lessons learned in Lawrence, where Flynn and other IWW leaders organized the strikers' children to counteract anti-strike propaganda in the public schools and to get strikers' children to support their parents. On Thursday, April 8, several hundred children marched to the Botany Mill. The police arrested six young strikers, four boys and two girls, ranging in age from twelve to seventeen. The next day the United Front Committee announced plans for a Saturday march of 20,000 children. When the police denied the march a permit, claiming that such a march would endanger the children, Weisbord called for children to stay away from school the following Monday in protest.[53]

The *New York Times* raised the specter of Weisbord leading the children out of public school into a "Communist school." The Passaic Board of Education threatened to invoke the Child Welfare Act of 1915 against those who "incited" children to picket if students missed five days of school. On April 10, children marched with signs, including "Don't Beat Our Fathers and Mothers" and "We Are Tired of Being Sick and Hungry." "Passaic children are sturdy pickets," Esther Lowell wrote for the Federated Press. "They know why their mothers and fathers, sisters and brothers are striking." After this march, the Communists' Textile Committee passed a motion directing "the Pioneers [to] hold Nuclei meetings, hikes, classes, carry on activities among the kids eating in the kitchens, social affairs and their primary business should be to counter the anti-strike sentiments in schools and among students."[54]

Women and children were a prominent part of the strikers' delegation to Washington.[55] Several children, aged four to fourteen years old, picketed the White House. "That wage cut took our milk away," read one sign. After ten minutes, Everett Sanders, President Coolidge's secretary, told them to stop because they were violating the capital's child labor law. In Trenton, thirty children and their mothers protested outside the State House against police attacks on strikers.[56] These protests threatened Governor Moore's image as "the kiddies' friend" that he had cultivated since his time in charge of Jersey City's parks under Mayor Hague.

The *Textile Strike Bulletin* carried letters by young workers and strikers' children. The March 22 issue carried a letter by "R.F.—entire family on strike—10" that denounced the police for attacking strikers' children. "When Chief Zober threw the bombs," the letter stated, "he threw them among the children, because he knows that the children can't fight." Another issue ran a letter from "F.L.", an eleven-year-old strikers' child describing the relief kitchens: "They give us very good food which we never ate when my father was working for Johnston & Huffmann's miserable death wages."[57]

The YWL and Young Pioneers urged youth to support their striking relatives. "The children are fighting side by side with their parents, with their sisters and brothers on the picket line, in the front line of the battle everywhere, as true young comrades," one article bragged. This included struggling against anti-strike propaganda in the schools. The article highlighted the case of Mike, the eleven-year-old son of a striker. "Mike has been active in strike and was expelled from his parochial school because of his activity" as "one of our bravest little fighters." Mike "told all his young comrades how the bosses kill the children with their wage cuts and the night work for the mothers, leaving their children uncared for, and the very low wages, which mean cold, damp homes."[58]

The *Young Comrade* emphasized what it called "the school struggle," battles between pro-Communist students and hostile teachers and administrators. While supporting public education and teachers' unionization, the paper denounced the school system's anti-strike stance. In an article addressed "To the Workers' Children of Passaic," the *Young Comrade* stated: "The war is on—between the workers and the bosses! And in order to smash the workers the bosses are bringing in their tools and servants to help them—the police and the public schools." Elsewhere the paper argued, "The board of education is also carrying on strike-breaking work in the schools where mostly workers' children go," thus proving that the schools "are just poison factories for the bosses to poison the minds of the workers' children." The paper demanded "that all anti-strike and anti-labor propaganda in schools should be stopped" and "that the schools should be supervised thru councils of parents and labor organizations" to "put a stop to the bosses using the schools against the workers." One thirteen-year-old student in Garfield whose parents were on strike wrote to the *Young Pioneer* to describe the anti-strike sentiment of the teachers. The letter ended, "I hope that the strikers win their struggle so that their children can get a better education, better food and better homes." (Some teachers supported the strike: the *Textile Strike Bulletin* reprinted a letter from the New York City teachers' union.)[59]

Given the school boards' function, and their members' professional backgrounds and links to the employers, their hostility to the strike was to be expected. J. Frank Andres, former secretary of the Wool Council, had been a member of the Passaic Board of Education until recently. At least two members of the Passaic Board of Education had links to the wool industry, and in Clifton, one commissioner of education had two sons who worked in Botany management, and was a long-time friend of William B. Davidson, the judge who sentenced many strikers. In Lodi, a long-time employee of United Piece Dye Workers was appointed a member of the school board in June 1926.[60]

Childcare and the Strike

In early March 1926 the *New York Times* reported that strikers raised funds to aid the first "strike baby," born to a striker the day before. This highlighted the challenge that strikers faced: How would they take care of their children during the strike? Opponents of the strike seized on the hardships that strikers' families suffered. Relief efforts attempted to lessen the strikers' suffering and to counteract such propaganda. Suffering children featured heavily in attempts to build support for the strike. "Nothing perhaps is more tragic of the faces of these long starved babies," Agnes de Lima wrote in an article published in *Justice*, the paper of the ILGWU. "Even the babies of two and three reflect the dreariness and misery that has surrounded them ever since they came so unwelcomed into the world." "The Children Look to You," read an advertisement for the Passaic Children Milk Fund in the same paper in October. "You cannot be deaf to the cry of these Passaic children."[61]

In May, with spring—and summer vacation—approaching, Communist leader Alfred Wagenknecht, in charge of the relief efforts during the strike, described "a special campaign for the relief of strikers children" in a letter to his wife. This campaign included "1 Milk for strikers children and 2 Shoes and clothes for them 3 Kitchens for them were they may eat a meal a day and 4 camps for them and boarding them out with sympathizers." The UFC opened milk stations "for the many sickly, underfed children, whose milk had been taken away from them" because of the wage cut; provided relief to 5,000 children daily; sent the children of strikers "to homes of sympathetic friends, where they could get better care"; and organized union-run camps for the children.[62]

The UFC emphasized the poverty of Passaic workers, claiming that thousands of working-class children went without milk. When the city's health officer objected, Wagenknecht stated that of a hundred strikers' children that doctors examined, half were underweight, malnourished, or suffering from anemia. In September supporters organized a "Passaic Children's Milk Fund."[63] During the summer, International Workers' Aid opened a 140-acre camp for children near Morristown, New Jersey, that could house twenty-seven children. It featured "a cement swimming pool, woods, beautiful country roads for hiking, open fields for sports of all kinds, and milk, *real milk*, all they can drink." The United Front Committee ran Victory Playground, in Saddle River, a Bergen County town not far from Passaic. Some 1,500 strikers' children were cared for at the playground while their parents were on the picket line. The eight-acre playground featured showers, swings, see-saws, and other amusements. Volunteers organized games for the children and staffed "a children's kitchen and milk station," the *Young Comrade* reported, "and the kids are given a nutritious meal and lots of milk during the day." The article continued: "Order is kept in various novel ways. One method is by song: 'Sit down, sit down, this is a union town' will invariably send the children squatting in the grass. Perfect discipline is maintained without ever a cross word from the leaders." The *Daily Worker* described the purpose of these activities was "to bring a little joy and sunshine into these young lives so darkened by the pall of oppression."[64]

A lurid article in the *Passaic Daily Herald* warned of "children five and six" at the playground who were supposedly "talking gloatingly of stabbings, shootings and clubbings; of strike breakers and strikers, and of hurling rocks at the heads of Cossacks—as they are taught to call the police." The *Passaic Daily News* denounced the camp: "The sinful thing in connection with it is the fact that children are not taken there to forget the strike, which would be the right thing, but remember it every moment." In response to the union playground, the city of Passaic installed a wading pool and showers at a municipal park. Officials also selected twenty boys as play leaders, who, the union alleged, were expected to spy on and intimidate pro-strike youth.[65]

Recalling the Lawrence strike, the UFC organized sympathetic workers outside of Passaic "to take strikers' children into their homes for as long a period as possible while the strike lasts." The *Daily Worker* explained, "This will help relieve the economic pressure on the parents and the relief organization, as well as give the benefit of a new environment, and wholesome meals." In late July a thousand children of Passaic strikers came to New York City on large trucks that carried them through the streets carrying signs in support of the strike. After being treated to sandwiches and ice cream by the Hotel Workers' Union, the children went to sympathetic families to spend the summer.[66]

The soup kitchens, playgrounds, milk stations, relief centers, and summer camps that the union organized as part of relief efforts implicitly raised the possibility of collectivizing the work traditionally done by the family, one of the goals of the Bolsheviks in Russia. This work drew on the tradition of ladies' auxiliaries that wives of skilled craft workers had organized since the 1890s, to support their husbands' unions. It also anticipated the union battles of the 1930s when industrial unions organized women's auxiliaries that staffed the union's commissary, nursed injured strikers, and provided clerical work in the union's headquarters during strikes. Unlike in some auxiliaries that confined women to the kitchen and nursery, in Passaic, women were drawn into all phases of the battle, in the relief work *and* on the picket line.[67]

The sign on the truck says "Saving the Passaic Textile Strikers' Children from the Greedy Mill Owners." In July 1926, a thousand strikers' children came to New York City on large trucks, and after being treated to lunch by the Hotel Workers' Union, went to sympathetic families to spend the summer. American Labor Museum/Botto House National Landmark.

During the strike, according to Jack Rubenstein, "the union declared a moratorium on rent and where a landlord put a worker out on the street for not paying rent the strikers would either move the furniture back into the vacated apartment or find a new apartment for these workers." Nobody would rent an apartment, Rubenstein recalled, if a striker had been evicted from it, and it "remained empty for the duration of the strike as the workers would see to it no one else would move into the place." The General Relief Committee prepared a housing department to deal with large-scale evictions when most workers stopped paying rent. In the context of a strike these actions tied tenant activism to the power of the union and expanded the legitimate concern of the union to include housing. This both reflected traditions of tenant activism (such as the 1907 Lower East Side rent strike) and anticipated Communist activities in the 1930s. Only fifteen families were evicted between January and August, since "landlords were cooperative, or at least philosophical where unpaid rent was concerned," as Siegel put it. In the fall, however, the eviction rate increased, with reportedly twenty families a day being evicted by November.[68]

Building Support among University Students

Even though in the 1920s most university campuses were conservative and most university students came from capitalist or professional families, strike leaders built support among students. In early March, at the height of police violence, the *New York Times* reported that "students of economics from several colleges are visiting the strike zone daily."[69]

Simon Gerson, son of an early member of the Communist Party and president of the Social Problem Club (SPC) at the City College of New York, organized students to aid the strike. Another Communist student at City College, sophomore Carl Weisberg, traveled to Passaic with other SPC members and spent the night in the UFC office, helping to protect it. The next morning, while visiting the picket lines, he was clubbed by the police. The *Campus*, the student publication at City College, detailed his saga; the SPC organized a meeting of 300 students to listen to Weisberg. (The City College administration tried to stamp down any support of the strike: first, administrators denied the SPC use of a room, so they met in the alcoves in the lunchroom. Then the editor of the *Campus* was removed for publishing Weisberg's account, according to the *Daily Worker*, at the instigation of the City College administration.)[70]

In late April the president of the SPC at Columbia University led a group of students from City College, Columbia, Barnard, and Washington Square College (the downtown college of New York University) to Passaic. The SPC organized a pro-strike meeting at Columbia's Teachers College in late April, where several hundred people listened to Weisbord, Stephen Wise, and Norman Thomas. In May, Hillman M. Bishop forwarded to Deak $155.15 collected "at a student mass meeting of all the colleges of New York City held last night in Columbia University." Two Columbia students defended master's theses sympathetic to the strike in 1927 and 1928, suggesting firsthand experience with the strike. In April members of Hunter College's Social Science Club traveled to Passaic to help Miriam Silverfarb, their former classmate.[71]

Justine Wise built support for the strike in New Haven. She spoke at a mass meeting at the Trades Council Hall in mid-March, and then several days later at the sympathetic Yale Liberal Club. Two Yale undergraduates visited Passaic in the spring and denounced the workers' "deplorable conditions" in the *Yale Daily News* (reprinted in the *Harvard Crimson*). Students built support at Harvard, including with the help of Henry Wadsworth Longfellow Dana, class of 1903 and scion of the Boston upper crust. The Harvard Liberal Club hosted Ella Reeve Bloor in April, and Weisbord in November.[72]

Another youth who was active in the Passaic strike was New Yorker Jack Rubenstein, a founding member of the U.S. Communist Party who was about eighteen years old at the start of the strike. He recalled that during the strike, he "took a trip to Passaic, just as one would casually go seeing a friend, [with] no intention of staying." He ended up staying seven months and became

THE PASSAIC TEXTILE STRIKE

1926-1927

By MARY HEATON VORSE

Pamphlet by Mary Heaton Vorse, one of the most famous labor journalists of the time, who oversaw strike publicity. General Relief Committee of Textile Strikers.

Weisbord's assistant, leaving only when it became clear "the police were making me a symbol" by arresting him at least thirty times during the strike. The *Passaic Herald and News* wrote in his obituary in 1989 that in the Passaic strike Rubenstein "discovered his reason for living."[73]

Even though for Communists the liberation of women and the liberation of youth required the replacement of the family, this point was absent from their propaganda. Instead, women's oppression was collapsed into youth oppression and class exploitation: young women and men workers were encouraged to fight for the liberation of the working class. Despite the lack of a conscious effort to integrate women into the highest levels of Communist leadership, the UFC and the CP incorporated women into all areas of the work during the strike, providing the basis for women's advancement within the workplace and the union had the strike won. Economist Theresa Wolfson, in a 1929 survey of women's trade-union activities, described the strike as "an epoch-making example of the ability of women workers to fight for what they consider their economic rights." The strike gave many women, like Nancy Sandosky, Ellen Dawson, and Anna Breznac, their first taste of politics—and political leadership. For Marxists, women workers were doubly oppressed—as workers in the mills and as women in the family. The UFC addressed the first form of oppression forcefully, but not the second. One can only imagine what the effect would have been on the strike, and its ability to consolidate women's support, had the strike leadership done so.[74]

9

The End of the Strike

In the autumn of 1926 the Trade Union Educational League published a pamphlet by William Z. Foster, *Strike Strategy*.[1] In the last chapter, "On Ending Strikes," Foster argued that it was "fundamental... for the left wing to learn when and how to settle, no less than when and how to strike," and warned that "settlement proceedings, whether before or after strike movements, constitute real danger spots, genuine tests of leadership." Foster contrasted the right-wing labor bureaucracy's interest in industrial peace to the left wing's aim to "secure better positions from which to go on prosecuting the class war more vigorously than ever." Foster stressed that while "the left wing must always fight for the best terms possible," leftists "must never rely upon these pieces of paper" but instead look to "powerful trade unions, clear-seeing and militantly led."

Foster, the leader of the defeated steel strike of 1919, understood that strikes often lost. After referring to the "nine months of bitter struggle" in Passaic, Foster wrote: "From time to time our forces will be so defeated that we will be confronted with little Brest-Litovsks," alluding to the treaty that Germany forced upon the young Soviet government in early 1918 in which it gave up much of its territory in exchange for peace. "But we must understand them as Lenin did his, as offering breathing spells during which we shall rally our shattered battalions for the next offensive." The danger of not recognizing a defeat, Foster warned, was "that many loyal workers, who have fought valiantly while there was even a slight chance to win the strike, are forced back to work with the odium of scab upon them" and "are largely lost to the trade union movement." Instead, leftists should "call off the strike officially when it is manifestly lost, and let the fragments of the defeated army go back to work with honor."[2]

Foster, the Communists' most experienced trade-union leader, was in the Soviet Union from when the strike started until May.[3] While Foster was in Moscow, the Comintern leadership passed a motion condemning "secessional movements and formation of parallel trade unions."[4] Starting in the summer Foster was key in orientating the party's labor work, including in Passaic. Since Foster's break with the IWW in the teens, a core of his philosophy was that radicals must work within the AFL and avoid "dual unions." *Strike Strategy* stressed that "the left wing must maneuver carefully to kill the dual union charge by moving for affiliation with the A. F. of L." Foster cited the Passaic strike, where "affiliation was actually brought about in the midst of the struggle and the A. F. of L. was compelled to endorse openly the strike which for seven months it had shamelessly sabotaged." He warned: "in carrying through such affiliation maneuvers the left wing must be careful to maintain its ideological and organizational control over the striking masses and to prevent a sell-out settlement by the right wing, for which the left wing would be held responsible by the workers."[5]

The end of the strike played out in almost exactly the way Foster had warned it would. In the summer the Communist Party forced the United Front Committee to dissolve and the workers to join the UTW. The UTW leadership then settled the strike piecemeal, on compromise terms that amounted to a defeat. This chapter argues that the real failure of the Communists was not that the strike lost or that the workers joined the UTW, but that the Communists downplayed the UTW leadership's betrayal and labeled the strike a victory. During the strike, the Communist Party sought to deflect anti-Communist attacks by reducing the party's profile in Passaic, which meant that the party had a weaker base to build upon during the last stages of the strike.

Botany Consolidated Mills reported net losses of more than $3.5 million— almost $51 million in today's dollars—for the first six months of 1926. The wool companies refused to settle with the UFC, accepting short-term financial disaster to avoid unionization. Thus, in early June they rejected the efforts by Frank P. Walsh, Stephen Wise, and Henry Hunt to negotiate.[6]

The UFC increased their efforts to get the rest of the labor movement to take up the strike. In early June the Federated Textile Workers organized a two-day conference in New York City. Forty-three delegates from fifteen independent textile unions from New England, New Jersey, and Pennsylvania pledged financial and moral support to the Passaic strikers. Foster summarized his perspective that the conference should make "definite plans . . . for the amalgamation of all the textile organizations" and "launch a general organization campaign in the textile industry." Foster advocated that "we definitely constitute the United Front Central Bureau and organize it in control of the left wing work in the textile industry."[7]

The independent textile unions at the conference rejected the UFC's program as "neither workable nor reasonable." When Weisbord and John J. Ballam advocated an immediate organizing campaign among northern textile workers, the unions objected, citing a slump in the textile industry. Instead, the conference set up a ten-person committee (including Weisbord and Ballam) to arrange another conference later in the month. The conference emphasized that the Passaic strikers were on their own.[8]

The AFL Bureaucracy's Anti-Passaic Campaign

On June 11, after seventeen weeks on strike, 12,000 fur workers in New York City under the leadership of Communist Ben Gold won a forty-hour week, a 10 percent wage increase, and an end to subcontracting. The *Textile Strike Bulletin* predicted that the wool workers would "score the next victory for the workers and lay the basis for the union in the textile industry, as powerful and effective as the furriers have built up in the needle trades."[9] By raising the specter of increased Communist influence in the labor movement, the furriers' victory frightened the mills and the AFL leadership.

William Green attacked the Passaic strikers for having no "relationship with the A.F. of L." and urged members of the federation not to "contribute funds to be used for the purpose of advancing the cause of a dual organization or to pay the salaries of Communist officials who are seeking the destruction of the A.F. of L."[10] Days later, Henry F. Hilfers, leader of the New Jersey State Federation of Labor, wrote an open letter to Michael J. O'Donnell, his counterpart in Massachusetts, that declared the strike would not win, had been doomed from the start, and did not have the support of the AFL.[11]

In a letter to Green, Weisbord and Deak denounced Hilfers's letter and added: "We have always indicated our readiness to affiliate with the A. F. of L." They proposed that the AFL executive council create a committee to meet with the UFC.[12] The next day Green defended his statements and reiterated his advice that "those who are members of the American Federation of Labor withhold support to outlaw, communistic organizations." He accused the relief campaign of being "used for the sole purpose of advancing the cause of Communism."[13]

In Passaic, opponents of the strike formed a Citizens' Committee in early July "to restore peace and prosperity to this community." This committee urged workers to abandon the strike. A full-page advertisement in the Passaic papers highlighted that "some of the Communist agitators who have been active in the Passaic Strike, either as leaders or propagandists." The advertisement contained a list of about 250 people who had joined the Citizens' Committee, including the Right Reverend Monsignor Thomas J. Kernan, rector of St. Nicholas Roman Catholic Church. The merchants' committee of the Passaic Chamber of Commerce quickly endorsed the Citizens' Committee. The Citizens' Committee seized on Hilfers's letter to O'Donnell, running full-page advertisements in the two daily Passaic newspapers, consisting of excerpts from the letter under the headline, "The Strike Is Lost."[14]

The Slavic Committee and the Lauck Committee

Meanwhile, the United Front Committee and the Associated Societies and Parishes of Passaic (the Slavic Committee) pressured the AFL to take over the strike. Senator Borah lobbied the AFL leadership. Weisbord telegraphed Borah on July 22: "We welcome your aid and I assure you if settlement can be secured I personally will do everything in my power to help even to the extent of completely stepping aside in settlement negotiations." Borah immediately telegraphed Charles F. H. Johnson, informing him of Weisbord's pledge and asking if Botany would be willing to negotiate.[15]

Johnson's three-sheet telegram in response insisted that "in addition to complete elimination of Weisbord the United Front Committee must be replaced by bona fide representation of actual workers" and denounced the UFC as "a communistic device and... a first step in the communistic program to overthrow this government." Johnson described the strike as "a seditious conspiracy" that was "instigated and financed to a considerable extent by communists."[16] Johnson's emphasis on Communism gave Borah and the Lauck Committee hope that once Weisbord left Passaic the strike could be settled easily.

On July 23 William Vaneck, of the Slavic Committee, met with Hilfers and Anna Neary (a bookbinder from the Baltimore Federation of Labor and the only woman organizer in the AFL). Given Borah's willingness to mediate the strike and Weisbord's willingness to leave Passaic, Hilfers and Neary agreed that when requested by the strikers, the AFL would take over the strike.

On July 26 Borah met in Washington with Weisbord, who reiterated his willingness to withdraw. Shortly afterward Johnson met with Borah, and then with AFL secretary Frank Morrison in the federation's headquarters. The headline of the July 30 issue of the *Textile Strike Bulletin* reflected the optimism that this would settle the strike: "For Unity—Through Affiliation with the American Federation of Labor."[17]

At a meeting of 12,000 strikers on July 31, Weisbord introduced a resolution that empowered a committee of W. Jett Lauck, Helen Todd, and Henry T. Hunt (with the support of Frank P. Walsh, who was out of town) to "represent us in the settlement of the strike through Senator Borah in Washington, or through any other mediation or adjustment agency." The resolution empowered the Lauck Committee to conduct an election to organize a union, and then "to negotiate and arrange with the United Textile Workers of America of the American Federation of Labor, for the admission of this duly organized union into the United Textile Workers of America." Weisbord agreed to step aside after "negotiations have reached such a point where the workers can join the United Textile Workers without any danger of the employers breaking their strike." He emphasized the strike faced two choices:

On the one hand there is a possibility of a speedy and honorable settlement of the strike on the basis of a recognition of the union of the workers if the workers affiliate themselves to the United Textile Workers of the American Federation of Labor. On the other hand, if there is no such affiliation, there is a certainty of a continued struggle for some time to come, and while I feel no doubt about the final outcome and that the workers . . . fighting independently will win this struggle, nevertheless I certainly feel that it is in the best interest of the workers and that it is my duty to tell them so, to advise them to join the United Textile Workers and thus bring the strike to a speedy and just end.[18]

The correspondence of Ballam, the National Textile Organizer of the Communist Party, and the Communist leadership indicate that the CP followed and approved of these negotiations.[19] On July 27, Ruthenberg telegraphed Ballam (in Washington) about these negotiations: "Approve with understanding that wage cut and other demands go to arbitration and that Albert's elimination applies only to negotiations and settlement and not to holding official position afterwards. Must insist on right to elect whom they see fit after settlement."[20] The leadership of the CP's District 2 (encompassing New York City and northern New Jersey) established a committee of five—Ballam, Benjamin Gitlow, George Ashkenudzie, Weisbord, and Wagenknecht—"to carry out party policies in Passaic" during this period. In early August, Ballam indicated that the Lauck Committee "work[ed] entirely under our direction," and later in the month Ruthenberg noted that "it is the understanding of the Political Committee that our committee approves all statements of the Lauck Committee before they are issued."[21]

The Unhappy Marriage of the UTW and the Passaic Strikers

Before the strike, McMahon derided the Passaic wool workers as unorganizable; during the strike, he feared that their organization would threaten his class-collaborationist outlook. Because the UTW had an estimated 30,000 members in 1926, the entrance of the Passaic workers as a mass would threaten McMahon's control. According to the minutes of the AFL executive council, when Rabbi Wise and Hilfers met with McMahon in late March, "President McMahon said at that meeting that they could not unload the strike, which has been lost, on their organization."[22] Even when national attention made it impossible to reject the Passaic strikers any longer, McMahon remained unhappy about welcoming thousands of unskilled workers, many of them immigrants and women, into the UTW.

On August 10, Hunt met with the UTW executive committee and Hilfers in the union's New York City headquarters for two and a half hours. Hunt reported to Walsh:

They were apparently fearful that they would be asked to take the strike over after it failed, with the result that they would be blamed for its failure and the alleged communistic leadership of the strike would escape without loss of prestige. They were also fearful that the support for the strike from labor unions not affiliated with the A.F. of L. and other citizens would be withdrawn as soon as the U.T.W. took it over. . . . The U.T.W. was also fearful that the strikers would not understand that their demands for a raise in wages, etc., might not be obtainable.[23]

On August 12, Lauck and his committee met with McMahon again to finalize the Passaic workers' entry into the UTW. McMahon stressed that the one non-negotiable condition was "the elimination of Albert Weisbord and his associates from any connection with the local union or unions of Passaic workers." The Passaic workers would need to apply as individuals, not an existing union. Strikers who remained unemployed would not have to pay an initiation fee or dues to the union, "but will be held morally responsible when they return to work to meet this obligation." Strikers who had found jobs elsewhere would pay a $1 initiation fee to the UTW. Once the Lauck Committee accepted these conditions, the UTW voted to accept the Passaic workers. Weisbord issued a statement "that upon the issuance of the charter by the U.T.W. of A. to the textile workers of Passaic and their formal affiliation with the U.T.W., I will withdraw from any participation in the affairs of the Passaic local union of the U.T.W."[24]

Immediately after the vote, Lauck telegraphed Borah, "My opinion is that our committee should obtain tactic [sic] understanding from mill owners that they will recognize new union as soon as reorganized." On August 14, Lauck and his committee wrote to Charles F. H. Johnson and Julius Forstmann informing them that Weisbord had agreed to withdraw and requesting that the mills negotiate with the UTW. On August 18 the *Textile Strike Bulletin* ran the headline "Up to Bosses Now," adding "Obstacles Are Removed from the Path of Settlement; Whole Labor Movement Awaits Action of Mill Owners."[25]

The Mill Owners Play Hardball

Johnson called a meeting of all Botany employees at 11:30 A.M. on August 19. He read a statement that rejected negotiations and added that the mill owners "have not and will not consult or confer with any committee now or hereafter which represents or claims to represent those who are no longer employed in the mill." Further, Johnson stated that the mills "have said frankly to the representatives of the American Federation of Labor that the situation was not one in which their services could be useful." He conceded that the workers had a right to elect representatives to bargain with management, but insisted this be done through a company union.[26]

The next day, August 20, Julius Forstmann followed suit and rejected any union for his company's workers. Instead Forstmann announced that the "F&H Representative Assembly"—the company union—would be refurbished, eliminating the open representatives of management. He announced a permanent mediation committee, consisting of three outside persons of "recognized standing in the community" and "unimpeachable reputation for character and integrity." Even though Forstmann claimed to have no objection to labor unions in theory, he asserted that "insurmountable technical difficulties" in "diverse and complex operations" such as his company's wool mills made unionization impossible. Forstmann announced that his mills would have regular wage scales, and concluded by giving striking workers until August 28 to return to work and keep their benefits and seniority. Forstmann even sent a Forstmann and Huffmann executive to Boise to convince Borah that the company was a model employer and an innocent bystander in the Passaic strike. (Borah refused to issue such a statement.)[27]

The mill owners' refusal to deal with the AFL shocked Lauck and Borah.[28] On August 27, Matthew Woll, vice-president of the AFL, denounced Senator Borah's attempts to mediate the Passaic strike, criticizing Borah's support of diplomatic relations with the Soviet Union and claiming that the senator's real aim was compulsory arbitration for all strikes. Not all of the AFL leadership agreed with Woll's attack on Borah; in late September, Green wrote to Rabbi Wise that "those engaged in the Passaic strike are in great need of the services of Senator Borah" and promised Wise time to address the upcoming AFL convention about the strike.[29]

The Communists and the Hand-Off to the UTW

The Passaic strikers' joining the UTW was the culmination of a months-long effort by the UFC and the Communist Party. As early as April 7 the CP's Trade Union Committee decided that Weisbord should withdraw from the negotiations to facilitate a settlement and that the UFC should agree to become a local in the UTW if the union offered.[30]

Within the Communist Party, Weisbord opposed his withdrawal from the strike. At a meeting of the Textile Committee in early August, Weisbord put forward a motion that "the proposal to join the UTW in form and manner decided is a retreat. Such a retreat is not a defeat but a retreat in order to facilitate a speedy and just settlement of the strike. If it was not a question of facilitating this kind of settlement we would not at this time in this manner join the UTW." John Ballam, the Communist in charge of work in the textile industry, put forward a counterproposal, "That the affiliation of the Passaic workers to the UTW is in line with the general policy of our Party (in the interests of the workers) for amalgamation and against dual unionism." Rather than a retreat for the workers, Ballam argued that "in view of the former attitude of the AF of L and UTW bureaucrats towards the Passaic strike, their present decision to open negotiations for our affiliation represents a retreat on their part and distinct victory for our policy and for the striking textile workers." The committee approved Ballam's motion.[31]

Nonetheless, there existed, Ballam acknowledged, "a very widespread misunderstanding of our policy among our Party members in the textile industry and of course also among our sympathizers." In New England, he reported, there was "a growing protest against the Passaic move into the UTW—some interpreting this as a betrayal of the workers to the AF of L and the bosses."[32]

When the CP leadership opted to dissolve the UFC and have the workers affiliate with the UTW, Weisbord followed discipline and carried out this decision. Publicly, Weisbord depicted his being forced out of the strike leadership as a victory: "The union had become so strong that, once it secured settlement or affiliation it could carry on without [Weisbord]. So the United Front Committee declared it was ready to accept even the humiliating conditions laid down to affiliate. This forced the hand of the A.F. of L. bureaucracy. They were compelled to take in the strikers."[33] But the decision rankled Weisbord.

For Weisbord, joining the UTW was a retreat if it meant that he had to leave the strike. For Ballam this was a victory, because it meant that the UTW was forced to accept the Passaic workers and accept the local leadership, which was largely Communist. This also reflected Ballam's fear that Weisbord was building his own prestige at the expense of following party policy. Ballam believed that the Communists, rather than being outmaneuvered by McMahon's demand that Weisbord leave, were outmaneuvering the UTW leadership, since Communist supporters would remain in the local leadership. "Weisbord cannot be elected as an official in the new union but there is nothing to prevent the new executive [committee] from engaging him and others as their organizer," Ballam wrote in early August.[34]

Later that month Ballam proposed measures "to safeguard the workers against the UTW expulsion policy." This included that "the United Front Committee and our Party Fraction...draw up a slate in advance" for the union's leadership, and begin "now to popularize those workers we want to elect, and to guarantee the election of our slate." Ballam saw the Passaic workers as the core of "a left wing and progressive bloc in the UTW" and advocated "the formation of a conscious left wing in Passaic" to begin "at once under the direction of our Party Fraction there."[35]

Ballam and other leading Communists saw entering the UTW as a launch pad for increased work in the textile industry, not a defensive maneuver: "The strike from now on assumes national and political importance as we draw close to the fall elections. Relief will be stimulated. All liberals and progressives will line up. The issue now becomes—the open shop and the company union versus collective bargaining and the right to organize in bona fide unions." The entrance of thousands of textile workers in Passaic, he wrote, "is our answer to the accusation of the bureaucrats of communists disrupting unions. We further put up to the A.F. of L. in concrete form the issue of organizing the unorganized and prove beyond question that it can be done. After Passaic, they will not be able to dodge this issue in other industries such as, steel, coal, rubber, automotive, chemical, metallurgical, etc." Ballam noted that "the Passaic local [was now] the biggest local in the UTW and the largest single local of textile workers in the United States."[36]

Later in September the party's Trade Union Committee instructed Ballam "to organize Party fractions in all the local [textile] unions and United Front Committees in which we have Party members." (This was carried out in October when the Political Committee established a National Textile Committee, which then called for a conference in December of "communist and left wing militants" to plan Communist work in the textile industry.)[37]

On September 3, as 10,000 strikers watched, Henry T. Hunt presented to Gustav Deak the charter for Local 1603, United Textile Workers of America. The workers—who had been on strike for 227 days—"cheered lustfully" for Weisbord's departing speech and presented him a gold watch, a silver loving cup, a traveling bag, and other gifts. "The platform from which he spoke," reported the *Passaic Daily Herald*, "was banked with roses, and a sigh went up from the densely packed crowd as they were presented." By then, the local had accepted 3,400 workers into membership and was processing another 4,000 applications. The Lauck Committee disbanded and Hunt became the local's attorney.[38]

Despite the purge of Weisbord and other Communist leaders, the CP did not quit Passaic. Deak became chair of the strikers' executive committee and the presumptive president of Local 1603. The other members of the executive committee were Eli Keller (secretary), Ellen Dawson (financial secretary), George Rusko (treasurer), along with Sam Latchuk, Frances Rivardo, and Joseph Bellene. In Ballam's words, "Deak, Dawson, Rusko and Latchuk are Party members, others sympathizers." Keller was likely a member of the Communist Party as well.[39]

According to the *Daily Worker*, after stepping down from leading the strike, Weisbord "remain[ed] in Passaic to fight the mill baron's attempts to railroad him to jail for his service to the workers," although in late September he went on a national speaking tour. Alfred Wagenknecht would remain to work on relief, while Lena Chernenko and Jack Rubenstein were "expected to remain in this city for some time assisting in the organization of the internal machinery of the new local of the United Textile Workers," according to the *Passaic Daily Herald*. Vera Buch also stayed in Passaic. Even the gifts given to Weisbord and other Communists had a political purpose, designed, in Ruthenberg's words, to cement Weisbord's role as strike leader and prevent "the danger that the U. T. W. will bring about a repudiation of Weisbord and our workers in the strike generally after the affiliation."[40]

After the handover to the UTW, Ballam outlined a plan for Communist work in Passaic. The "Party Committee of Five" was to meet regularly (with Deak replacing Weisbord), and the "Party Fraction [was] to meet twice a week." One goal was "the building of a left wing in the UTW local," based on what he claimed were 60 Communist Party members, 35 Young Workers' League members, and 1,100 "non-party (sympathizers)." The sympathizers included 450 members of the United Council of Working-Class Housewives, 700 members of the International Labor Defense, 40 members of the Italian Anti-Fascist Alliance, 200 block committee executives, and 120 members of the United Front Committee, in addition to 2,000 Young Pioneers. Ballam proposed to keep several organizers in Passaic for six months to oversee women's work, youth work, defense work, and three language groups.[41]

In its efforts to deflect accusations of having used the strike to build the Communist Party, the party had neglected to build a strong base among the union. In 1952, at the height of the Cold War, the *Passaic Herald-News* recalled that "the United Front Committee did not ask the Passaic strikers to join the Communist Party." While the union leadership was largely Communist, the rank-and-file was not. In October 1926 Lovestone complained that "so called progressives in the trade unions" had "all said that we have gone even too far in hiding our communist face in Passaic." Lovestone added: "I am also told that at one time or another instructions were given to keep the Daily Worker out of Passaic. I hope these reports are untrue but if they are not, then we have made some very grievous errors in the campaign."[42]

In late January 1927, Emil Gardos, the local organizer, criticized the "mistake" that "we did not have from the beginning the machinery for party work" in Passaic. He estimated that there were eighty members of the Communist Party in Passaic; the CP organized fortnightly forums, the first of which drew over 700 people. He called the ILD "our political mass organization" and noted that it had nine branches, ranging from a 30-strong Russian branch to the 560-strong Hungarian branch. Gardos underlined that "the future of the party movement in Passaic depends largely on the future of the union," but "that the organizations we built and the vanguard we developed will not only be more or less preserved, but will be a guarantee for the maintenance of the union under the present unfavorable circumstances." Ballam was less optimistic. "The Party membership is composed of unreliable forces, young, immature and irresponsible comrades who today speak for the Party and tomorrow will rob the office." He added: "There are no steady, mature, and reliable workers in the Party fraction." By August 1927, according to Gardos, the Passaic membership had dropped to forty-one.[43] More than a thousand workers had joined the ILD or other pro-Communist organizations during the strike, indicating that many were open to Communism. In the wake of the strike's defeat, the CP was not able to consolidate these workers.

Because Weisbord symbolized Communist leadership in the public's eyes, it was a retreat to agree to his removal from the strike leadership on terms dictated by the AFL. Many leading Communists were probably happy to see Weisbord's back. "The impression of all the comrades here is that he is an ego centrist and has a distinctly anti-Leninist slant," Ballam wrote in January 1927. Gardos quipped in March that "com. Weisbord needs a lot of experience, a lot of political development to become what he thinks he is today." This personal animosity does not negate Weisbord's importance. Weisbord, whom the strikers nicknamed "Jecusko," or little Jesus, connected with and inspired the strikers in a way that other Communist leaders did not. At a congress of the New Jersey State Federation in mid-September, Hilfers acknowledged that Weisbord "has accomplished what probably others couldn't accomplish under the same circumstances" and " has kept these strikers out for a solid eight months."[44]

The UTW Runs the Strike

On September 11 the strike leadership and the Slavic Societies organized a mass parade to celebrate joining the AFL. From the dais McMahon declared, "We are here to build, not to destroy." He continued: "We must put an end to the personal abuse of employers and the heckling on the street. We are utterly opposed to the destruction of mill owners' property. We cannot make headway with such tactics. Workers reap far more benefit from intelligent understanding of their problems than through physical force."[45]

McMahon depicted the strike as a mess to clean up, not an opportunity to organize workers: "Our first task is to undo the harm that has been done." He promised to "aid and assist in improving working conditions and gaining recognition of our union" though "every constructive and helpful means within our power." Creating a stable union was the overriding goal, McMahon emphasized. "I would rather establish this local with ten men who clearly understand the conditions than with ten thousand who do not—in fact I would refuse a charter to the later group."[46]

That the UTW leadership viewed the Passaic strike as a burden was driven home at the UTW's twenty-fifth convention two days later in New York City. Because the Passaic local had been members for less than three months, Deak and other representatives were seated as observers, without voice or vote.[47] McMahon tried to ignore the Passaic strike altogether, but pressure from delegates forced him to address the strike on the third day of the convention. In a rambling speech, McMahon claimed that one week into the strike, he had "received an urgent call from the labor movement in Passaic to get there as soon as possible." Upon arrival, McMahon claimed, he "realized that the strike was just, if ill-advised." McMahon asserted that although the workers wanted to join the UTW, he refused to accept them into membership because they were members of the UFC and a number of them were unemployed when they joined the UFC. He criticized the strikers' conduct:

> After seven months of vilification and abuse, of kicking and cuffing and shooting, after getting the other fellow down, not only punching him and kicking him but stamping his heels in his face, you come in to us and ask for recognition of the union and waive all other claims but recognition of the union. We said, "We will try to do that, but if we fail, we come to you, and we will tell you honestly. But you must stop these proceedings, if you expect the men that you kicked, the men who are the employers who must say 'Yes, we agree to the recognition of your union,' and if you do wish to tie our hands, you will cease all of that kind of stuff."[48]

After violence-baiting the strikers and attacking the strike, McMahon reportedly predicted that the Passaic local would not last a year.[49]

In the face of this snub, delegates insisted that Deak speak. He stressed that "our strike has been conducted according to the best traditions of the A.F. of L., and the American labor movement," and noted that "at all times our Strike Committee and our leaders have counseled us to refrain from violence." He warned that "any public statements blaming the Passaic strikers for the violence in Passaic will hurt our cause and will be misinterpreted so as to absolve the mill owners and the city, county, and police officials who alone are responsible for all the violence and unlawful attacks upon persons and property of the Passaic textile strikers." He continued: "In joining the United Textile Workers, we wish to assure your convention that we did so without reservation." He emphasized "our single-minded and whole-hearted loyalty to the principles of the American Federation of Labor and the United Textile Workers." In conclusion Deak noted: "Passaic is a milestone on the road to the complete organization of the textile industry within the U.T.W.... The U.T.W. can win undying glory by leading us to victory and the recognition of our union.... We do not expect impossibilities, but we want the United Textile Workers to assume complete responsibility and take full charge of the situation."[50] Wagenknecht, who was allowed to speak at the convention, emphasized that "so far as the textile strikers are concerned and their present leadership and former leadership, their policy has always been to join the main body of the American labor movement, namely, to join the American Federation of Labor through the United Textile Workers." A Local 1603 statement, "U.T.W. Convention Calls on A.F of L. Unions to Aid Passaic Strikers," did not mention any disputes and implied that the UTW had solidly backed the strike.[51]

The Detroit Convention of the AFL

The CP's approach of downplaying defeat in their approach to the American Federation of Labor framed their approach to the AFL's forty-sixth annual convention, which opened in Detroit on September 29. The convention stressed anti-Communism, patriotism, and cooperation with employers. At one point, the *New York Times* proclaimed, "Never has a convention of the American Federation of Labor witnessed such an excoriating attack on Communist attempts to 'bore from within and seize, control and wreck the American labor movement' as marked today's session." In an anti-Communist tirade, John L. Lewis pointed to William Z. Foster, seated in the convention gallery, calling him "the arch priest of communism in the United States" who regularly traveled to Moscow to conspire against the AFL.[52]

No delegate was an open Communist or TUEL supporter, although Foster and other leading Communists attended as observers. The front page of the *Daily Worker* printed a TUEL "program for building the trade unions," directed at the convention, that demanded a campaign to organize the unorganized; fight against company unions and injunctions; fight against oppression of Black workers, women, and children; organize a labor party; freedom for political prisoners; struggle against American imperialism; amalgamation of craft unions and democracy within the AFL. The Passaic strike was a central axis of Communist intervention into the convention. In the lead-up to the convention, Local 1603 wrote a letter to Green, urging "that the American Federation of Labor, thru its president and Executive Council should make an immediate attempt to bring about a settlement."[53]

The *Daily Worker* claimed that McMahon had invited Ellen Dawson to address the convention. Although this proved to be false, Ballam prepared a speech for her, and Ruthenberg vetted it. The draft shows the pressure to present the strike as compatible with the AFL bureaucracy. It asserted that the strike "demonstrated that not only can the textile workers be mobilized for resistance to inhuman conditions, but that they can be organized under the banner of the American Federation of Labor." Later the draft speech stated, "The American Federation of Labor has a glorious record for advancing the well-being and happiness of millions of American workers by lowering hours, increasing wages, and bettering working conditions." Ruthenberg deleted two sections of the speech that went too far in adapting to the AFL leadership. The first asserted, "Communism was never an issue in the strike"; the second, that "those who use or counsel violence are usually in the wrong."[54]

As Green promised, the convention allowed Rabbi Wise to speak, which meant that the convention's discussion of the strike was framed by his liberal anti-Communism.[55] Wise recalled "that in the hour in which that strike began I most solemnly and earnestly counseled the leaders to withdraw and to turn over the leadership of the strike to the United Textile Workers of the American Federation of Labor." The speech contained jibes against the Communists and flattery for the AFL. According to Wise, "The young man who led the strike for a time has vanished from the picture and the strikers are under the command and leadership of the wise and well led United Textile

Workers," At the end of his speech, Wise stated: "Hail to the American Federation of Labor! You are the friends of the Republic, you are among its bravest, finest and truest supporters!"[56]

J. Louis Engdahl, a Communist leader at the convention, criticized Wise's speech, "which was supposed to be the first big gun for Passaic." Instead, "Wise went out of his way, not only to attack us, but to take a swipe at the Soviet Union." Engdahl added: "With his speech over everything else went flat."[57] No doubt the Communists could have been more energetic, but the fundamental problem was not how they comported themselves in Detroit, but the Communists' illusions that their leadership role in Passaic would force Green and the AFL to listen to them.

Neither Green nor McMahon wanted to use the Passaic strike to start a national campaign to organize the textile industry and other non-unionized mass-production industries. This would have upset their dedication to craft unionism and a partnership between workers and capitalists. And they did not want a reinvigorated left wing rallying around the Passaic struggle. Instead, they sought to bury the Passaic strike, and the Communists with it. The rest of the Communist Party's leadership did not share Engdahl's pessimism. The front page of the *Passaic Textile Strikers Relief Bulletin*, published by the General Relief Committee, declared, "A.F. of L. Convention: Huge Rally for Passaic" and claimed there had been "a rousing discussion of the Passaic situation." At a postconvention political committee meeting, Ruthenberg put forward a motion "to instruct the Passaic committee" to capitalize on "the movement in Passaic among the workers on the basis of the endorsement of the AF of L."[58]

The End of the Strike

In late October, Ballam described "a steady dribbling into the Botany at the rate of about 10 workers a day," as some workers returned to work "in order to get two or three weeks wages and then quit again." Botany Mills and New Jersey Spinning had secretly restored the 10 percent wage cut that had precipitated the strike. While there were strikebreakers working at all the struck mills, these represented no more than a third of the pre-strike workforce (at Botany) and as little as 15 percent (at Forstmann and Huffmann). Ballam concluded, "after 9 months of struggle . . . the strike is still on effectively." The aid provided by the relief campaign, Ballam underlined, was crucial in maintaining the strike.[59]

In late October, Passaic mayor John H. McGuire organized a "Committee of Five" to broker a settlement. It comprised himself, Judge Cabell, Reverend Kernan, Reverend Michael Sotak, and Reverend Talbott. UTW vice president James Starr met with Cabell, Mayor McGuire, editors of the Passaic newspapers, and representatives of the mills. Borah visited Passaic to meet with the mill owners. On October 21 a union committee approached Governor Moore at a political meeting in Garfield and urged him "to use his influence as governor to settle the strike." In a discussion in his car, Moore told the group "that since Reds are out and the AFL is conducting the strike, that he will do anything in his power to bring about a settlement." After meeting with the mills' representatives in Passaic on November 4, Moore announced that they were willing to allow workers in their mills to join the UTW, but opposed a closed shop. Botany and the smaller mills were willing to settle with the union, but Forstmann and Huffmann remained determined to break the strike.[60]

On November 11, through the help of the Committee of Five, the UTW reached an agreement with the Passaic Worsted Mills, a smaller firm. The agreement did not guarantee a closed shop, but recognized the workers' right "to organize in a legitimate organization," their right to collective bargaining to resolve grievances, arbitration by a third party, that strikers would be "taken back without discrimination," and that "no outside help employment after date of settlement until strikers re-employed." The mill rehired 100 workers and promised to hire another other 600 workers as soon as possible. McMahon hailed the settlement as a victory, claiming that management "had conceded the right of collective bargaining as well as the right to belong to the legitimate American Labor Movement, and further conceded the right of workers to have representatives of their own choosing meet with the management when the workers with in the mills and the management fail to agree on any grievance brought forward by the workers." The strikers approved the settlement unanimously.[61]

Noting that this was the "first mill in the Passaic district which has ever signed an agreement with a labor union," a Local 1603 press release celebrated "a very important landmark in the stormy labor history of this region." The *Daily Worker* hailed "the greatest labor victory of the year" and "a triumph of unorganized workers against strongly entrenched exploiters." Ballam described the settlement as "a distinct victory." He added that "Passaic Worsted Mills now hires only thru the main union office," and not at the gate, so "a closed shop is practically in effect." Nonetheless, he warned that the lack of a formal closed shop was "detrimental to the workers interests" and "the basis for betrayal in Passaic by the UTW machine."[62]

It is possible that a strike for union recognition could fall short of this goal and still establish the basis for successful struggle. This was the case in the New York City hospital workers' strike in 1959, which did not result in immediate recognition but was crucial in forging a fighting union that forced the employers to negotiate.[63] But this requires that the workers maintain their militancy and unity. This did not happen in Passaic: many workers were exhausted, the leading Communist was forced out of the union, and the UTW leadership had no intention of continuing the struggle.

Ballam observed that "the UTW officials, particularly Mr. Starr, work in secret" and did not consult the local leaders. Ballam warned that Starr and the UTW leadership advocated "that the scabs in the Botany be organized within the mill and that they should then settle with the Botany." Further, the UTW "issues a charter to each mill as it settles," which meant that "the present Local 1603 will eventually become a local of the unemployed and blacklisted textile workers," who will be unable to pay dues "and will consequently disappear or be officially dissolved." Ballam urged his comrades that "a *first class* man be sent in ... for stiffening up our fraction, because of the necessity for quick action in mobilizing the Passaic strikers against an attempt to betray the strike by the McMahon machine."[64]

Later in November, Botany Mills publicly rescinded the 10 percent cut that had precipitated the strike in January. While welcoming the move, Deak underlined that "the major demand of the strikers, however, is the recognition of the union, and no satisfactory cessation of the struggle can be had until this demand is met." After the wage increase, Starr wanted to call off the strike; the Communists, Ballam reported, mobilized to fight this.[65]

Upon hearing of Botany's retreat, Ballam wired Ruthenberg that "this will create [a] critical condition" and stated that the Local 1603 executive committee would meet with McMahon and demand that the UTW and AFL go on the offensive. Ballam's somewhat cryptic telegram states: "If they refuse we will claim partial victory basis restoration wage cut increase ten percent and right to organize defeated on recognition union collective bargaining and blame reactionaries for failure to act and issue statement calling strike off this is Passaic Brest Qitovisk [*sic*] retreat saving union and our machinery and claiming partial victory or demoralization complete rout."[66] In insisting that the young Soviet Republic accept the Brest-Litovsk treaty in order to survive, Lenin did not sugarcoat the treaty, emphasizing its "unprecedentedly severe, immeasurably oppressive, predatory terms."[67] In contrast, Ballam wanted to "claim partial victory" while agreeing to terms that amounted to a defeat. In order to prepare for future struggle, it is necessary to make an honest assessment of previous strikes. The terms of unity with the UTW, the workers' weariness, and the CP's own exhaustion prevented this in Passaic.

On November 29 the *Daily Worker* ran a front-page article, "The Passaic Mill Owners Can Be Beaten." The paper warned, "The mill owners of Passaic, undoubtedly with the advice and aid of their agents in the labor movement, are making strenuous efforts to settle the strike without conceding the right to organize to the great majority of the workers." The article stated that "the task of the U.T.W. officials in charge of the strike is to explain this to the workers, start a new offensive against the mill owners by intensifying and extending the strike and put forward the demand" of the right to unionize for all the workers. The article called "for an end to the playing of politics in the ranks of the two capitalist parties in Washington" and concluded that if "President Green of the American Federation of Labor and President McMahon of the United Textile Workers come to the Passaic battlefield, pledge the full support of the trade union movement to a mass meeting of the strikers, carry out this pledge in letter and sprit ... the strike will be won."[68]

In early December, Ballam reported more strikebreakers working in several mills. He added: "In Forstmann-Huffmann we were steadily losing ground" since "six spinners went back there and each spinner means production for 150 unskilled workers." Seventy to 80 percent of the strikers had obtained jobs in other industries, and "only old women and a few old men are on the picket lines." He estimated there were "about 1000 active strikers in Passaic." Furthermore, "Lodi is completely lost," with 2,000 out of 3,500 workers back at work in the silk-dyeing mills.[69]

In December, Botany and Garfield mills (both owned by Botany Consolidated Mills) settled. The agreement guaranteed workers the right to join the UTW and to bargain collectively, and stipulated that the mills would not discriminate against union members and would hire strikers before outside workers. "The closed shop was not asked," the Federated Press noted, "and both workers and mill owners agree to arbitrate future differences." A week later, Dundee Textile Co. agreed to the same terms.[70]

Local 1603 issued a statement, "Another Victory for Passaic." Ballam, in the TUEL's new journal, *Labor Unity*, called this "a signal victory in the most stubbornly fought and longest strike in the history of the textile industry." In an internal report, Ballam was less sanguine. He noted that that Botany management, and not the union, controlled who was hired—and that McMahon and Starr had collaborated in this policy. The Communists in Passaic, Ballam observed, lacked "sufficient power to fight it openly against the mill."[71]

Forstmann and Huffmann refused to deal with the union, even after Borah visited Julius Forstmann in Passaic in late October. In November, Forstmann dismissed "the suggestion now advanced that the company deal with the union and discriminate in favor of union men, regardless of their ability." On January 19 Forstmann wrote to the Committee of Five that his firm did not object "to the membership of employe[e]s in legitimate outside organizations, whether religious, social, or otherwise." He added, "As soon as business conditions will permit us to re-employ still more of our former workers than we have already done so far, the Company will select its employe[e]s according to their individual fitness, without discrimination on account of membership in legitimate outside unions."[72]

Forstmann's statement did not recognize the union or accept collective bargaining, but left open the possibility that the union could organize without overt company hostility. Starr and the UTW leadership wanted to settle the strike on the basis of Forstmann's statement, and refused to negotiate any more. The Forstmann and Huffmann committee of Local 1603, led by Ellen Dawson, rejected Forstmann's letter.[73]

The Communist leadership in Passaic decided (in Ballam's words) "that we could not assume the responsibility for continuing the strike in the face of the refusal of McMahon to carry on any further negotiations with F&H as instructed by the strikers, since we could hold out no hope to the workers, and would be ourselves compelled to call the strike off later." After debate, the Communists agreed to advocate settlement while continuing to highlight the weakness of Forstmann's letter. On February 1, about 500 workers voted by secret ballot whether to return to work: 35 voted to end the strike, 70 voted to continue, and the rest abstained. After McMahon declared the ballot invalid, the workers voted again the next day: 84 workers voted for the Communists' proposal, 242 against, and 200 abstained. This created "a very serious and difficult situation," Ballam reported, since "we are now on record for calling off the strike, with the workers turning down our resolution." Ballam thought the strike could not win: "The workers insist on carrying on the strike, while at the same time they refuse to picket, and the gates of the F&H Co. are stormed every morning with strikers seeking to go back to work. We cannot maintain an effective picket line and there is in reality no strike in progress."[74]

Only on the third vote—held on February 15—did the union membership agree to return to work based on Forstmann's letter. "I said at the last meeting and I can only repeat this afternoon that I don't see any possible chance of getting any further concession from Mr. Forstmann," Deak stated. According to the union press release, Forstmann's letter, "while not conceding recognition of the United Textile Workers union," was "a distinct concession to the strikers, and a qualification of the former anti-union attitude of the Forstmann-Huffmann Company."[75]

Gera Mills and New Jersey Worsted, the remaining two wool mills, agreed to settle on the same terms as Forstmann and Huffmann shortly afterward. The union membership first rejected returning to work, but voted to accept them on March 1. The same day, the union ended the strike of silk dye workers at United Piece Dye Works in Lodi after "the management gave a verbal agreement that no union members would be discriminated against," in the words of the Federated Press. "While this was a defeat of the Lodi strikers," Deak said in a speech to 250 workers, "it is our aim and ambition to build a union from the inside of the mill and drop the battle of the picket line." Again, in an internal report, Ballam was more blunt: "The United Piece Dye Works refuse to deal with the workers in any way, claiming they have enough workers and do not want anything to do with the union."[76]

Despite their agreements, the mill owners fired and blacklisted militants and laid off many workers. Ballam observed in January that "the present policy of the Passaic settled mills is to demoralize the workers and to break the hold of the union and the local leadership over them." The UTW leadership refused to defend its members. The Communist leadership did not have enough support to maintain pressure on the UTW leaders. In early February, Ballam estimated that 10,000 workers had applied to the UTW, but "not over 200 are today actually dues-paying members of the union." Two weeks later, he estimated the membership had grown to 800, and by early March, to 1,000 workers. By July he estimated there were 1,176 members in the six different

UTW locals in the former strike zone. This was more union members than before the strike, but the union did not organize the majority of the workers at any of the mills, and none of the mills had signed a union contract.[77]

On March 11 the new UTW locals in Passaic, Garfield, Lodi, and Clifton organized a Textile Council of Passaic and Vicinity, with Deak as its president, Keller as general secretary, and Dawson as secretary-treasurer. This turned out to be a rearguard action.[78] Many workers deserted the UTW because they left the industry altogether or because they could not afford the initiation fees and dues, or out of disgust with the union leadership.

The Passaic Chamber of Commerce's September 1927 *Bulletin* bragged, "In the majority of industries in Passaic the labor is not unionized." The writer added, "Unions have been formed in the woolen textile mills, but as far as can be learned, not very much progress can be made."[79] As far as the mill owners and their supporters were concerned, this was the strike's epitaph.

10

After the Strike

In Passaic the strike ended with a whimper, not a bang. Over a period of months, the struck mills reached individual agreements with the United Textile Workers, each falling short of a union contract. Strikers trickled back to the mills, although fewer than had worked a year earlier. This chapter examines to what extent the defeat of the strike resulted from the Communist Party's policy of seeking unity with the American Federation of Labor. It also examines the legacy of the strike—on Passaic, on the labor movement more broadly, and finally, on the Communist Party.

As James P. Cannon later wrote to Theodore Draper, the strike "under all ordinary circumstances should have a resulted in a resounding victory." He added: "The bosses were too strong, had too many financial resources and were too determined to prevent the consolidation of a radical union organization."[1] Both the strike leaders and the textile companies saw the strike as more than a battle over wages; it reflected the broader class struggle. Perhaps reflecting their origins in Germany, where the textile industry had pioneered employer associations (*Arbeitgeberverbände*) and where Communists had gained a mass base in the labor movement, the mill owners sacrificed immediate economic losses to perceived longer-term class interests.[2]

Rather than bring defeat, the strike's Communist leadership allowed the workers to persevere as long as they did. As Marxists, the Communists emphasized that the strike would be won or lost on the picket line; at the same time, they sought allies and sought to bring the Passaic struggle to the broader labor movement. Communists pressured labor leaders, radical intellectuals, and liberal politicians to take up the strike, but had no illusions that the capitalist government would bring victory to the wool workers. Communists built

Black workers join the walkout of silk-dyers in Lodi. The United Front Committee stressed solidarity and the common struggle of the working class against exploitation and oppression. Such solidarity was central in the industrial union battles a decade later. American Labor Museum/Botto House National Landmark.

solidarity networks that helped sustain the workers amid repression and hunger; at the same time, they generalized the political importance of the strike, transforming it from a local fight for higher wages into a broader struggle for the entire working class.

Even though the strike benefited from Communist leadership, it highlighted weaknesses in the CP's approach to the labor movement, which had been developed by William Z. Foster. During the steelworkers' and meatpackers' strikes in

1919, Foster eschewed forming new unions and pushed for existing AFL unions to work together and organize the unorganized and amalgamate into industrial unions. After joining the Communist Party, Foster maintained this perspective through the TUEL, a pan-union organization opposed to dual unionism. The initial United Front Committees, organized before the Passaic strike, focused on different sectors of the textile industry in various states, and reflected the TUEL approach: coordinating left-wing militants in the textile unions, calling to organize the unorganized, and advocating amalgamation of the textile unions.[3]

In Passaic the UFC had faced new challenges: rather than being an opposition group within established unions, Communist militants had to organize a union where none existed. The UFC became a union even as it denied it was doing so—violating Foster's hostility to organizing new unions. "The action at Passaic did indeed violate both the letter and spirit of Fosterite trade-union policy," James P. Cannon recalled decades later, after he had become a Trotskyist.[4] The UFC was not a classical dual union: the UTW claimed theoretical jurisdiction over all textile workers everywhere, but they had long disdained to organize the unskilled wool workers. Organizing the unorganized required a vehicle outside the AFL—something that Foster was not willing to countenance. Especially after he returned to the United States in the summer of 1926, Foster strove to reorient the Passaic strike, demanding that the striking wool workers join the AFL.

While Foster's theoretical objection to organizing a new union may have been dogmatic, in practical terms it recognized that the Communist Party in 1926 did not have the social weight to set up a rival labor federation, especially after the Associated Silk Workers and other unions refused to extend the Passaic strike. A small Communist-led textile union would have been unlikely to defeat the mills. In this situation, the Communists' attempt to seek support from the UTW and AFL was preferable to abandoning the Passaic workers or leading them into demoralization and defeat. Cannon stressed in 1930: "To say that the affiliation amounted to a betrayal of the workers is childish nonsense that ignores all the facts. The strike was virtually at an end at the time. It had been prolonged for eight or ten months, and the workers were simply worn out.... The greatest error was the opportunistic manner in which the affiliation was carried out. This was particularly noticeable in the publicity of the strike committee, which began to be tainted with defeatist apologies to the labor fakers."[5] Affiliation with the UTW did not result in union recognition or collective bargaining and meant that the UTW's bureaucracy dictated that Weisbord, despite his popularity with the strikers, leave Passaic. But joining the UTW left open the possibility that there would be the foundation upon which to build a union when the next struggle broke out. Rather than stage an orderly retreat, the UFC and the CP depicted the UTW's taking over the strike as a victory. Presenting the formation of a new union in Passaic not just as impossible in the concrete circumstances, but as unprincipled in *all* situations, meant that joining the UTW was the only possible end to the strike. It is not a crime to be defeated, but the pretense that the defeat was a victory demoralized the workers, undermining their discipline and the militancy necessary for future struggle.

Passaic after the Strike

The companies attempted to refurbish their image after the strike. In early March 1927, Robert M. Reinhold, director of employment and industrial relations for Forstmann and Huffmann, resigned. Reinhold had organized the company union, and many workers saw him as the architect of the company's anti-union campaign. Later that month the Industrial Council of Passaic Wool Manufacturers (the so-called Wool Council) disbanded. In early summer, Botany overhauled its management, discharging many foremen and department heads. Along with the increased wages, the company abandoned its company union, improved sanitary conditions, and instructed foremen to be less arbitrary. Colonel Johnson resigned from Botany and moved to Europe, leaving the company in the hands of Max Stoehr. The Passaic Chamber of Commerce (which counted the mills as prominent members) began publishing an attractive monthly bulletin celebrating the region.[6]

After the strike, the mills blacklisted union militants, laid off workers, and slashed wages. The number of wool and worsted workers in New Jersey fell from 17,838 in 1923 to 9,197 in 1929. In April 1927 the union noted that "thousands of textile workers are without jobs because of the slump in the woolen industry" and that "most of the mills are working only part-time days and have cut out the night shift altogether." The union estimated that less than a third of textile workers were working.[7]

Emil Gardos called the union "very weak" and unlikely to survive the increasing unemployment. He estimated that "present membership is less than a thousand with many unemployed members." That month the union helped organize a conference "to request the city to start work at once on construction and repairs in order to furnish work for the jobless." The mayor, Chamber of Commerce, and local unions created the Federal, State, Municipal Employment Bureau, which tried to match unemployed residents with companies looking for (often temporary) workers. Eli Keller, a Communist leader in the textile union, sat on the board.[8]

A year later, in April 1928, Gera Mills cut wages by 20 percent and sped up production. "If things that are taking place in the mills in Passaic continue," Deak warned, "no one can stop a repetition of 1926." *Labor Unity*, the newspaper of the TUEL, reported that the mills had rehired only several thousand workers, many part-time at reduced wages, and concluded, "It is evident that the bosses are trying to smash the union." According to the journal, the national UTW leadership and Botany management had agreed at the end of the strike to blacklist militants and suspected Communists. In August, Passaic Worsted Spinning Company declared bankruptcy.[9]

Conditions worsened in the Great Depression. Full-time weekly wages for the state's wool and worsted workers declined from an average of $27.83 in 1928 to $22.83 in 1932. In December 1929 Deak told the *Daily Worker* that only 6,000 of the 16,000 strikers had been able to find work in the mills. The next month *Labor Unity* reported layoffs at the United Piece Dye Works and Botany Mills, and a shortened workweek at Forstmann and Huffmann. In 1929, Colonel Johnson returned from Europe to run Botany. To modernize production, he scrapped almost 2,000 looms from the late nineteenth century, but Botany Consolidated Mills still filed for bankruptcy in August 1935.[10]

In his short story "Life along the Passaic River" (1938), William Carlos Williams—a poet who was chief of pediatrics at Passaic General Hospital during the strike—had a character expound on the strike's futility:

> When they had the big strike at the textile mills, and that bright boy from Boston came down and went shooting off his mouth around the streets here telling us what to do: Who paid for having their kids and women beat up by the police? Did that guy take a room down on Monroe St. and offer his services for the next ten years at fifty cents a throw to help straighten out the messes he helped get us into? He did not.[11]

Although the poor condition of Passaic workers in the Great Depression would seem to confirm Williams's pessimism, workers in the Passaic area had increased what the Communists would refer to as their class consciousness. A Passaic native, writing in the *New York Times* fifty years after the strike, underlined: "What the strikers had gained was recognition of their right to organize, a consciousness of their own power and the sharing of a profound experience." Columbia University historian James P. Shenton was born in Passaic in 1925 and lived there his entire life. "It was a world in which class was real, a world of immigrants and their work," he told a campus publication in 1996. "The one thing I still cannot do is cross a picket line."[12]

The Passaic Strike and the Communist Party

In Passaic the Communist Party fought for the entire working class as the rest of the labor movement retreated. Along with the subsequent Sacco and Vanzetti campaign, the strike highlighted the CP's potential strength. The tragedy of American Communism is that this potential was not realized as the party became increasingly subordinated, politically and organizationally, to the Stalinist Comintern. Although Cannon and a small number of supporters fought against this degeneration in solidarity with Leon Trotsky's Left Opposition, Lovestone, Foster, and other leading Communists believed that their role was, not to make a revolution in the United States, but to champion the current line from Moscow. Even as the CP embraced the Stalinist program of socialism in one country (which subordinated the interests of the international proletariat to the defense of the Soviet bureaucracy's own privileged position), cadres active in the strike would play important roles in future labor battles.[13]

In the aftermath of the strike, the Communist Party tried to increase its influence and support in the strike zone. In April and May 1927, Weisbord and fellow Communists Simon E. Bambach (a mill worker and UTW local officer) and Simon Smelkinson (a member of the ILGWU) ran for Passaic city commissioners—running against not only against Mayor McGuire and Commissioner Preiskel, but Justice Cabell and the Slavic Committee's William Vanacek. The Communist candidates demanded freedom for Sacco and Vanzetti and proclaimed as their platform "Not a bosses' government or a businessmen's government but a workers' government." The campaign "created an enthusiasm that we only had at the best day of the strike," according to one report. An estimated 4,000 people came to hear Weisbord speak during the campaign; he received more than a thousand votes, and his comrades on the tickets around 400 votes.[14] That fall, Gustav Deak, Felix Penarisi, and John Di Santo ran for the Garfield city council on the "United Labor Party" ticket. (Deak received 18 percent of the votes in his ward, and the other two much less.)[15]

The New Bedford Strike and the National Textile Workers Union

In July 1927 the Comintern seemed to draw upon the Passaic strike in reformulating its labor policy:

> The Party should not limit itself to work the existing trade unions. The
> reactionary policies of the bureaucracy who in many instances refuse to
> organize workers, and the increasing will of the unorganized masses to
> struggle, demand that the Party, after examining all the circumstances, and
> exhausting all possibilities to force the A.F. of L. to organize the unorganized,
> especially in connection with definite struggles against the employers, should
> pursue with the greatest energy the task of organizing the unorganized. Having
> founded such new organizations, every effort must be made to link them up
> with the existing trade unions and at the same time to insist on the right of the
> workers themselves to administer the unions.[16]

The party pursued a different policy in New Bedford, Massachusetts, where from April to October 1928 some 30,000 workers struck against a 10 percent wage cut. Veterans of the Passaic strike—including UTW Local 1603 leaders Dawson, Keller, and Deak—traveled to New Bedford. In August 1928, Communists (led by Weisbord) denounced the "strike-breaking" activities of the UTW in New Bedford, and called on textile workers to leave the AFL and "take things in their own hands and build a national textile union that will be a real workers' union." This "real workers' union" was the newly formed National Textile Workers Union (NTWU), led by the Communist Party. When the Passaic UTW local supported this call, the McMahon national leadership ousted two Passaic delegates at the UTW's national convention. The Passaic union left the AFL and joined the NTWU. Deak and Dawson became vice presidents of the new union, and Weisbord secretary-treasurer.[17]

Unlike the UFC in Passaic, the NTWU sought to split workers from the UTW and other established textile unions. In New Jersey the NTWU focused on the Paterson silk industry, including, in 1928, a 3,000-strong silk workers' strike, in which NTWU leaders competed with the Associated Silk Workers for leadership. Despite support from leaders of the wool workers in Passaic, the NTWU never gained a foothold among the workforce. In February 1929 the NTWU had 3,097 members, 2,647 of whom were in good standing; the Passaic local had 43 members, only 3 of whom were in good standing. The NTWU's most famous struggle was the strike at the Loray Mill in Gastonia, North Carolina, later in 1929.[18]

The formation of the NTWU reflected the shift in the Communist Party's trade-union work—abandoning its emphasis on working within the AFL and instead forming Communist-led unions. This was a domestic reflection of the zigzags in Stalin's policies in Russia and abroad. As yesterday's heroes became today's traitors per Stalin in Moscow, the political balance sheet of the Passaic strike was subordinated to party factionalism. In the United States, Communists used the role of the AFL in the Passaic strike to justify this turn.[19] The Communist Party was never able to fully grapple with the Passaic strike. Depending on the political context, writers sympathetic to the Communist Party painted the strike a victory or a compromise.[20]

The Lovestoneite Exodus and the Passaic Strike

During the factional warfare that accompanied the rise of Stalinism in the Communist Party in the United States, the Ruthenberg faction—the Lovestone faction after Ruthenberg died in March 1927—used the Passaic strike to bolster their trade-union credentials against accusations of being petit bourgeois "City College boys." In the lead-up to the party's Fifth National Convention in 1927, internal correspondence in the Lovestone faction labeled Weisbord "our best mass leader, a potential foil to Foster" on the central committee. In the region as a whole, support for Lovestone's faction was more than three times greater than for Foster's, and in Passaic it was more than six times greater.[21]

In 1929 the CP expelled Lovestone and about 300 of his followers, who soon organized the Communist Party (Majority Group). Within a decade Lovestone and his remaining followers would become agents in the crusade against Communism by the AFL bureaucracy and the U.S. government.[22]

Jack Rubenstein, a founding member of the Communist Party in the United States, was 18 years old at the start of the strike. He became Weisbord's assistant and was arrested multiple times; later he was active in the New Bedford strike and in the National Textile Workers Union. He was expelled from the Communist Party in 1929 and eventually became a trade-union official in New York. International Workers' Aid.

Those expelled included Benjamin Gitlow and Bert Miller, who helped oversee the party's labor work in New Jersey; and Ellen Dawson, Eli Keller, Jack Rubenstein, and Myriam Silvis, who had been active on the ground in Passaic. Lovestone's *Revolutionary Age* claimed that the expulsion of Lovestone's followers brought "ruin" to the party in Passaic, causing the branch to decline from eighty members to seven and leaving the CP with "no organization at all among the militant textile workers of Passaic."[23]

The Fate of Albert Weisbord and Other Strike Leaders

In late 1929 the Communist Party purged Albert Weisbord and Vera Buch. After flirting with the Lovestoneites, in the fall of 1930 they formed the Communist League of Struggle and declared themselves followers of Trotsky (although enemies of Cannon and Trotsky's other followers).[24] Weisbord would never again play as prominent a role in the labor movement as he had during the textile industry during the 1920s, even as his self-constructed cult-of-personality grew.

Weisbord was a product and a victim of the degenerating Communist Party. The cynicism of Stalinism, particularly under Lovestone, accentuated Weisbord's worst traits. Sixty years after the strike, Deak recalled Weisbord as "an egomaniac." In his later writing, Weisbord's hostility to other Communists in the 1920s seems almost pathological, especially his insinuation that most of the leadership was in the service of the U.S. and Soviet intelligence services.[25] The Weisbords continued the Communist League of Struggle through the mid-1930s. Albert Weisbord died in 1977 and Vera Buch Weisbord a decade later.[26]

Blacklisted from the textile industry after the strike, Deak eventually got a job with AT&T, where he worked for more than thirty years. By 1932 Deak had left the Communist Party; the next year he ran, again unsuccessfully, for Garfield city councilman. This time he was a representative of the Garfield Taxpayers Association, which advocated smaller city budgets, including lower wages for municipal employees. Throughout the Depression he focused on local politics, advocating a city manager system and criticizing elected officials. In 1939 he won election to the Garfield city council, and over the next decades he briefly held a variety of elected posts. In 1974 he became city manager, essentially mayor. In his political career, Deak did not hide his role in the strike, although he did deny he had been a member of the Communist Party.[27] Deak died in May 1987, at age eighty-two; obituaries in several local papers recounted his political career in Garfield, but only one mentioned the strike.[28]

Ellen Dawson, who became politicized through the Passaic strike, rose to prominence in the Communist Party and the NTWU until, in early 1929, she became a member of the party's Central Executive Committee and then an activist in the Gastonia strike. Months later, the CP and the NTWU expelled her during the anti-Lovestoneite purge. The Lovestoneites elected her to their national council and the editorial board of *Revolutionary Age*. David McMullen, in his biography of Dawson, concluded: "Although the exact date is not clear, it appears highly probably that Ellen's life as a radical activist ended at some point during the early 1930s." He added: "She simply labored as a weaver and returned to being an anonymous American worker." In December 1965 she retired from Samuel Hird and Sons in Garfield. In April 1967, while in Florida, she died suddenly, most likely from a lung condition contracted during her years of textile work. The Paterson *News* and the *Passaic Herald-News* ran obituaries (under the name Mrs. Louis Kanki), but neither noted her activity in the strike.[29]

The Communist Party expelled Jack Rubenstein, Weisbord's much-arrested assistant, in August 1929 because he "openly solidarized . . . with Lovestone . . . and his anti-Party and anti-working class activities." In 1933 he was an organizer in a 20,000-strong silk dyers and finishers strike in Paterson. He eventually became an official in the Textile Workers Union of America, and then vice president of the New York AFL-CIO. "My husband was a union man till the day he died," his widow, Ruth Rubenstein, was quoted as saying in his *Passaic Herald-News* obituary, after he died in 1989, aged eighty-four.[30]

In late 1929 the Communist Party purged Eli Keller, a former Botany worker and officer in UTW Local 1603 and then a leader of the NTWU, because he "refused to take an uncompromised stand against Ellen Dawson."[31]

He became a leader in the Paterson silk workers' union (which rejoined the UTW), including during the 1934 nationwide textile strike. He resigned from the union in early 1935 and became a merchant in suburban Newark until he retired in 1971. Upon his death in 1985, the *Passaic Herald-News* ran a short obituary, which misspelled his first name and did not mention his history as a weaver or union leader.[32]

Not all Communists involved in the strike were Lovestone supporters, of course. Elizabeth Gurley Flynn, after almost a decade of inactivity, became a leading Communist in the 1930s until her death in 1964. Robert Dunn helped organize the pro-Communist Labor Research Association in 1927 and remained a Communist until he died in 1977. Sophie Melvin, a Communist youth activist in Passaic and then Gastonia, returned to Passaic in 1930 to work with the unemployed textile workers. She married Si Gerson, another leading Communist who had been to Passaic. In 1953 the Justice Department tried to revoke her citizenship and deport her to the Soviet Union. She remained in the CP for the rest of her life.[33] Martha Stone, another young Communist militant, eventually became the leader of the Communist Party in New Jersey (and, under her married name, Martha Stone Asher, a target of the Smith Act in the 1950s).[34]

Alfred Wagenknecht continued to organize relief work during Communist-led strikes, and remained a leading Communist until his death. His daughter, Helen Allison, also remained in the CP for life; in 1927 she married Carl Weisberg (better known as Carl Winter), the City College student whom the police beat up in the strike. Both became organizers for the Communist Party; Winter spent five years in federal prison under the Smith Act.[35] Lena Chernenko, a Communist organizer in Passaic, remained with the CP for the rest of her life. According Art Shield's obituary for her in the CP's *Daily World*, she was a district organizer of the CP in New Jersey in the 1930s, and then an official in the New York State Communist Party. She died in 1979, at age seventy-eight, bequeathing $1,000 each to the Socialist Republic of Vietnam and the *Daily World*.[36]

The Impact of the Passaic Strike on the Broader Labor Movement

The Passaic strike highlighted the AFL leadership's opposition to organizing mass-production industries. In some cases this stemmed directly from personal corruption: After Henry Hilfers was voted out of his leadership position in the New Jersey Federation of Labor shortly after the strike, it was discovered that during his tenure he had accepted $100,000 from anti-union companies—supposedly for advertisements in the union journal he ran, but more likely, his enemies alleged, as bribes to leave those companies unorganized. (The state federation did not pursue the charges, and Hilfers remained active in the New Jersey labor movement until his death in 1932.)[37]

Against refrains that workers like the Passaic mill hands could not be orga-nized, the strike showed that workers in the United States, given the opportu-nity and a leadership prepared to lead class struggle, could overcome ethnic and religious divisions and fight in the interest of all workers. The UFC's focus on mass picket lines and organizing unskilled mass-production workers, including women and immigrants, presaged the labor battles of 1930s.[38]

In September 1934 about 400,000 textile workers struck from Maine to Alabama in one of the biggest strikes in U.S. history. Unlike the UFC's insis-tence in 1926 on mobilizing the workers in their own interest, the UTW looked to the capitalist state to solve industrial problems; the UTW orga-nized no publicity, opened no soup kitchens, and paid no strike benefits. The strike ended in defeat, with most locals destroyed and tens of thousands of militants fired and blacklisted. The UTW leadership bears responsibility for this defeat—but the formation of the NTWU meant that there was no sig-nificant Communist opposition within the UTW.[39]

That same year there were three highly successful labor battles that paved the way for the success of the Congress of Industrial Organizations (CIO): the longshoremen's strike in San Francisco, the automobile parts workers' strike in Toledo, and the truck drivers' strike in Minneapolis. These strikes—not the defeated UTW strike—were the true progeny of the Passaic strike. They sought to organize the unorganized and relied on the power of the workers and their picket lines instead of the government and its arbitrators. Each became a social movement, not just a strike to improve economic conditions. Each sought sup-port and solidarity from the entire working class. Each had a leadership that saw itself as revolutionary and saw the need to organize workers independently of the capitalists' state and their Democratic or Republican parties.

Even though the UTW supported the CIO, its leadership was incapable of and uninterested in organizing mass-production workers. When the CIO leadership turned to organize textile workers, they saw the discredited UTW leadership as an obstacle. In 1937 the CIO formed the Textile Workers Organ-izing Committee (TWOC), under the leadership of Sidney Hillman.[40] The TWOC was a pale imitation of the UFC, based on Hillman's trust in the capitalist Roosevelt administration and the New Deal National Labor Rela-tions Board to protect textile workers. Hillman kept Communists and other radicals out of the TWOC.[41] McMahon's purge of Weisbord and the UFC thus set the mold for the later failure of textile unionism, even when it was carried out under the auspices of the CIO.

The Passaic Workers in the 1930s

The Lodi silk dye workers had been the last to return to work and the first to strike again. They were among the estimated 20,000 textile dyers and finish-ers in Brooklyn and North Jersey who struck for two months and won union recognition, forming the Federation of Dyers, Finishers, Printers, and Bleachers of America. In October 1934 the dye workers joined the national textile strike (against the wishes of the UTW leadership) and returned to work in December, having won a shorter workweek and higher wages, although not a closed shop.[42]

By the time of the 1934 strike, only 2,500 woolen workers, out of 24,000 in the area, were working, and none under union contract. During that strike the UTW vice president, William F. Kelly, called upon the tradition of the earlier strike to mobilize workers. "Your strike in 1926 was a sectional strike," he told a meeting of 600 workers, "but this war embraces the entire country." John Salmond, in his history of the 1934 strike, speculates that the Passaic workers' "memories of 1926, perhaps, were not positive ones" and highlights "strong evidence that most of the town's workers had no interest in joining the strike." The mayor of Passaic, John R. Johnson, promised to allow picketing outside the city's mills if picketers allowed open access to the mills. Soon, however, Johnson banned picketing outright, and in an echo of 1926, police broke up picket lines. When Eli Keller tried to lead 900 Paterson silk workers to picket the Botany Mill, police clubbed the picketers and arrested Keller and another union leader.[43]

In April 1937, a decade after the defeat of the Passaic strike, the TWOC began a campaign to organize the Passaic mills. At Botany, Charles F. H. Johnson tried to defeat the TWOC through harassment, intimidation, and spying. When the TWOC's successor, the Textile Workers Union of America (TWUA), finally won a National Labor Relations Board election in 1940 to represent thirty-two wool trappers and sorters, Botany refused to deal with the union. In December 1943 the majority of 3,855 eligible workers voted to be represented by the TWUA—despite having been forced to attend fourteen anti-union speeches by Johnson and told to vote against the union the day before the election. In June 1944 about 600 Botany workers engaged in a sit-down strike for almost a week. Only then did Botany Worsted Mills sign a contract with the TWUA, providing 4,500 workers company-paid social insurance, paid vacations, double time for Sunday, and medical and maternity leave.[44]

Julius Forstmann died in 1939, and his company (called Forstmann Woolen Company since 1931) passed into the hands of his son, Curt E. Forstmann. In June 1944 almost two-thirds of Forstmann workers in Passaic signed cards to join the TWUA, and in August the company and the union signed a contract that provided social insurance coverage and equal pay for men and women.[45] In late July 1946, after the TWUA lost its second election to organize the 2,500 workers at New Jersey Worsted Mills in Garfield and Gera Worsted Mills in Passaic, the New Jersey Worsted workers struck for higher wages, and Gera workers struck in solidarity. During the six-week strike, the workers voted to be represented by the TWUA.[46]

Twenty years after the Passaic strike was defeated, the wool workers accomplished their goal: union recognition. The companies accepted unionization only begrudgingly, and the workers struck several times, including a six-week strike at the Botany, Gera, and Forstmann mills in 1951. In early 1952, Botany and Gera mills announced that due to poor conditions in the wool industry, they were not going to renew their union contract, although the companies eventually signed another contract with the TWUA.[47]

In May 1952 Colonel Johnson died, and his son, Charles F. H. Johnson Jr., took over Botany. In late 1955 Botany Mills quit the textile industry. It set up an affiliate company, Clarence Worsted, that took over its last textile operation, a dyeing and finishing plant in Passaic that employed 150 people. "With the disposal of the plan," wrote the *New York Times*, "Botany becomes primarily a real estate and licensing company." The company continued in different locations under various owners and names (including Botany Finishing and Stervo Dyeing and Finishing). In February 1970 the company went into receivership, and Richard G. Stoehr, the company's president and the scion of Botany's founder, told the plant's seventy-five employees to remain home "until further notice." That March the bankruptcy court auctioned off the company's assets.[48]

In 1957 J. P. Stevens textile company bought Forstmann Woolen Company and closed its mills in New Jersey. Theodore J. Forstmann, grandson of Julius Forstmann, later became a billionaire financier specializing in leveraged buyouts. (Among other things, he was famous for having a brief affair with Diana, Princess of Wales.)[49] Also in 1957, United Piece and Dye Works closed its plant in Lodi, laying off 800 people. By then the company had moved much of its production to York, Pennsylvania; Charlotte, North Carolina; and Los Angeles, California.[50] This was part of a long-time shift of textile production from the Northeast (largely to the South).

The Lessons of Passaic and the Working Class Today

Later, textile manufacturers moved to Asia and Latin America; between 1994 and 2005, the United States lost 900,000 textile and apparel jobs. Since then, in response to labor militancy and higher wages in these countries, many textile companies returned to the United States, but the companies now employ many fewer people: there are only about 366,000 employees in the textile industry once farming and growing jobs are discounted. In 2017 there were 520 textile, apparel, and furnishing workers in New Jersey.[51]

Nonetheless, Passaic today is not much different from how it was ninety years ago. Its residents are likely to be immigrants working in light industry. In 2011 more than 18,500 people in Passaic County worked in manufacturing, a greater number than in any other sector except healthcare and retail.[52] The industries have changed, and the workers are more likely to speak Spanish than Polish or Hungarian.

In many ways the late 2010s appear similar to the 1920s: many workers are discontent with stagnant wages and poor jobs, while union leadership looks to the government, not to their members' strength. Between 1954 and 2018, the proportion of the national workforce that belonged to unions declined from 35 percent to 10.5 percent—not far off from the 7.5 percent of workers who belonged to unions in 1930. In 2017 the number of strikes involving more than a thousand workers was the lowest since the Bureau of Labor Statistics started tracking such numbers after the Second World War. For most workers, real wages are lower now than in the 1970s, and workers find themselves working long hours for low wages and few benefits. In 1928, income inequality peaked in the United States—unmatched until 2013.[53]

The politics of the 2020s differ in many ways from the 1920s. One of the most notable is that many workers and intellectuals in the 1920s, motivated by the Bolshevik Revolution, saw their struggles as part of a broader effort for socialism; today, the idea that capitalism can be replaced with a social system based on collective ownership and production for use is seen as obsolete or impossible by most intellectuals, workers, and oppressed peoples. Nonetheless, like in the 1920s, many workers today are angry about increasing exploitation and oppression—and are willing to struggle against it.

In 2018 more workers went on strike than in any year since 1986.[54] These included tens of thousands of teachers in Arizona, California, Oklahoma, West Virginia, and elsewhere who struck for higher pay and better conditions. For more than a month in 2019, almost 50,000 automobile workers struck against stagnant wages, unequal pay, and the growth of long-term "temporary" jobs. As in Passaic, immigrant and women workers are often central to today's labor battles. The task of organizing the unorganized remains outstanding, and, as in the 1920s, the current labor leadership seems unwilling and unable to do this. The lessons of the Passaic strike—the need for militancy, mass picket lines, bravery in the face of state and company violence, and, above all, an understanding of the fundamental hostility between labor and capital and the danger of relying on politicians from either the Democratic or Republican capitalist parties—are as important now as in the 1920s. What is lacking is the kind of leadership the Communist Party provided in Passaic—willing to draw on these lessons, combining audacity and a dedication to mobilize workers' power, not only for immediate economic needs but for the interests of the entire multiracial and multiethnic working class in sweeping away capitalism altogether through socialist revolution.

Acknowledgments

Writing a book is based on collective labor, even if it appears that there is only the solitary scholar in the hidden abode of production. This book, which took several years to write, has directly and indirectly benefited from the assistance of scores of people. If there is anything valuable in this book, I cannot take sole credit. I do, however, take responsibility for any errors that may have slipped in despite all the help I received. I also apologize to anyone whose name I have inadvertently left out from these acknowledgments.

Several friends and colleagues took the time to read earlier drafts of this book and provided invaluable comments. These include Don Andrews, Bruce Chadwick, Paul Cooperstein, Alison Dundy, Michael Goldfield, Edith Gould (who also saved me from way too many typographical errors), Carla Leshne, Norman Markowtiz, Jason Martinek, Jonathan Piper, Francis Ryan, Jeff Taylor, and Skye White. Karen Walter and her Russian readers' circle helped translate several *Pravda* articles about the strike.

I benefited from assistance from many scholars who answered my queries, offered advice, or otherwise helped me. These include Jennifer Armiger, Kamika Bennett, Kasper Braskén, Kevin Brownlow, Russell Campbell, Tim Davenport, Glenn Gebhard, Elizabeth Grey, Will Guzmán, Donna Haverty-Stacke, Michael Jameson, Jacob Kramer, Paul Le Blanc, David L. McMullen, Jonathan Michaels, Annelise Orleck, Bryan Palmer, Carol Smith, Randi Storch, Lara Vapnek, and Daniel Walkowitz.

This book would have been impossible without the assistance of the staff at libraries and institutions who shared their resources and expertise, sometimes in person but often through correspondence. These include Alexander Library, Rutgers University; American Labor Museum—Botto House; Clifton Public Library; Episcopal Diocese of Newark; Guarini Library, New Jersey City University; High Point (North Carolina) Museum; Hoover Institution, Stanford

University; Houghton and Schlesinger Libraries, Harvard University; Kheel Center, Cornell University; Library of Congress; Lodi Public Library; Longfellow House—Washington Headquarters; Museum of Modern Art; Newark Public Library; New Jersey Room, Jersey City Free Public Library; New York Public Library; Passaic City Clerk's Office; North Bergen Public Library; Passaic Public Library; Paterson Public Library; Prometheus Research Library; Msgr. William Noé Field Archives and Special Collections, Seton Hall University; Tamiment Library, New York University; Harry Ransom Center, University of Texas at Austin; Walter Reuther Library, Wayne State University; and United States Senate Historical Office.

In particular I want to thank Timothy Johnson and Michael Koncewicz at Tamiment Library, both of whom encouraged and facilitated my research in numerous ways, including by pointing out materials that I might have otherwise overlooked and allowing me to present my ongoing research; also at Tamiment, Peter Filardo and the late Michael Nash continually assisted me over the last twenty years on my research on Communism in the 1920s, which not only was invaluable for my previous book but also helped the current book. The same is true of Dale Reed at the Hoover Institution at Stanford. I want to thank the New York Public Library, one of the great institutions in the United States, for irreplaceable expertise and resources (including electronic). Susan Kriete helped track down obscure genealogical information on people involved in the strike. At New Jersey City University's Guarini Library, James Brown, Michele Hoban, and Fred Smith provided advice on obtaining resources and helped get necessary material, as did the staff at the Brigham Library in Lawrenceville. Finally, the Prometheus Research Library in Manhattan has provided a home away from home, and without its facilities and staff—Don Andrews, Helene Brosious, Alison Dundy, Richard Genova, and Edward Kartsen—I would never have been able to conceive of this book, much less write it.

Many people kindly allowed me to interview them or corresponded with me about relatives who were involved in the strike, or otherwise provided their expertise. These include Michele Artt (Carl Winter's daughter); Mark Auerbach (Passaic City historian); Brian Chenensky (grandnephew of Lena Chernenko); Judith R. Ehrenfeld (Martha Gartenlaub's daughter-in-law); Deborah Gerson (daughter of Simon Gerson); Carol Luparella (parish secretary of St. Stanislaus's Koostak Roman Catholic Church); Ingrid McLoughlin (granddaughter of Colonel Charles F. H. Johnson); William Zame (son of Herbert Zam and Miriam Silverfarb). At Rutgers University, I must thank Norman Markowitz. It would not be an overstatement to say that professor Markowitz has aided me at every step of my career as a historian, starting when I took his class as an undergraduate and extending through helping me obtain permission for graphics for this book. He has also served as an inspiration as an academic who has remained loyal to his vision of the struggle of the working class (however much our visions differ).

I owe many thanks to Jerry Ardimento, Frank Cadden, François Diacono, Bruce Mishkin, and Joe Semien for helping me with the photos, which give the reader a deeper sense of the strike. Without their masterful assistance in selecting and preparing the photos, the book would have been much less attractive or useful. I also want to acknowledge the American Labor Museum/ Botto House, and C. J. Atkins, managing editor of the *People's World*, for permission to use photographs.

I want to thank the History Department at New Jersey City University: John Bragg, Patricia Catrillo, Bruce Chadwick, Jason Martinek, José Morales, Rosemary Thurston, and Tim White. The department has provided encouragement and assistance in numerous ways. Jennifer Musial, in the Women's and Gender Studies Department, gave me moral support while I navigated the tenure track at NJCU.

My editor at Rutgers University Press, Peter Mickulas, helped guide this book from conception to final product. I thank the entire staff at the Press, as well as Wendy Nelson for copy editing the manuscript.

Finishing this book coincided with the emergence of the crisis caused by the COVID-19 pandemic, and it became difficult to keep healthy, much less sane. I wish to thank my neighbors Mariel López-Mota, Joe Semien, Doris Altmann, and Michael Jameson, who made it possible for us all to keep connected while maintaining appropriate social distance.

Finally, I want to thank my family for their support: my wife, Bleida (*para quien todavía no hay palabras*); and my children, Luis, Leidis, and Bernadette (*ya tienes una biblioteca casi tan grande como la de tu papá*). I want to thank my parents, Robert and Mary Zumoff, for their continuing and continuous support. As I was finalizing the manuscript, my uncle Philip C. Ruddy passed away. He will be sorely missed, and I will miss the opportunity to discuss this book over wine and bratwurst at Lake Michigan.

Some material in this book appeared in different form in *American Communist History*; *Journal for the Study of Radicalism*; and the *Academic Forum of New Jersey City University*. I am grateful for permission to republish this material here. I also wish to acknowledge the anonymous peer reviewers at these journals. The research for this book benefited from a Separately Budgeted Research grant from the Provost's Office of New Jersey City University and release time from the William Maxwell College of Arts and Sciences at NJCU.

While I was working on this book, several friends and comrades died. Each helped shape my understanding of the working class, class struggle, and workers' leadership—themes central to this book. They include Corky Benedict, Bonnie Breen, Edward Cliffel, Victor Granovsky, Lisa Gruber, and James Robertson. I dedicate this book to their memory and hope that the vision of the world that they struggled for is reflected in these pages.

Abbreviations Used in Notes

Newspapers

APEN	*Asbury Park Evening News*
APP	*Asbury Park Press*
BCN	*Bridgewater Courier News*
BDE	*Brooklyn Daily Eagle*
BER	*Bergen Evening Record*
BG	*Boston Globe*
DHN	*New Brunswick Daily Home News*
DW	*Daily Worker*
JJ	*Jersey Journal* (Jersey City)
LD	*Labor Defender* (International Labor Defense)
LL	*Federated Press Labor Letter*
NL	*New Leader* (Socialist Party)
NM	*New Masses*
NTW	*New Textile Worker* (ATWA)
NYDN	*New York Daily News*
NYEP	*New York Evening Post*
NYHT	*New York Herald Tribune*
NYT	*New York Times*
NYW	*New York World*
PCN	*Plainfield Courier News*
PDH	*Passaic Daily Herald*
PDN	*Passaic Daily News*
PHN	*Passaic Herald-News*
PIA	*Progresso Italo-Americano*
PMC	*Paterson Morning Call*

RA	*Revolutionary Age* (published by supporters of Jay Lovestone)
TET	*Trenton Evening Times*
TSB	*Textile Strike Bulletin*
TW	*Textile Worker* (published by UTW)
WSJ	*Wall Street Journal*
YC	*Young Comrade*
YW	*Young Worker*

Archives

ACLU papers	American Civil Liberties Paper, Mudd Library, Princeton University*
AFL papers	American Federation of Labor papers, Meany archives, Silver Spring, Maryland*
AFPS papers	American Fund for Public Service papers, New York Public Library*
AUF	Archive Union Files, Kheel Center, Cornell University.
BLSCBA	Bureau of Labor Statistics Collective Bargaining Agreements, Kheel Center, Cornell
Bell papers	Daniel Bell papers, Tamiment Library, New York University
Borah papers	William E. Borah papers, Library of Congress
Comintern	Archives of the Communist International, Russian Institute for Contemporary History, Moscow, Tamiment Library, New York University*
Consumers papers	Consumers' League of New Jersey papers, Special Collections, Rutgers University
Coolidge papers	Calvin Coolidge papers, Library of Congress*
Dana papers	H.W.L. Dana papers, Longfellow National Historic Site, Cambridge, Mass.
Draper papers	Theodore Draper papers, Hoover Institution, Stanford University
Dunn papers	Labor Research Association papers, Tamiment Library, New York University
Ernst papers	Morris Ernst papers, University of Texas at Austin
ILGWU papers	International Ladies' Garment Workers' Union/Charles Zimmerman papers, Kheel Center, Cornell University
Lovestone papers	Jay Lovestone papers, Hoover Institution, Stanford University
Magliacano papers	Joseph Magliacano papers, Tamiment Library, New York University

McMullen papers	David Lee McMullen papers, Tamiment Library, New York University
Morgue	*Newark Evening News* morgue, Newark Public Library*
NAACP papers	NAACP papers, ProQuest Digital History Vault*
Oral History	Passaic Strike Oral History Project, American Labor Museum, Haledon, NJ
Ordinances	Ordinances of City of Passaic, City Clerk's Office, Passaic City Hall
Polier papers	Justine Wise Polier papers, Schlesinger Library, Harvard University
PRL	Prometheus Research Library, New York, NY
Socialist papers	Socialist Party papers, Duke University*
Tamiment Ephemera	Printed Ephemera Collection (PE.029), Box 16, Passaic Textile Strike, Tamiment Library, New York University
Vertical file	Passaic Strike Vertical File, Forstmann Library, Passaic
Villard papers	Oswald Garrison Villard papers, Houghton Library, Harvard University.
Vorse papers	Mary Heaton Vorse papers, Walter Reuther Library, Wayne State University, Detroit
Wagenknecht papers	Wagenknecht/Winter family papers, Tamiment Library, New York University
Walsh papers	Frank P. Walsh papers, New York Public Library
Wise papers	Stephen S. Wise papers, Brandeis University*
Zimmerman papers	Charles Zimmerman papers, Tamiment Library, New York University

*Consulted on microfilm or electronic copy

Notes

Introduction

1 On the condition of workers in this period, see Irving Bernstein, *The Lean Years: A History of the American Worker, 1920–1933* (Boston: Houghton Mifflin, 1960).

2 U.S. Department of Labor, *Handbook of Labor Statistics, 1924–1926* (Washington, DC: U.S. Government Printing Office, 1927), 570 (table 2).

3 John Kenneth Galbraith, *The Great Crash* (Boston: Houghton Mifflin, 1961), 180; Gene Smiley, "The U.S. Economy in the 1920s," *EH.Net Encyclopedia*, ed. Robert Whaples (2004), http://eh.net/encyclopedia/the-u-s-economy-in-the-1920s/; Michael Goldfield, *The Decline of Organized Labor in the United States* (Chicago: University of Chicago Press, 1987), 8.

4 James O. Morris, "The AFL in the 1920's: A Strategy of Defense," *ILR Review* 11, no. 4 (July 1958): 571–590.

5 Information taken from a search on newspapers.com.

6 Robert H. Zieger, "Pennsylvania Coal and Politics: The Anthracite Strike of 1925–1926," *Pennsylvania Magazine of History and Biography* 92 (April 1969): 244–262; Philip S. Foner, *History of the Labor Movement in the United States*, vol. 10 (New York: International, 1994), chap. 2.

7 Irwin M. Marcus, James P. Dougherty, and Eileen M. Cooper, "Confrontation at Rossiter: The Coal Strike of 1927–1928 and Its Aftermath," *Pennsylvania History* 59, no. 4 (1984): 310–326; Leigh Campbell-Hale, "Remembering Ludlow but Forgetting the Columbine: The 1927–1928 Colorado Coal Strike" (PhD diss., University of Colorado, 2013).

8 *NYT*, August 16, 1924; *APP*, November 22, 1924; Martha Glaser, "Paterson, 1924: The ACLU and Labor," *New Jersey History* 94, no. 4 (Winter 1976): 160–162.

9 On the 1925 Connecticut strike, see Jamie H. Eves, "David Moxon's Forgotten Files: The American Thread Company Strike of 1925," www.millmuseum.org /history/sweat-of-their-brows/strike/.

10 The furriers' and cloakmakers' strikes are discussed in Foner, *History of the Labor Movement*, vol. 10, chaps. 4–7. See also Jonathan Michaels, "Servants of Two Masters: The Dilemma of Grassroots Communist Leaders in the Cloakmakers' Strike of 1926" (unpublished paper).

11 Melvyn Dubofsky and Warren Van Time, *John L. Lewis: A Biography*, abridged ed. (Urbana: University of Illinois Press, 1986), 110; see also David Montgomery, "Thinking about American Workers in the 1920s," *International Labor and Working-Class History* 32 (Fall 1987): 9.

12 Thomas Y. Owusu, "Economic Transition in the City of Paterson, New Jersey (America's First Planned Industrial City): Causes, Impacts, and Urban Policy Implications," *Urban Studies Research* 3 (September 2014): 1–9; Bonnie Stepenoff, "Child Labor in Pennsylvania's Silk Mills: Protest and Change, 1900–1910," *Pennsylvania History* 59, no. 2 (April 1992): 101–121.

13 See Michael Goldfield, *The Southern Key: Class, Race, and Radicalism in the 1930s and 1940s* (New York: Oxford University Press, 2020), chap. 3.

14 Albert Weisbord, *Passaic: The Story of a Struggle against Starvation Wages and for the Right to Organize* (Chicago: Daily Worker, 1926), 6.

15 See, for example, Bert Cochran, *Labor and Communism: The Conflict That Shaped American Unions* (Princeton: Princeton University Press, 1977), 32–33.

16 For example, see *Pravda* (Moscow), May 23, 1926, and March 9, 1927; *L'Humanité* (Paris), December 28, 1926.

17 This process of Stalinization is beyond the current book, but it is examined in Jacob A. Zumoff, *The Communist International and US Communism, 1919–1929* (Leiden: Brill, 2014). See also Bryan D. Palmer, *James P. Cannon and the Origins of the American Revolutionary Left, 1890–1928* (Urbana: University of Illinois Press, 2007).

18 See Weisbord, "Passaic Reviewed," http://www.weisbord.org; and Michael H. Ebner, "The Fiftieth Anniversary of the Passaic Textile Strike," *International Labor and Working-Class History* 11, no. 9 (1977): 9–10.

19 Benjamin Gitlow, *I Confess: The Truth about American Communism* (New York: Dutton, 1940).

20 James P. Cannon, *The First Ten Years of American Communism: The Report of a Participant* (New York: Lyle Stuart, 1962).

21 Vera Buch Weisbord, *A Radical Life* (Bloomington: University of Indiana Press, 1977), chap. 5.

22 For examples of scholars' treatment of the Passaic strike, see Cochran, *Labor and Communism*, 30–34; Theodore Draper, *American Communism and Soviet Russia: The Formative Years* (New York: Vintage, 1986 [1960]), 223–233; Elizabeth Faue, *Rethinking the American Labor Movement* (New York: Routledge, 2017), 88; Foner, *History of the Labor Movement*, vol. 10, chap. 10; Dee Garrison, *Mary Heaton Vorse: The Life of an American Insurgent* (Philadelphia: Temple University Press, 1989), 196–203; Palmer, *James P. Cannon*, 255–260; Philip Taft, *The AFL from the Death of Gompers to the Merger* (New York: Harper and Brothers, 1959), 8–9; Leo Troy, *Organized Labor in New Jersey* (Princeton, NJ: Van Nostrand, 1965), 93–97; Zumoff, *The Communist International*, 189–197.

23 Paul L. Murphy, David Klaassen, and Kermit Hall, eds., *The Passaic Textile Strike of 1926* (Belmont, CA: Wadsworth, 1974).

24 The two-part, hour-long program is available at http://www.talkinghistory.org/cohen.html.

25 See Raymond H. Groff, "The Passaic Textile Strike of 1926" (master's thesis, Columbia University, 1927); Sara Fanny Simon, "The Passaic Strike—A Study in Left Wing Leadership" (master's thesis, Columbia University, 1928); Esther E. Liberman, "The Influence of Left-Wing Radicalism in the Paterson Silk Strikes of 1912–1913, and Passaic Woolen Strike of 1926" (unpublished paper, 1965); Steven R.

Irwin, "Conflict Resolution and the Development of Law: The Passaic Textile Strike of 1926 and the New Jersey State Riot Act" (bachelor's thesis, Rutgers University, 1976); Annick Des Roches, "Women United in Defense of the Family: The Public Battle for Improved Domestic and Workplace Conditions during the Passaic Textile Strike of 1926" (master's thesis, Hunter College, 2006); Kamika Bennett, "Passaic Negro Workers Strike: The Passaic Strike of 1926 and the Making of a Radical and Multi-Racial Struggle" (master's thesis, Rutgers University Newark, 2020). All manuscripts were consulted in the special collections of the libraries of the institutions for which they were written, except for Liberman's paper, which is at the Rutgers University library, and Bennett's thesis, which was provided by its author.

26 Morton K. Siegel, "The Passaic Textile Strike of 1926" (PhD diss., Columbia University, 1953).

27 Theodore Draper, *The Roots of American Communism* (New Brunswick, NJ: Transaction, 2003 [1957]); and Draper, *American Communism*.

28 David Lee McMullen, *Strike! The Radical Insurrections of Ellen Dawson* (Gainesville: University Press of Florida, 2010).

29 I especially used scrapbooks in the Walsh papers and the ACLU papers and databases for the *New York Times* and the *Daily Worker* (available at the New York Public Library through ProQuest) and newspapers.com.

30 The role of ethnicity and race, and the press and the strike deserve more attention, including from foreign-language and international sources. Bennett, "Passaic Negro Workers Strike," examines the role of Black workers in the strike.

Chapter 1   Passaic, New Jersey

1 See "Passaic Industrial Park Sold for $10 Million," *NorthJersey.Com*, July 1, 2013, http://archive.northjersey.com/news/passaic-industrial-park-sold-for-10-million-1 .616612; "Police Shut Down Large Synthetic Pot Manufacturing Operation in Passaic," *NorthJersey.Com*, November 10, 2015, http://archive.northjersey.com /news/police-shut-down-large-synthetic-pot-manufacturing-operation-in-passaic-1 .1452338; "New Jersey Police Recover $1 Million in Stolen Goods during Cargo Theft Bust," *Land Line* March 15, 2018, http://www.landlinemag.com/story.aspx ?storyid=71931.

2 Brainhard H. Warner Jr., "German Textile Factories in America," December 13, 1899, in *Consular Reports: Commerce, Manufactures, Etc.*, vol. 62 (Washington, DC: U.S. Government Printing Office, 1900), 334; *NYT*, March 17, 1918; *The News' History of Passaic* (Passaic, NJ: News Publishing Co., 1899), 281; *Alien Property Custodian Report* (Washington, DC: U.S. Government Printing Office, 1919), 129; Alfred D. Chandler Jr., *Scale and Scope: The Dynamics of Industrial Capitalism* (Cambridge, MA: Harvard University Press, 1990), 454; Mary H. Blewett, "The Dynamics of Labor Migration and Raw Materials Acquisition in the Transatlantic Worsted Trade, 1830–1930," in *Connecting Seas and Connected Ocean Rims: Indian, Atlantic, and Pacific Oceans and China Seas Migrations from the 1830s to the 1930s,* ed. Dirk Hoerder and Donna R. Gabaccia (Leiden: Brill, 2011), 338–370; Sven Beckert, "Migration, Ethnicity, and Working-Class Formation in Passaic, New Jersey, 1889–1926," in Dirk Hoerder and Jörg Nagler, eds., *People in Transit: German Migrations in Comparative Perspective, 1820–1930* (Cambridge: Cambridge University Press, 1995), 348–349. On Kammgarnspinnerei Stöhr & Co., see Sean Dobson, *Authority and Upheaval in Leipzig, 1910–1920:*

The Story of a Relationship (New York: Columbia University Press, 2001), 112. On Stöhr, see his entry in John William Leonard, *History of the City of New York, 1609–1909* (New York: Journal of Commerce and Commercial Bulletin, 1910), 779. David Jenkins, "The Western Wool Textile Industry in the Nineteenth Century," in *The Cambridge History of Western Textiles*, ed. David Jenkins (Cambridge: Cambridge University Press, 2003), 2:778, 781, 786. For a comprehensive overview of the American textile industry in a global context, see Michael Goldfield, *The Southern Key: Class, Race, and Radicalism in the 1930s and 1940s* (New York: Oxford University Press, 2020), chap. 6.

3 Morton Siegel, "The Passaic Textile Strike of 1926" (PhD diss., Columbia University, 1954), 9.

4 Beckert, "Migration, Ethnicity," 350–351; Siegel, "Passaic Textile Strike," 8; William Starr Myers, *Prominent Families in New Jersey* (Baltimore: Genealogical Publishing Co., 2002 [1945]), 1:318; Peter J. Buckley and Brian R. Roberts, *European Direct Investment in the U.S.A. before World War I* (New York: Palgrave Macmillan, 1982), 49–50; Leonard, *History of the City of New York*, 797. The Forstmann family history is detailed in Willy Fleischer, *Werdener Tuchmacher: Die Familien Forstmann und Huffmann und andere Tuchhersteller* (Essen: Nobel, 2001). On the two plants, see the Bill of Complaint in *Forstmann and Huffmann Company v. The United Front Committee of Textile Workers* (1926) in Vorse papers, box 116. On the Forstmann mansion in New York City, see *NYT*, July 27, 2008.

5 *NYT*, October 10, 1915; Richard D. Margrave, "The Role of the Paterson, N.J., Silk Industry in the 19th-Century Atlantic Economy," *Northeast Historical Archaeology* 4 (1975): 54; See James B. Kenyon, *Industrial Location and Metropolitan Growth: The Paterson-Passaic District* (Chicago: University of Chicago Department of Geography, 1960), 61–62.

6 For a regional overview, see B. M. Selekman, Henriette R. Walter, and W. J. Crouper, *The Clothing and Textile Industries in New York and Its Environs: Present Trends and Probable Future Development* (New York: Regional Plans of New York and Its Environs, 1925). On broader pressures in the textile industry, see Gladys L. Palmer, "The Mobility of Weavers in Three Textile Centers," *Quarterly Journal of Economics* 55, no. 3 (May 1941): 460–487; Martin C. Mooney, "The Industrial Workers of the World and the Immigrants of Paterson and Passaic, New Jersey, 1907–1913" (master's thesis, Seton Hall University, 1969), 7, 14; Shelley G. Herochik, "Yours for the Good Fight: The Effects of Industrial Decline in the Hatting, Textile, and Machine Tool Industries on Orange and Paterson, New Jersey, in the 1920s" (EdD diss., Rutgers University, 1986), 198; David J. Goldberg, *A Tale of Three Cities: Labor Organization and Protest in Paterson, Passaic, and Lawrence, 1916–1921* (New Brunswick, NJ: Rutgers University Press, 1989), 20–21.

7 Richard W. Hunter et. al., *Cultural Resource Investigation of the Allied Textile Printing Site, Paterson, NJ* (Princeton, NJ: Hunter Research, 2010), 1:50–51; *American Silk Journal*, July 1912; *NYT*, September 12, 1912; Steve Golin, *The Fragile Bridge: Paterson Silk Strike, 1913* (Philadelphia: Temple University Press, 1988), 73.

8 Information from stock offering notice by Lehman Brothers, *BDE*, February 8, 1928. Stevens, *New Jersey Manufacturers*, 23–24; Albert Weisbord, *Passaic: The Story of a Struggle against Starvation Wages and for the Right to Organize* (Chicago: Daily Worker, 1926), 22; Giuseppe Iannarelli, *Lo Sciorpero dei Tessitori di Seta di Paterson New Jersey* (New York: Nicoletti Brothers, 1916), 8; *Norwich (Connecticut) Bulletin*, May 22, 1917; ACLU, "Synopsis of Testimony regarding the Passaic Textile Strike," undated [March 1926?], in ACLU papers, vol. 302.

9 J. Magliacano, "The Passaic Textile Strike—1926" [undated, but after 1972], in Magliacano papers, box 2, folder 10, p. 2; Vera Buch Weisbord, "Italian Strikers in Lodi, N.J., 1926," *La Parola del Populo*, https://www.marxists.org/archive /weisbord/Lodi.htm; *New York Tribune*, October 26, 1890; *PCN*, May 2, 1902; *NYT*, June 19, 1902; *Janesville* (Wisconsin) *Daily Gazette*, October 9, 1905; *BDE*, May 20, 1913; Golin, *Fragile Bridge*, 26–27.

10 Blewett, "Dynamics of Labor Migration," 352; Jenkins, "Western Wool Textile Industry in the Nineteenth Century," 787.

11 Leonard, *History of the City of New York*, 797.

12 Stuart Chase, "Memorandum of Finances for Botany Consolidated Mills, Inc.," in Borah papers, box 213, first Passaic strike folder; Mira Wilkins, *The History of Foreign Investment in the United States, 1914–1945* (Cambridge, MA: Harvard University Press, 2004), 115–116.

13 Selekman, Walter, and Crouper, *Clothing and Textile Industries*, 28; Herochik, "Yours for the Good Fight," 7.

14 William W. Scott, *History of Passaic and Its Environs* (New York: Lewis Historical, 1922), 1: 497. The figures are taken from the 1920 Census. Goldberg, *Tale of Three Cities*, 49, 53; Michael Ebner, "The Passaic Strike of 1912 and the Two I.W.W.s," *Labor History* 11, no. 4 (1970): 452–456. See Siegel, "Passaic Textile Strike," 19–22, for an extensive discussion of the immigrant background of the Passaic population. The *Passaic Chamber of Commerce Bulletin* (April 1929) included a detailed breakdown of the population by place of birth; Beckert, "Migration, Ethnicity," 354–361. Because the Census listed immigrants by citizenship of origin and not ethnicity or language, exact figures are difficult to establish.

15 Weisbord, *Passaic*, 18–19. In testimony to the Senate in May 1926, Henry Hunt repeated the statement, which he credited to Henry Hilfers, head of the AFL in New Jersey; see *Hearing before the Committee on Education and Labor, United States Senate . . . Pursuant to S. Res 177* (Washington, DC: U.S. Government Printing Office, 1926), 20.

16 Alice Barrows Fernandez, *The Problem of Adult Education in Passaic, New Jersey* (Washington, DC: U.S. Government Printing Office, 1920); Women's Bureau, U.S. Department of Labor, *The Family Status of Breadwinning Women: A Study of Material in the Census Schedules of a Selected Locality* (Washington, DC: U.S. Government Printing Office, 1922), 11; Justine Waterman Wise, "Passaic," May 1925, draft manuscript in Polier papers, box 1, folder 16.

17 Helena Flam called Paterson in the late nineteenth and early twentieth centuries a "laborite democracy," which underlines the influence that workers had in local politics. See Helena Flam, "Democracy in Debt: Credit and Politics in Paterson, N.J., 1890–1930," *Journal of Social History* 18, no. 3 (1985): 439–462; Mooney, "Industrial Workers of the World," 41; George H. Rice, "How the Passaic (N.J.) Police Force Handle Labor Problems," *National Police Journal* 5, no. 3 (December 1919): 14; Rich Cohen, "The Ghost in the Gulfstream," *Vanity Fair*, February 2013, http://www .vanityfair.com/news/2013/02/memoirs-teddy-forstmann-billionaire-ghostwriters; Mary Heaton Vorse, *The Passaic Strike, 1926–1927* (Passaic, NJ: General Relief Committee of Textile Workers, 1927), 3; Fernandez, *Problem of Adult Education*.

18 Arthur Harrison Cole, *The American Wool Manufacture* (Cambridge, MA: Harvard University Press, 1926), 2:107–110; Paul F. Brissenden, *Earnings of Factory Workers, 1899 to 1927: An Analysis of Pay-Roll Statistics* (Washington, DC: U.S. Government Printing Office, 1929), 76. On the wage divisions based on sex, see Beckert, "Migration, Ethnicity," 357.

19 *Passaic Chamber of Commerce Bulletin*, September 1927; Beckert, "Migration, Ethnicity," 365; Michael H. Ebner, "Socialist and Progressive Political Reform: The 1911 Change-of-Government in Passaic," in *Socialism and the Cities*, ed. Bruce M. Stave (Port Washington: Kennikat Press, 1975), 116–140; Goldberg, *Tale of Three Cities*, 3; Daniel J. Saposs, *Left Unionism: A Study in Radical Policy and Tactics* (New York: International, 1926), 138; Clete Daniel, *Culture of Misfortune: An Interpretive History of Textile Unionism in the United States* (Ithaca, NY: Cornell University Press, 2001), 18–20, 24; Kathleen Banks Nutter, *The Necessity of Organization: Mary Kenney O'Sullivan and Trade Unionism for Women, 1892–1912* (New York: Garland, 2000), 112–113. The best overview of the UTW's history up to the 1930s is Robert R. R. Brooks, "The United Textile Workers of America" (PhD diss., Yale University, 1935); Marion Dutton Savage, *Industrial Unionism in America* (New York: Ronald Press, 1922), 250; Thomas F. McMahon, May 26, 1926, in *Hearing before the Committee on Education and Labor, United States Senate . . . Pursuant to S. Res 177* (Washington, DC: U.S. Government Printing Office, 1926), 7.

20 *Daily People*, March 26, 1912; *Charlotte* (North Carolina) *News*, April 5, 1912; *New York Sun*, April 6, 1912; Ebner, "Passaic Strike of 1912," 452–466; Goldberg, *Tale of Three Cities*, 60–61.

21 Siegel, "Passaic Textile Strike," 25; Goldberg, *Tale of Three Cities*, 63.

22 *NYT*, November 25, December 9 and 15, 1916.

23 On the Silk Association, see *NYT*, October 4, 1913; Herochik, "Yours for the Good Fight," 154; *PCN*, March 22, 1916. On the Crimmitschau textile strike and the Arbeitgeberverbände, see Dieter Groh, "Intensification of Work and Industrial Conflict in Germany, 1896–1914," *Politics & Society* 8, nos. 3–4 (1978): 371–375.

24 J. Frank Andres, "The New Passaic Council," *Bulletin of the National Association of Wool Manufacturers* 47 (July 1917): 232–239. See Goldberg, *Tale of Three Cities*, 64–65.

25 Sidney Howard and Robert Dunn, *The Labor Spy* (New York: Republic, 1924), 91–92. The original article is in the *New Republic*, March 16, 1921. See William Hard, "Learn from Passaic," *New Republic*, April 14, 1920, 213–215; *World Tomorrow*, April 1920; *NYT*, March 24, 1920; *NTW*, February 28 and March 13, 1920. Robert Dunn obtained a copy of instructions for spies in Passaic; see Dunn papers, box 8, New Jersey Labor Spies folder.

26 *Alien Property Custodian Report*, 129.

27 *NYT*, March 16, 17, and 30, 1918; April 1, 6, and 8, 1918; *WSJ*, April 1, 1918.

28 Florence Kelley, *Wage-Earning Women in War Time: The Textile Industry* (New York: National Consumers' League, 1919), 7. Eloise Shellabarger, "The Shawled Women of Passaic," *Survey* 44 (July 3, 1920), 464, identifies this mill as Botany. Robert W. Dunn and Jack Hardy, *Labor and Textiles: A Study of Cotton and Wool Manufacturing* (New York: International, 1931), 147–149. During the strike the Workers' Health Bureau examined 404 strikers and found that 6 percent had tuberculosis—which was 12 times the rate of policy holders of the Metropolitan Life Insurance Company, 6 times the rate of garment workers, and 3 times the rate of furriers. See *LL*, June 23, 1926.

29 *Wilmington* (Delaware) *Morning News*, December 12, 1918; *Stoehr v. Wallace*, 255 U.S. 239 (41 S.Ct. 293, 65 L.Ed. 604); *NYHT*, March 30, 1921. On Johnson, see *TSB*, March 15, 1926; *PCN*, February 17, 1916; *New York Herald*, March 30, 1921. See Johnson's obituary in *PHN*, May 10, 1952. Arthur H. Cole, "The Domestic and Foreign Wool Manufactures and the Tariff Problem," *Quarterly Journal of Economics* 36, no. 1 (November 1921): 102–135 (quotes on 29 and 117).

30 Siegel, "Passaic Textile Strike," 26; *APP*, April 1 and July 28, 1919; David J.
Goldberg, "Immigrant Workers and Labor Organizations, 1912–1926: Lawrence,
Massachusetts, and Passaic, New Jersey," in *Work, Recreation, and Culture: Essays
in American Labor History*, ed. Martin Henry Blatt and Martha S. Norkunas
(New York: Routledge, 1996), 216–217; David J. Goldberg, "Twentieth-Century
Textile Strikes," in *The Encyclopedia of Strikes in American History*, ed. Immanuel
Ness et al. (Armonk, NY: Sharpe, 2009), 333–334.

31 *NTW*, April/May 1923; on the ATWA, in addition to *New Textile Worker*, see
Goldberg, *Tale of Three Cities*; Brooks, "The United Textile Workers," 232–245;
Savage, *Industrial Unionism in America*, 250–276. On the ATWA and Hillman,
see Steven Fraser, *Labor Will Rule: Sidney Hillman and the Rise of American
Labor* (New York: Free Press, 1991), 157–160; *NYT*, December 4, 1921; Shella-
barger, "Shawled Women," 466–467; *NTW*, May 22, 1920.

32 Robert W. Dunn, *Company Unions* (New York: Vanguard Press, 1927), 50–56;
Dunn, "Company Union Fights Passaic Strike," in *NL*, May 1, 1926; see also
notes on interview of Albert F. Francis, April 18, 1925, in Polier papers, box 1,
folder 16.

33 Agnes de Lima, *Night-Working Mothers in Textile Mills: Passaic, New Jersey*
(Newark: National Consumers' League, 1920); *Family Status of Breadwinning
Women*, 4, 7, 26; Charles H. Weeks, New Jersey Deputy Commissioner of Labor,
to Katherine G. T. Wiley, Consumers' League, May 2, 1923, in Consumers papers,
box 46, folder 16.

34 De Lima, *Night-Working Mothers*; Siegel, "Passaic Textile Strike," 67.

35 Shellabarger, "Shawled Women," 466.

36 ACLU, "Synopsis of Testimony regarding the Passaic Textile Strike," undated
[March 1926?], in ACLU papers, vol. 302.

37 *BCN*, January 31, 1922; *TET*, January 31 and March 14, 1922.

Chapter 2   The Strike Begins

1 *NYT*, April 6 and 7, 1925; *APP*, April 6, 1919. Forstmann and Huffmann's
management denied Wise's charges; see her account in "Passaic," a draft manuscript from May 1925, in Polier papers, box 1, folder 16. In his *The Labor Spy* (New
York: Republic, 1924), Sidney Howard claimed that espionage was "followed by
the majority of our great employers."

2 Notes on interview with William G. Andrews, no date [April 16, 1925], and notes
on interview with Albert F. Francis, no date [April 18, 1925], both in Polier papers,
box 1, folder 16.

3 "Account of Meeting of John Sherman, 40 Spencer Place, Garfield, New Jersey,
with Dr. Stephen S. Wise," spring 1926, Wise papers, box 71 (microfilm reel
74-49); copy in Polier papers, box 1, folder 16.

4 Mary Heaton Vorse, *The Passaic Strike of 1926–1927* (Passaic, NJ: General Relief
Committee of Textile Workers, 1927), 7–8. See Stuart Chase, "Memorandum of
Finances, Botany Consolidated Mills, Inc." (1926?), in Borah papers, box 213,
general office files, first Passaic strike folder; Max W. Stoehr to William Blair and
Co., December 24, 1924, quoted in ACLU, "Synopsis of Testimony regarding the
Passaic Textile Strike," ACLU papers, vol. 302; Arthur H. Cole, "The Domestic
and Foreign Wool Manufactures and the Tariff Problem," *Quarterly Journal of
Economics* 36, no. 1 (November 1921): 102–135; Morton Siegel, "The Passaic Textile
Strike of 1926" (PhD diss., Columbia University, 1954), 29–33.

5 Raymond H. Groff, "The Passaic Textile Strike of 1926" (master's thesis, Columbia University, 1927), 10; Siegel, "Passaic Textile Strike," 136; Vorse, *The Passaic Strike*, 4; *YW*, May 1, 1926.

6 Groff, "The Passaic Textile Strike," 10; Siegel, "Passaic Textile Strike," 136; Vorse, *The Passaic Strike*, 4; *NYT*, April 15, 1925; Melvin Urofsky, *A Voice That Spoke for Justice: The Life and Times of Stephen S. Wise* (Albany: SUNY Press, 1982), 232. Solon De Leon and Nathan Fine, eds., *The American Labor Yearbook, 1926* (New York: Rand School of Social Science, 1926), 223–224.

7 *NYT*, September 26, 1925.

8 Although Deak has been described as born in Hungary, both the 1920 Census and the 1940 Census list him as being born in New York, in 1905 and 1906, respectively; both list his parents as Hungarian-born; information taken from https://familysearch.org.

9 *APP*, November 14, 1925. Deak later denied he was a Communist, but in 1927, J. Louis Engdahl included Deak on list of trade-union supporters of the Lovestone faction, indicating that he was a member of the CP; in Comintern, 495:37:12.

10 *TSB*, March 15, 1926; *DW*, January 31, 1926. On Johnson's response to the workers, see Vorse, *The Passaic Strike*, 11; Albert Weisbord, *Passaic: The Story of a Struggle against Starvation Wages and for the Right to Organize* (Chicago: Daily Worker, 1926), 23; Siegel, "Passaic Textile Strike," 171.

11 The material on the early days of the strike in the following paragraphs is taken from: *PDN*, January 26, 27, 28, 29, and 31, 1926, and February 2 and 3, 1926; *NYT*, January 26 and February 3, 1926; *PMC*, January 26, 28, and 29, 1926. See also *DW*, January 31 and February 4, 1926. An overview of the first month of the strike can be found in J. O. Bentall, "The Passaic Strike Encounters the Courts," *LD*, April 1926, 57–58. See also Siegel, "Passaic Textile Strike," 173–174.

12 *DW*, February 5, 1926; *PMC*, February 5, 1926; Weisbord, *Passaic*, 28; *PDN*, February 6, 1926.

13 *DW*, February 7, 1926.

14 *PDN*, February 8 and 9, 1926; *NYT*, February 10, 1926.

15 *PDN*, February 15, 1926.

16 *PDN*, February 10, 1926.

17 "An Ordinance concerning Disorderly Persons," February 14, 1926, in Ordinances.

18 *PDN*, February 6, 1926; Sara Fanny Simon, "The Passaic Strike—A Study in Left Wing Leadership" (master's thesis, Columbia University, 1928), 88–89; *NYT*, February 12, 1926.

19 *NYDN*, February 12, 1926; *PDN*, February 15, 16, and 17, 1926; *NYT*, February 18, 1926.

20 *PDN*, February 18 and 20, 1926; *NYT*, February 20, 1926.

21 *NYT*, February 14, 1926; *PDN*, February 15, 1926.

22 *PDN*, February 25, 1926; *NYT*, February 26, 1926.

23 *NYT*, February 28, 1926.

24 *NYT*, March 4, 1926.

Chapter 3 The Communist Party and the Start of the Passaic Strike

1 C. E. Ruthenberg, "The Achievements of Our Party," no date [November 1926], in Comintern, 515:1:923; Anthony Bimba, *The History of the American Working Class* (New York: International, 1937 [1927]), 308; "Synopsis of Testimony regarding the Passaic Textile Strike," undated [March 1926?], ACLU papers, vol. 302.

2 James P. Cannon, "Passaic Strike Anniversary: Some Lessons in Militant Labor Leadership for the Future," *Militant*, February 22, 1930, reprinted in James P. Cannon, *The Left Opposition in the U.S., 1928–31* (New York: Monad, 1981), 241.

3 Martha Stone Asher, "Recollections of the Passaic Textile Strike of 1926," *Labor's Heritage* 2, no. 2 (1990), 8. Michael Goldfield labels this type of solidarity "associative power"; see Michael Goldfield, *The Southern Key: Class, Race, and Radicalism in the 1930s and 1940s* (New York: Oxford University Press, 2020), chap. 3.

4 V. I. Lenin, "Economic and Political Strikes," May 31, 1912, in *Collected Works* (London: Progress, 1975), 18:87.

5 Albert Weisbord, *Passaic: The Story of a Struggle against Starvation Wages and for the Right to Organize* (Chicago: Daily Worker, 1926), 6.

6 *PDN*, March 22, 1926.

7 William Z. Foster, *History of the Communist Party of the United States* (New York: International, 1952), 250.

8 *People's World*, April 24, 1986.

9 Philip S. Foner, *History of the Labor Movement in the United States*, vol. 10 (New York: International, 1994), chap. 10; on the UFC and TUEL, see 143, 147.

10 The classic account is Theodore Draper's two-volume study of the Communist Party, vol. 1, *The Roots of American Communism*, and vol. 2, *American Communism and Soviet Russia* (New York: Viking, 1957). James P. Cannon, *The First Ten Years of American Communism: Report of a Participant* (New York: Lyle Stuart, 1962), comprising letters to Draper, is a useful account. Recent scholarly studies include Bryan D. Palmer, *James P. Cannon and the Origins of the American Left, 1890–1928* (Urbana: University of Illinois Press, 2007); Jacob A. Zumoff, *The Communist International and US Communism, 1919–1929* (Leiden: Brill, 2014). See also the introduction to *James P. Cannon and the Early Years of American Communism* (New York: Prometheus Research Library, 1992). The following paragraphs are drawn from these sources.

11 *The Fourth National Convention of the Workers (Communist) Party* (Chicago: Daily Worker, 1925), 37, 39.

12 Readers interested in factionalism and Stalinism (and my analysis of them) are directed to Zumoff, *The Communist International*. The term "Stalinism" is used to refer to the degeneration of the Soviet Union due to isolation, poverty, and the defeat of revolutions in Germany and elsewhere, leading to the rise of a bureaucracy led by Stalin that opposed the original Bolshevik program of international revolution in favor of "socialism in one country." This process—in the Soviet Union and in the Comintern—was neither overnight nor obvious at the time to many Communists. For the classic analysis of the rise of Stalin, see Leon Trotsky, *The Revolution Betrayed: What Is the Soviet Union and Where Is It Going?* (New York: Doubleday, 1937); on the Communist International, see Leon Trotsky, *The Third International after Lenin* (New York: Pioneer, 1936). For the effects of Stalinism on the American Communist Party, see Palmer, *James P. Cannon*, and Zumoff, *The Communist International*.

13 *Brooklyn Daily Eagle*, December 28, 1918; biographical information from Albert Weisbord, *Passaic Reviewed* (San Francisco: Germinal Press, 1976), available at http://www.weisbord.org/Reviewed.htm. *Trow's New York Partnership and Corporation Directory for Manhattan and the Bronx*, January 1919, 456, listed a "Jacob Weisbard" as the owner of the Good Made Shoulder Pad Company, located on East Fourth Street in Manhattan. The claim that Weisbord was fired for organizing his father's workers is from the *PDN*, March 9, 1926. On Weisbord's

chess activity, see *NYT*, January 1 and December 26, 1918, and January 30, 1920; and *American Chess Bulletin* 17 (1920): 30.

14 *PDN*, March 9, 1926; the article was reprinted from the previous day's *Newark Evening News*. Interview of Martha Stone Asher by Kevin Brownlow, May 24, 1988, copy in author's possession. I wish to thank Kevin Brownlow for providing me with a copy of this interview.

15 John J. Ballam to Herbert Benjamin, January 10, 1927, in Comintern, 515:1:1197.

16 Greetings from Albert Weisbord, December 10, 1922, in *Souvenir Program, Young People's Socialist League National Convention, December 30, 31, 1922 and January 1, 1933, Fitchburg, Mass.*, in Socialist papers, reel 81.

17 Memorandum on Albert Weisbord by J. Edgar Hoover, in Albert Weisbord FBI file, file NY-61-6137-1, McMullen papers; *DW*, November 22 and 24, 1924.

18 On Weisbord's early Communist activity, see his letter to Theodore Draper, August 26, 1959, http://www.marxists.org/archive/weisbord/Draper.htm.

19 Albert Weisbord, *Passaic Reviewed*, 1–21.

20 Weisbord, *Passaic Reviewed*. Quote about not receiving help is from *PHN*, October 18, 1976, in vertical file.

21 *PDN*, March 9, 1926.

22 The TUC minutes, March 24, 1926, refer to "our fraction in Paterson." On fractions, see the "Guidelines on the Organizational Structure of Communist Parties on the Methods and Content of Their Work," adopted by the Third Congress of the Comintern, 1921, *Prometheus Research Series* no. 1 (New York: Prometheus Research Library, 1988); *DW*, September 19, 1925. The article describes the constitution as a proposal.

23 "Proposal for a Left Wing Program in the Associated Silk Workers of Paterson," October 1925, Comintern, 515:1:573. In the original the demands are in block capitals.

24 TUC minutes, January 3, 1926, PRL.

25 Emil Gardos, "Report on Party Work in Passaic," January 27, 1927, in Comintern, 515:1:1173.

26 Cannon, *The First Ten Years*, 141.

27 On the city central committees in the New York region, see Chas. Krumbein to C. E. Ruthenberg, May 12, 1925, Comintern, 515:1:489. On the membership, see the monthly "Summary Branch Report for District 2" for 1924, Comintern, 515:1:380. For a rough sense of the organization in New Jersey, see "Minutes of the New Jersey State Conference of the Workers Party Held in Newark," April 5, 1925, Comintern, 515:1:550; see also Jack Stachel, "New Jersey: One Year after Reorganization," *Party Organizer* 1, no. 1 (April 1927): 13–15.

28 On the Newark Communists, see Warren Grover, "The Newark Communist Party: 1919 to the New Deal," presentation at the Newark Historical Society, December 3, 2012, http://www.newarkhistorysociety.org/resources.html. On the restaurant workers, see *NYT*, August 14, 1926.

29 The numbers are from "Summary Branch Report for District 2," for March and June 1924, Comintern, 515:1:380. The outgoing correspondence for the district organizer (first Charles Krumbein and then William Weinstone) for 1924–1925 is in Comintern, 515:1:489. This includes regular lists of new industrial nuclei. On the existence of a Communist group, see statement by Jacob S. Bailin, secretary of Passaic CCC, included in Molly [Siegel] to Jay Lovestone, January 27, 1926, Comintern, 515:1:747.

30 On the CP election campaign in New Jersey, see "Minutes of the Special D.E.C. Meeting," February 12, 1925, Comintern, 515:1:545; "Minutes of the New Jersey

State Conference of the Workers Party," April 5, 1925, Comintern, 515:1:550. For the election results, see official *Statement of the Result of the Election* (1926), http://www.state.nj.us/state/elections/1920-1970-results/1925-general-election .pdf. On the CP in Passaic, see also Morton Siegel, "The Passaic Textile Strike of 1926" (PhD diss., Columbia University, 1954), 148–150.

31 On Communist interest in the textile industry, see Siegel, "Passaic Textile Strike," 139–142.

32 John J. Ballam, "Report on Trade Union Educational League; Trade Union Fractions; Industrial Composition of Party in District One (Boston)," December 23, 1925, Comintern, 515:1:544. On Communist organizing among textile workers in Massachusetts, see also Theodore Draper, *American Communism and Soviet Russia* (New York: Random House, 1986 [1960]), 223.

33 On the strike, see Grace Hutchins, *Labor and Silk* (New York: International, 1929), 147–150; see also the *Newark Evening News*, August to October 1924; file "Strikes—Paterson Silk Workers, 1911–1924" in Morgue, reel S-55. See *Newark Evening News*, October 8 and 16, 1924, for the activity of Communist leader H. M. Wicks, a supporter of Ruthenberg, during the strike. W. Z. Foster to "Comrade Zimmerman," November 11, 1924, ILGWU papers, box 45, folder 6; Joseph Manley, report on Paterson CCC meeting on February 6, 1925, and Charles Krumbein, "Minutes of the Special DEC Meeting," February 14, 1925, both in Comintern, 515:1:545. On New Jersey, see "Report of the National Committee Needle Trades Section, TUEL" [April/May] 1925. On the 1925 silk strike (and mention of Communist activity), see Bert Miller, "Report of the District Industrial Organizer, District 2, from September 1, 1925, to January 15, 1926"; Miller, "Report of the Industrial Organizer, District 2," September 28, 1926; and Miller, "Industrial Activity, District 2," October 25, 1925; all in Lovestone papers, box 220, folder 3.

34 Bert Miller, "Report of the Industrial Organizer, District 2, Paterson Situation," October 15, 1925, Comintern, 515:1:548; minutes of the Meeting of the Political Committee [of District 2], October 23, 1925, Comintern, 515:1:547; minutes of DEC Meeting, October 25, 1925, Comintern, 515:1:545.

35 For Weisbord's articles, see *DW*, July 6 and August 27, 1925. On September 17, 1925, Bert Miller wrote to C. E. Ruthenberg (Comintern, 515:1:490): "We have made absolutely no preparation for the Textile Conference Called here for Sunday, September 20. I have received no instructions other than the first mimeographed notice. . . . I don't know whether anything is being done about it all."

36 *DW*, October 8, 24, 29, and 30, 1925; November 4 and 6, 1925. On the Hungarian federation and Passaic, see Thomas L. Sakmyster, "A Communist Newspaper for Hungarian Americans: The Strange Case of *Új Előre*," *Hungarian Studies* 32, nos. 1–2 (2005): 47–48.

37 "Industrial Activity District 2" [by Bert Miller?], October 25, 1925, in Comintern, 515:1:548.

38 Bert Miller to C. E. Ruthenberg, October 31, 1925, Comintern, 515:1:490; Albert Weisbord, "Crucial Moments in Textile Strikes," *Class Struggle* (June 1931), http://www.weisbord.org.

39 *DW*, November 2 and 3, 1925.

40 The best coverage of the Hillcrest strike can be found in the *Jersey Journal* and the *Hudson Dispatch* from October through December 1925. The "Nel Campo del Lavoro" column of New York's *Il Progresso Italo-Americano* ran articles about the strike in October–December 1925; see in particular November 20 and 25, 1925.

The strike is covered in a series of articles in the *Daily Worker*, several written by
Weisbord; see October 30, 1925; November 1, 12, 17, and 21, 1925; December 8, 15,
16, and 29, 1925. The *New York Times* ran an article on the strike on November 18,
1925. See also *New Brunswick Home News*, October 26, 1925. On the injunctions,
see Albert Weisbord to Bert Miller, December 21, 1925, Comintern, 515:1:490. On
the North Carolina plant, see *Albemarle* (North Carolina) *Press*, February 26,
1925. I am grateful to Cynthia T. Harris and John Beekman of the New Jersey
Room of the Jersey City Public Library, Chelsea Neary of the North Bergen
Public Library, and Marian Inabinett, of the High Point (North Carolina)
Museum, for information on the Hillcrest plant.

41 *DW*, December 24, 1926.

42 TUC minutes, January 4, 1926, PRL.

43 Report by Gitlow on meeting of CEC Textile Committee at Passaic, February 2,
1926, PRL.

44 William Z. Foster, *Organize the Unorganized* (Chicago: Trade Union Educational
League, 1926?), 10, 15–16.

45 Draper, *American Communism*, 215–223.

46 Bert Miller to C. E. Ruthenberg and J. W. Johnstone, January 15, 1925, Comintern,
515:1:490. The Miller-Ruthenberg correspondence is in Comintern, 515:1:490;
Weisbord's regular reports to Miller are in Comintern, 515:1:549; Miller to
Ruthenberg, October 31, 1925, Comintern, 515:1:490. W.W. Weinstone to Jack
Johnstone, November 2, 1925, Comintern, 515:1:549.

47 Ruthenberg to Bert Miller, November 6, 1925, Comintern, 515:1:490.

48 Bert Miller to "Dear Comrade," November 13, 1925, in Comintern, 515:1:490. Albert
Weisbord, undated document on UFC, Comintern, 515:1:549; C. E. Ruthenberg
to Bert Miller, November 17, 1925, Comintern, 515:1:490.

49 Bert Miller to C. E. Ruthenberg, November 20, 1925, and Bert Miller, "Dear
Comrades," November 23, 1923, both in Comintern, 515:1:490.

50 C. E. Ruthenberg to Bert Miller, November 25, 1925, Comintern, 515:1:490.

51 Bert Miller to C. E. Ruthenberg, December 5, 1925; C. E. Ruthenberg to Bert
Miller, December 8, 1925; Albert Weisbord to Bert Miller, December 21, 1925; all
in Comintern, 515:1:490.

52 *DW*, January 4 and 6, 1926; see also Siegel, "Passaic Textile Strike," 163–164.

53 The description of the mechanism of strike leadership is from Simon, "Passaic
Strike," 31–33; and Siegel, "Passaic Textile Strike," 324–325.

54 Siegel, "Passaic Textile Strike," 152–155.

55 TUC minutes, February 3, 1926, PRL.

56 TUC minutes, February 10, 1926, PRL.

57 TUC minutes, February 13, 1926, PRL.

58 TUC minutes, February 17, 1926, PRL.

59 Grigorii Zinoviev, report to Sixth Plenum of the Executive Committee of the
Comintern, February 20, 1926, http://www.marxisthistory.org/history
/international/comintern/1926/0220-zinoviev-reportecci6.pdf; American
Commission at Sixth Plenum of the Executive Committee of the Comintern,
quoted in Draper, *American Communism*, 228–229. The broader context is dealt
with in Palmer, *James P. Cannon*, and Zumoff, *The Communist International*.

60 Report on CEC Textile Committee meeting, March 3, 1926; meeting of the CEC
Textile Committee, March 10, 1926; minutes of Political Committee, March 11,
1926; meeting of the CEC Textile Committee, March 13, 1926; all
in PRL.

Chapter 4 Bringing Passaic to the Labor Movement

1 Michael Goldfield has called this "associative power": see Goldfield, *The Southern Key: Class, Race, and Radicalism in the 1930s and 1940s* (New York: Oxford University Press, 2020), chap. 3.

2 On the 1924 presidential campaign, see Jacob A. Zumoff, *The Communist International and US Communism, 1919–1929* (Leiden: Brill, 2014), chap. 6. On liberalism in the 1920s, see Arthur S. Link, "What Happened to the Progressive Movement in the 1920s?," *American Historical Review* 64, no. 4 (July 1959): 833–851.

3 Carmen Brissette Grayson, "W. Jett Lauck: Biography of a Reformer" (PhD diss., University of Virginia, 1975), 274.

4 Morton Siegel, "The Passaic Textile Strike of 1926" (PhD diss., Columbia University, 1952), 128. This is based on McMahon's testimony before Congress in 1926.

5 Siegel, "Passaic Textile Strike," 131; *TW*, March 1926.

6 *TW*, February 1926.

7 *TW*, March 1926.

8 *PDN*, March 5, 1926.

9 Thomas F. McMahon to Elizabeth Gilman, March 12, 1926, in Vorse papers, box 58, January–March 1926 Correspondence.

10 *TW*, March 1926; C. J. Walsh, Passaic Trades and Labor Council, to Elizabeth Gilman, March 20, 1926, in Vorse papers, box 58, January–March 1926 Correspondence; *TW*, March 1926.

11 *Union Labor Messenger*, reprinted in *PDN*, March 24, 1926.

12 Political Committee minutes, March 20, 1926, PRL.

13 Albert Weisbord to AFL Executive Council, March 25, 1926, printed in *PDN*, March 26, 1926. The letter is appended to the minutes of the AFL Executive Council, March 23–29, 1926, AFL papers.

14 *PDN*, March 26, 1926.

15 *PDN*, March 26, 1926.

16 *PDN*, March 27 and 29, 1926; William Green to Albert Weisbord, March 29, 1926, printed in *TW*, April 1926.

17 TUC minutes, April 7, 1926, PRL; UFC to McMahon, no date, in Comintern, 515:1:912. McMahon to Weisbord, April 22, 1926, Weisbord to McMahon, April 27, 1926, and McMahon to Weisbord, April 30, 1926, all in Comintern, 515:1:912.

18 *PDN*, March 9, 1926; *APP*, March 6, 1926; *PMC*, March 4, 1926.

19 *Handbook of American Trade-Unions* (Washington, DC: U.S. Government Printing Office, 1929), 151–152; Robert R. R. Brooks, "The United Textile Workers of America" (PhD diss., Yale University, 1935), 254–258.

20 *PDN*, February 12, 1926; *APP*, March 6, 1926; *PMC*, March 6, 1926.

21 *PMC*, February 5, 1926.

22 *NYT*, March 15, 1926; *Baltimore Afro-American*, June 12, 1926; J. Magliacano, "The Passaic Textile Strike—1926," in Magliacano papers, box 2, folder 10; *LL*, August 18, 1926. See Kamika Bennett, "Passaic Negro Workers Strike: The Passaic Strike of 1926 and the Making of a Radical and a Multi-Racial Struggle" (master's thesis, Rutgers University Newark, 2020) for a history of Black workers in Lodi.

23 *NYT*, March 11, 1926; *NYHT*, March 11, 1926; summary of Weisbord's report at CEC Textile Meeting, March 13, 1926, PRL; *PIA*, March 11, 1926. Both the *PIA*

and the *Paterson Evening News* (March 10, 1926) termed the march in Lodi an invasion—or its Italian equivalent, *calata*.

24 *NYT*, March 12, 1926; *LL*, August 18, 1926.

25 *PIA*, March 14, 1926; Report on CEC Textile Committee Meeting, March 13, 1926, PRL; Siegel, "Passaic Textile Strike," 195–196.

26 *PIA*, March 16, 1926; *NYT*, March 16, 1926.

27 *PDN*, March 13, 1926.

28 *PDN*, March 27, 1926.

29 *PDN*, March 27, 1926; *NYT*, March 27, 1926.

30 Solon De Leon and Nathan Fine, *American Labor Year Book, 1926* (New York: Rand School, 1926), 223–224; *PDN*, March 8, 1926; *BG*, March 8, 1926.

31 *BG*, March 22 and 27, 1926; *NYT*, March 29, 1926; undated leaflet, "Police Terror in Passaic," calling for protest in Lowell, signed by UFC, with cover letter from G. Siskind to J. O. Bentall, April 15, 1926, in Vorse papers, box 116, "Passaic Strike Correspondence 1926."

32 Siegel, "Passaic Textile Strike," 202; *NYEP*, May 24, 1926, in Walsh scrapbook 74.

33 Ransom E. Noble Jr., *New Jersey Progressivism before Wilson* (Princeton: Princeton University Press, 1946), chaps. 1, 7.

34 Stephen Wise, *Challenging Years: The Autobiography of Stephen Wise* (New York: Putnam's Sons, 1949), 56–81; A. James Rudin, *Pillar of Fire: A Biography of Rabbi S. Wise* (Lubbock: Texas Tech University Press, 2015), 121–144; Melvin Urofsky, *A Voice That Spoke for Justice: The Life and Times of Stephen S. Wise* (Albany: SUNY Press, 1982), 92; Mordechai Ben Massart, "A Rabbi in the Progressive Era: Rabbis Stephen S. Wise, Ph.D., and the Rise of Social Jewish Progressivism in Portland, OR, 1900–1906" (master's thesis, Portland State University, 2010); Siegel, "Passaic Textile Strike," 275–276.

35 See, for example, the report of a speech Justine Wise made at a mass meeting in early March in Passaic, in *NYEP*, March 2, 1926, clipping in Polier papers, box 1, folder 15. On Wise and the ACLU, see Carl Hermann Voss, *Rabbi and Minister: The Friendship of Stephen S. Wise and John Haynes Holmes* (Buffalo, NY: Prometheus Books, 1980), 232–236; Stephen Wise to A. J. Muste, February 24, 1926, and Stephen Wise to Felix Frankfurter, February 24, 1926, both in Wise papers, reel 74-749. On Frankfurter's efforts against the injunction, see *NYDN*, April 26 and November 7, 1926. See also Siegel, "Passaic Textile Strike," 217. When Frankfurter was appointed to the U.S. Supreme Court by Franklin Roosevelt, his putative association with Weisbord was raised as part of a red-baiting attack on his appointment. See *Nomination of Felix Frankfurter: Hearings before a Subcommittee on the Judiciary, United States Senate, Seventy-Sixth Congress, First Session* (Washington, DC: U.S. Government Printing Office, 1939), 34.

36 Richard A. Greenwald, *The Triangle Fire, the Protocols of Peace, and Industrial Democracy in Progressive Era New York* (Philadelphia: Temple University Press, 2005); Jacob Kramer, *The New Freedom and the Radicals: Woodrow Wilson, Progressive Views of Radicalism, and the Origins of Repressive Tolerance* (Philadelphia: Temple University Press, 2015), 6, 130.

37 Telegram from Stephen Wise to Justine Wise, February 24, 1926, in Polier papers, box 1, folder 15; telegram from Stephen Wise to Justine Wise, February 26, 1926, in Wise papers, reel 74-49.

38 Albert Weisbord to Stephen Wise, February 25, 1926, in Wise papers, reel 74-49.

39 Stephen Wise telegraph to Justine Wise, March 3, 1926, in Polier papers, box 1, folder 15; notes on Weisbord's report to the Meeting of the CEC Textile Committee,

March 3, 1926, PRL; Stephen Wise telegram to Sidney Hillman on March 5, 1926, in Wise papers, reel 74-49. The description of the proposed committee is from notes on Weisbord's report at meeting of the CEC Textile Committee on May 3, 1926, PRL.

40 "Statement of Conditions Made by Mr. Albert Weisbord, Chairman of the United Front Committee of the Passaic Textile Strikers," March 4, 1926, in Wise papers, reel 74-49. The discussion among the Communist leadership took place at the March 3, 1926, CEC Textile Committee Meeting, PRL; Clarke A. Chambers, *Paul U. Kellogg and the Survey: Voices for Social Welfare and Social Justice* (Minneapolis: University of Minnesota Press, 1971); Tay Hohoff, *A Ministry to Man: The Life of John Lovejoy Elliott, a Biography* (New York: Harper, 1954). The obituary of William Howard Melish is in *NYT*, June 16, 1986.

41 "To the Strikers in the Textile Industries of America," by John Lovejoy Elliott, Paul U. Kellogg, John Howard Melish, and Stephen S. Wise, March 5, 1926, in Wise papers, reel 74-49; copy in Polier papers, box 1, folder 15.

42 *PDN*, March 6, 1926; Albert Weisbord and Gustav Deak, for the United Front Committee of Textile Workers of Passaic, N.J., and Vicinity, to Stephen Wise, March 7, 1926, and undated letters to "Gentlemen" (mill owners) by John Lovejoy Elliott, Paul U. Kellogg, John Howard Melish, and Stephen S. Wise, all in Wise papers, reel 74-49; *NYT*, March 8, 1926; Wise to Elliott, Kellogg, and Melish, March 26, 1926, in Wise papers, reel 74-49; *New York Sun*, March 8, 1926, clipping in Wise papers, reel 74-49.

43 Stephen Wise to Justine Wise, March 3, 1926, quoted in Urofsky, *Voice That Spoke for Justice*, 232.

Chapter 5   Enter the Politicians

1 *NYT*, February 14, 1926; *PDN*, February 15 and 17, 1926; *NYW*, May 4, 1926, Walsh scrapbook 74.

2 *PDN*, February 25, 1926; *NYT*, February 26 and 28, 1926.

3 See Maria Eucharia Meehan, "Frank P. Walsh and the American Labor Movement" (PhD diss., New York University, 1962); Jacob Kramer, *The New Freedom and the Radicals: Woodrow Wilson, Progressive Views of Radicalism, and the Origins of Repressive Tolerance* (Philadelphia: Temple University Press, 2015), 131, 138, 144.

4 Report on meeting of CEC Textile Committee, March 13, 1926, PRL; report of the CEC Textile Committee, March 13, 1926, PRL; Mary Heaton Vorse, *The Passaic Textile Strike, 1926–1927* (Passaic, NJ: General Relief Committee of Textile Workers, 1927), 28; Carmen Brissette Grayson, "W. Jett Lauck: Biography of a Reformer" (PhD diss., University of Virginia, 1975), 279.

5 *Fourteenth Annual Report of the Secretary of Labor for the Fiscal Year Ended June 30, 1926* (Washington, DC: U.S. Government Printing Office, 1926) 26–27; Vorse, *The Passaic Textile Strike*, 29.

6 *PDN*, special edition, March 16, 1926.

7 *PDN*, March 17, 1926.

8 *PDN*, March 17, 1926.

9 Harold G. Aron, General Counsel of Botany Worsted Mills, telegram to Everett Sanders, March 17, 1926, in Coolidge papers, series 1, file 89 (microfilm reel 62).

10 *PDN*, March 17, 1926; see also *Fourteenth Annual Report of the Secretary of Labor*, 27; letter to James J. Davis, Secretary of Labor, March 17, 1926, in Walsh papers, box 25, second Passaic strike folder; statement by Eight Passaic Strikers to James J. Davis, March 17, 1926, in Walsh papers, box 25, second Passaic folder.

11 See Leroy Ashby, *The Spearless Leader: Senator Borah and the Progressive Movement in the 1920s* (Urbana: University of Illinois, 1972), 85–89. Haywood was found not guilty, and much of the labor movement saw his prosecution as a frame-up; *PDN*, March 15, 1926; Grayson, "W. Jett Lauck," 279.

12 *PDN*, March 16, 1926.

13 Walsh to American Fund for Public Service, March 22, 1926, Vorse papers, box 116, "Passaic Strike Correspondence, 1926." Walsh to Edward N. Nockels, Chicago Federation of Labor, March 18, 1926, and Nockels to Walsh, March 19, 1926, both in Walsh papers, box 25, first Passaic strike folder.

14 *PDN*, March 19, 1926.

15 *PDN*, March 19 and 22, 1926.

16 *PDN*, March 19, 1926; Albert Weisbord, telegram to William E. Borah, March 18, 1926, in Borah papers, box 213, first Passaic strike folder; reprinted in *PDN*, March 19, 1926.

17 Sidney Hillman, telegram to Senator William E. Borah, March 19, 1926; American Civil Liberties Union, telegram to Borah, March 19, 1926; and Norman Thomas, telegram to Borah, March 19, 1926; all in Borah papers, box 213, first Passaic strike folder. Walsh to American Fund for Public Service, March 22, 1926, in Vorse papers, box 116, folder "Passaic Strike, 1926 Correspondence."

18 *PDN*, March 19, 1926.

19 *Congressional Record*, Senate 67, no. 80 (March 20, 1926): 5749–5754; *PDN*, March 22, 1926.

20 *Plainfield Courier-News*, September 22, 1924; *NYHT*, March 21, 1926.

21 See telegrams: Cornelia J. Brown to Borah, March 20, 1926; G.W.B. Cushing, president Consumers' League, to Borah, March 23, 1926; Lawrence F. Labrie, secretary treasurer Federated Textile Union of America, to Borah, March 23, 1926; Carolina B. Lamonte to Borah, March 24, 1926, Augusta T. Lappan to Borah, March 24, 1926; and Fred Hoelscher, secretary of Associated Silk Workers of Paterson, March 26, 1926; all in Borah papers, box 213, first Passaic strike folder. *NYHT*, March 21, 1926; Stephen Wise to Honorable Edward I. Edwards, March 22, 1926, in Polier papers, box 1, folder 15; Senator Edward Edwards to Rabbi Stephen S. Wise, March 23, 1926, in *PDN*, March 24, 1926, original in Wise papers, reel 74-49; *PDN*, March 25, 1926; *Washington Post*, March 21, 1926. See Mary Heaton Vorse to Frank P. Walsh, undated [March 20, 1926], in Walsh papers, box 25, first Passaic strike folder; *PDN*, March 23, 1926.

22 *PDN*, March 29, 1926; *NYT*, April 1, 1926; *NYDN*, April 1, 1926; *New York Telegram*, April 1, 1926.

23 See, for example, Pauline Clark to Walsh, March 23, 1926, Clark to Walsh, March 31, 1926, La Follette to Walsh, March 27, 1926, and Clark to Walsh, April 13, 1926, all in Walsh papers, box 25, first Passaic strike folder.

24 *JJ*, April 21, 1926.

25 The Polish National Catholic Church split from the Roman Catholic church in the 1890s in Scranton, Pennsylvania.

26 *PDN*, March 11, 1926; *PMC*, March 11, 1926; Stephen Wise to Justine Wise, March 16, 1926, in Polier papers, box 1, folder 15; *PDN*, March 12, 1926.

27 Notes on Weisbord's presentation, Report of CEC Textile Committee, March 13, 1926, PRL.

28 Elizabeth Fones-Wolf and Ken Fones-Wolf, "Lending a Hand to Labor: James Myers and the Federal Council of Churches, 1926–1947," *Church History* 68, no. 1 (March 1999): 70.

29 Joseph Magliacano, "Legacy of Memories," July 2, 1991, in Magliacano papers, box 2, folder 18.

30 See Edwin S. Lines to Stephen Wise, March 5, 1926, in Wise papers.

31 Michael Bourgeois, *All Things Human: Henry Codman Potter and the Social Gospel in the Episcopal Church* (Urbana: University of Illinois Press, 2004), 154–167. On the Episcopal Church and labor reform, see William A. Mirola, *Redeeming Time: Protestantism and Chicago's Eight-Hour Movement, 1866–1912* (Urbana: University of Illinois Press, 2015), 37; Marta Cook and John Halpin, *The Role of Faith in the Progressive Movement* (Washington, DC: Center for American Progress, 2010), 6.

32 *Literary Digest*, September 30, 1922.

33 *Fifty-Second Annual Convention of the Diocese of Newark, Trinity Cathedral, Newark, N.J., May 18, 1926* (Newark, NJ: Diocesan House, 1926), 67–68. The book is in the collection of the Episcopal Diocese of Newark.

34 *Baltimore Afro-American*, June 12, 1926; *Chicago Defender*, July 24, 1926; *New York Amsterdam News*, September 29, 1926; William Pickens, for National Organization of Colored People, telegram to Senator William E. Borah, July 29, 1926, in NAACP papers, pt. 2, William Pickens personal correspondence. On the Black population in Paterson, see Graham Hodges, *Black New Jersey* (New Brunswick, NJ: Rutgers University Press, 2019), 115. On Black workers and the strike, see Kamika Bennett, "Passaic Negro Workers Strike: The Passaic Strike of 1926 and the Making of a Radical and Multi-Racial Struggle" (master's thesis, Rutgers University Newark, 2020).

35 On Jewish Communists in Paterson, see Robert Snyder, "The Paterson Jewish Folk Chorus: Politics, Ethnic Identity and Musical Culture," *American Jewish History* 74, no. 1 (September 1984): 27–44.

36 *PDN*, March 15 and 21, 1926. Kernan, who was born in Scotland, was rector of St. Nicholas Church, which was an English-speaking parish and likely did not have many workers among its parishioners. See Kernan's obituary in *BER*, February 18, 1933.

37 *NYT*, March 29, 1926. On Lyons, see William Starr Myers, ed., *Prominent Families of New Jersey*, vol. 1 (Baltimore: Genealogical Publications, 2000), 1107.

38 Stephen Wise to Justine Wise, April 13, 1926, Polier papers, box 1, folder 15; *Survey* [April 1926], clipping in Polier papers, box 1, folder 15.

39 Stephen Wise to Justine Wise, April 16, 1926, in Polier papers, box 1, folder 15.

40 Steven Hart, *American Dictators: Frank Hague, Nucky Johnson, and the Perfection of the Urban Political Machine* (New Brunswick: Rutgers University Press, 2013), 50–51.

41 Richard J. Connors, *A Cycle of Power: The Career of Jersey City Mayor Frank Hague* (Metuchen, NJ: Scarecrow Press, 1971), 99; Dayton David McKean, *The Boss: The Hague Machine in Action* (New York: Russell and Russell, 1967), 183; Leonard F. Vernon, *The Life and Times of Jersey City Mayor Frank Hague* (Charleston, SC: History Press, 2011), 98; Hart, *American Dictators*, 122.

42 *Report of the Proceedings of the Thirty-Sixth Annual Convention of the American Federation of Labor Held at Baltimore, Maryland, November 13 to 25, Inclusive* (Washington, DC: Law Reporter Printing Co., 1916), 185–187.

43 *New York Daily Mirror*, April 15, 1926, in Walsh scrapbook 73. See Joseph Mahoney's entry on Moore in *The Governors of New Jersey: Biographical Essays*, eds. Michael J. Birkner, Donald Linky, and Peter Mickulas (New Brunswick: Rutgers University Press, 2014); *PDN*, March 8, 1926.

44 *NYEP*, April 15, 1926, clipping in Walsh scrapbook 73, Walsh; *JJ*, April 15, 1926.

45 Lauck telegram to Walsh, April 15, 1926, in Walsh papers, box 25, folder 1; *New York Evening World*, April 15, 1926, clipping in Walsh scrapbook 73; Stephen Wise to Justine Wise, April 15, 1926, in Polier papers, box 1, folder 15.

46 *New York Sun*, April 17, 1926, in Walsh scrapbook 74.

47 "Minutes of Trade Union Committee of the C.E.C.," April 7, 1926, in Bell papers, box 9, folder 2.

48 The above information, which will be dealt with in more detail in chapter 6, is taken from *PDN*, April 17 through 19, 1926, and clippings from the metropolitan press in Walsh scrapbook 74.

49 *NYT*, April 18, 1926.

50 *New York Sun*, April 19, 1926, in Walsh scrapbook 74.

51 Michael D. Doubler, *I Am the Guard: A History of the Army National Guard, 1636–2000* (Collingdale, PA: Diane Publishing, 2003), 103.

52 *NYHT*, April 20, 1926; *NYW*, April 20, 1926, in Walsh scrapbook 74; *NYT*, April 20, 1926.

53 *New York American*, April 21, 1926; *New York Sun*, April 21, 1926; *NYHT*, April 21, 1926; *New York Telegram*, April 21, 1926; *NYEP*, April 22, 1926; *New York Daily Mirror*, April 22, 1926; all clippings in Walsh scrapbook 74.

54 *New York Daily Mirror*, April 24, 1926, clipping in Walsh scrapbook 74.

55 *New York Telegram*, April 22, 1926, *NYHT*, April 22, 1926, and *New York American*, April 22, 1926, all clippings in Walsh scrapbook 74.

56 *New York Telegram*, April 21, 1926, and *New York Sun*, April 22, 1926, both clippings in Walsh scrapbook 74; *NYT*, April 22, 1922. See Hunt's obituary in the Cincinnati *Enquirer*, March 1, 1956. *NYDN*, April 21, 1926, and *NYEP*, April 22, 1926, both clippings in Walsh scrapbook 74.

57 *NYDN*, April 26, 1926, *NYEP*, April 26, 1926, *New York Evening Journal*, April 27, 1926, *New York Daily Mirror*, April 27, 1926, *New York Evening Post*, April 27, 1926, and *New York Sun*, April 27, 1926, all clippings in Walsh scrapbook 74.

58 *NYHT*, April 29, 1926, clipping in Walsh scrapbook 74.

59 Pauline Clark to Walsh, May 4, 1926, in Walsh papers, box 25, folder 1. The telegram is not in Moore's papers in the New Jersey State Archives. *NYW*, May 4, 1926, in Walsh scrapbook 74. I wish to thank Mary Baumann, of the U.S. Senate Historical Office, for information on "senatorial courtesy" in the 1920s.

60 Norman Thomas and Stephen Wise, telegram to Senator Borah, April 28, 1926, in Borah papers, box 213, first Passaic strike folder.

61 W. Jett Lauck to Walsh, May 4, 1926, in Walsh papers, box 25, folder 1.

62 Vorse, *The Passaic Textile Strike*, chap. 12; *LL*, May 19, 1926; *Daily Mirror*, April 17, 1926, Walsh scrapbook 74; CEC Textile Committee minutes, April 27, 1926, in Comintern, 515:1:814.

63 *New York Herald*, May 5, 1926, in Walsh scrapbook 74.

64 *New York Sun*, May 5, 1926, and *NYDN*, May 6, 1926, both clippings in Walsh scrapbook 74; *NYT*, May 6, 1926.

65 *NYT*, May 6 and 14, 1926; *NYDN*, May 14, 1926; *LL*, June 2, 1926; Morton K. Siegel, "The Passaic Textile Strike of 1926" (PhD diss., Columbia University, 1953), 220–222.

66 See the two letters from Stephen Wise to Justine Wise, both dated May 18, 1926, in Polier papers, box 1, folder 15; *LL*, May 5 and 19, 1926. Benjamin Gitlow speculated that "Hillman's concern about the Passaic Strike . . . is due to his concern about the Left Wing in his own organization" and warned that "it would be a mistake for us to have him become the champion of the Left Wing move to organizer the

unorganized" (letter to C. E. Ruthenberg, May 7, 1926, in Comintern, 515:1:713); Stephen Wise to Justine Wise, June 1, 1926, in Polier papers, box 1, folder 15.

67 Telegram from Garfield City Council to Senator Borah, May 19, 1926, in Borah papers, box 213, first Passaic strike folder.

68 *NL*, May 22, 1926; *LL*, May 26, 1926; Vorse, *The Passaic Textile Strike*, chap. 12; Weisbord telegram to Walsh, May 17, 1926, and Walsh to Dunn, May 19, 1926, both in Walsh papers, box 25, folder 1. Vorse and Weisbord describe the Slavic Committee's Washington delegation as thirty-strong.

69 *Hearing before the Committee on Education and Labor, United States Senate . . . Pursuant to S. Res. 177* (Washington, DC: U.S. Government Printing Office, 1926); Lauck to Walsh, May 26, 1926, in Walsh papers, box 25, folder 1.

70 *NL*, May 29, 1926.

71 Stephen Wise to Borah, June 4, 1926, in Borah papers, box 213, first Passaic strike folder, copy in Polier papers, box 1, folder 15.

72 Undated statement [June 5, 1926?], marked "Return at Once," in Polier papers, box 1, folder 15.

73 Stephen Wise to Borah, June 5, 1926, in Borah papers, box 213, first Passaic strike folder.

74 Stephen Wise to Hillman, June 5, 1926, and Stephen Wise to Justine Wise, June 8, 1926, both in Polier papers, box 1, folder 15.

Chapter 6   Repression and Class-Struggle Defense

1 *PDN*, January 15, 1926; *BDE*, January 15, 1926.

2 On violence and repression, see Larry J. Griffin, Michael E. Wallace, and Beth A. Rubin, "Capitalist Resistance to the Organization of Labor before the New Deal: Why? How? Success?," *American Sociological Review* 51, no. 2 (April 1986): 147–167. On the legality of picketing, see Ken I. Kersch, "How Conduct Became Speech and Speech Became Conduct: A Political Development Case Study in Labor Law and the Freedom of Speech," *Journal of Constitutional Law* 8, no. 2 (March 2006): 255–297. On the use of injunction, see P. F. Brissenden, "The Campaign against the Labor Injunction," *American Economic Review* 23, no. 1 (March 1933): 50–51; Holly McCammon, "'Government by Injunction': The U.S. Judiciary and Strike Action in the Late 19th and Early 20th Centuries," *Work and Occupations* 20, no. 2 (May 1993): 174–204. The classic study on injunctions is Felix Frankfurter and Nathan Greene, *The Labor Injunction* (New York: Macmillan, 1930).

3 For corruption and crime in Passaic during this time, see Bob Rosenthal's novel *Bootleggers, Mobsters, and My Mom: A True Passaic Story* (Hagerstown, MD: Star-L, 2011), which is based on substantial research in local newspapers, if prone to conspiracy theories. On Bergen County, see Frank Lombardi, "Bootleg Booze and Sewer Bonds," *Hackensack Record*, January 7, 1973. On Zober, see *NYDN*, March 23, 1927, and July 5, 1931; *BER*, April 12, 1934. Eventually the New Jersey Supreme Court reversed the convictions because the judge had not instructed the jury correctly; *BER*, February 6, 1937. On Preiskel, see *NYDN*, November 1, 1927; *NYT*, December 3 and 20, 1927; *BER*, February 3, 1930; *NYDN*, October 9, 1941.

4 James P. Cannon, memorandum on defense committee, April 22, 1926, in Comintern 515:1:915; Cannon, "The United Front at Passaic," *LD*, June 1926.

5 ACLU memorandum [April 1926?] on "Brutality of the Police," and ACLU memorandum, "Police Violence," [May 1926?], both in ACLU papers, vol. 302.

6 Sara Fanny Simon, "The Passaic Strike—A Study in Left Wing Leadership" (master's thesis, Columbia University, 1928), 61–62. The AFPS papers and Ernst papers provide lists of arrests and bail for portions of the strike. At the end of the strike, Wagenknecht estimated there had been 1,000 arrests; *LL*, March 9, 1927. Current equivalents taken from Bureau of Labor Statistics CPI Inflation Calculator for November 2019 values.

7 Cyril Briggs, "Rally Labor for Passaic Strike Prisoners," *LD*, May 1927.

8 Philip S. Foner, *The History of the Labor Movement in the United States*, vol. 4 (New York: International, 1965), 360–361; Robert Justin Goldstein, *Political Repression in Modern America from 1870 to 1976* (Urbana: University of Illinois Press, 2001), 90–91; George H. Rice, "How the Passaic (N.J.) Police Force Handle Labor Problems," *National Police Journal* 5, no. 3 (December 1919): 14–18.

9 *New Textile Worker*, April 10, 1920; "An Ordinance Regulating Street Parades, Processions, Street Assemblies, and Public Meetings in the City of Passaic," April 6, 1920, in Ordinances; *New Textile Worker*, March 27 and April 10, 1920. See also William Hard, "America in Passaic," *New Republic*, April 7, 1920, 182–185; Lewis S. Gannett, "The Constitution by Candlelight," *Nation*, April 3, 1920, 425–427; Laura Weinrib, *The Taming of Free Speech: America's Civil Liberties Compromise* (Cambridge: Harvard University Press, 2016), 133–134; Arthur T. Vanderbilt II, *Changing Law: A Biography of Arthur T. Vanderbilt* (New Brunswick, NJ: Rutgers University Press, 1976), 47–53. See also the pamphlet *"Unlawful Assembly in Paterson": The Trial and Conviction of Roger N. Baldwin and Seven Silk Strikers under a Law Passed in 1796* (New York: ACLU, 1925).

10 *DW*, April 22, 1926.

11 *PDN*, January 25 and 26, and February 6, 1926.

12 *DW*, February 7 and 8, 1926.

13 *PDN*, February 8, 1926; *BER*, February 9, 1926; *PDH*, February 9, 1926.

14 James P. Cannon, "The Second Annual Conference of the International Labor Defense," *LD*, October 1926.

15 *LD*, June 1926; Reminiscences of Roger Nash Baldwin (1954), Columbia University Oral History Project, 108, 125. See also Baldwin's obituaries in *NYT*, August 27, 1981, and *St. Louis Post-Dispatch*, August 27, 1981; Weinrib, *Taming of Free Speech*, 7–11.

16 *LD*, January 1926, October 1926; John J. Ballam, "Special Textile Report of Organizational Basis for Building Left Wing and Party in Passaic," September 4, 1926, in Comintern, 515:1:913.

17 *LD*, January 1926. The *Labor Defender*'s editor, Max Shachtman, claimed the journal was "the first left-wing pictorial magazine in the country." Reminiscences of Max Shachtman (1963), Columbia University Oral History Project (NXCP87-A1249), 116.

18 *PDN*, February 10, 1926. Brodsky's obituary and several reminiscences are in *DW*, July 30, 1947. On Feder, see William W. Scott, *History of Passaic and Its Environs* (New York: Lewis Historical, 1922), 1:415–416; Jennifer R. Uhlmann, "The Communist Civil Rights Movement: Legal Activism in the United States, 1919–1946" (PhD diss., University of California Los Angeles, 2007), 117–118.

19 Marc Lendler, *Gitlow v. New York: Every Idea an Incitement* (Lawrence: University Press of Kansas, 2012); Gloria Garrett Samson, *American Fund for Public Service: Charles Garland and Radical Philanthropy, 1922–1941* (Wesport, CT: Greenwood, 1996), 160; Mary Anne Trasciatti, "Elizabeth Gurley Flynn, the Sacco-Vanzetti Case, and the Rise and Fall of the Liberal-Radical Alliance, 1920–1940," *American Communist History* 15, no. 2 (2016): 193–194.

20 David Montgomery, "Thinking about American Workers in the 1920s," *International Labor and Working-Class History* 32 (Fall 1987): 16; Emily Zackin, "Popular Constitutionalism's Hard When You're Not Very Popular: Why the ACLU Turned to Courts," *Law & Society Review* 42, no. 2 (2008): 378; Morton Siegel, "The Passaic Textile Strike of 1926" (PhD diss., Columbia University, 1954), 271–272.

21 For the Communist view of the state, see V. I. Lenin, *The State and Revolution: The Marxist Theory of the State and the Tasks of the Proletariat in the Revolution* (1917), in *Collected Works* (Moscow: Progress, 1964), vol. 25; J. O. Bentall, "The Passaic Strike Encounters the Courts," *LD*, April 1926.

22 Although Cannon would later become one of the most prominent supporters of Leon Trotsky in the United States, during most of his time leading the ILD he had not yet reached Trotsky's conclusion that the Soviet Union had degenerated since Lenin's time.

23 Robert Cottrell, *Roger Nash Baldwin and the American Civil Liberties Union* (New York: Columbia University Press, 2001), 145–148; Uhlmann, "Communist Civil Rights Movement," 89–90.

24 Roger N. Baldwin to James P. Cannon, May 26, 1926, in ACLU papers, vol. 303. On Abramovitch and the CP, see Tony Michels, "The Abramovitch Campaign and What It Tells Us about American Communism," *American Communist History* 15, no. 3 (2016): 283–291; Baldwin to Cannon, August 31, 1926, in ACLU papers, vol. 303; James P. Cannon, "Who Can Save Sacco and Vanzetti?," *LD*, January 1927.

25 *LD*, April 1926; *PDN*, February 11 and 15, 1926; *NYDN*, May 16, 1926; Jack Rubenstein interview by Martha Asher, February/March 1987, in Tamiment Ephemera. I wish to thank Timothy Johnson for drawing this interview to my attention. See also Rubenstein's obituary in the *North Jersey Herald and News*, July 8, 1989; George Ashkenudse to C. E. Ruthenberg, October 5, 1926, in Comintern, 515:1:713. There is a list of people arrested in AFPS papers, reel 16.

26 *PDH*, February 12, 1926.

27 *PDN*, February 16 and March 8 and 18, 1926; *PDN*, March 19, 1926; *PDN*, March 24, 1926; *DW*, August 10, 1926; Siegel, "Passaic Textile Strike," 180.

28 *PDN*, February 20 and 22, 1926; *NYDN*, February 21, 1926.

29 *PDN*, February 23 and 25, 1926.

30 *PDN*, March 1, 1926.

31 *PDN*, March 3, 1926.

32 *PDN*, March 3, 1926; *TSB*, March 3, 1926.

33 Minutes of CEC Textile Committee, March 3, 1926, PRL; C. E. Ruthenberg to J. J. Ballam, September 10, 1926, in Comintern, 515:1:713.

34 *PDN*, March 6, 1926; *NYDN*, March 6, 1926; *NYT*, March 6, 1926; *NYDN*, March 7, 1926; *NYT*, March 7, 1926. The *Passaic Daily Herald* (March 6, 1926) wrote that Katz "was arrested several months ago by Chief of Police Richard O. Zober, on a Boonton complaint" but did not elaborate.

35 Siegel, "Passaic Textile Strike," 183–185.

36 *PDN*, March 8, 10, 11, and 19, 1926.

37 *PDN*, March 10, 1926.

38 *PDN*, March 12, 1926.

39 *PDN*, March 11, 1926; *NYT*, August 16, 1924; Judith Deveson, "The Ku Klux Klan in New Jersey in the 1920s" (1972), unpublished paper in Special Collections, Alexander Library, Rutgers University.

40 *PDN*, March 10 and 12, 1926.

41 *New York Mirror*, March 15, 1926; *NYEP*, March 15, 1926; clippings in Walsh scrapbook 73. On Nimmo's anti-labor reputation, see Steven R. Irwin, "Conflict Resolution and the Development of Law: The Passaic Textile Strike of 1926 and the New Jersey State Riot Act" (bachelor's thesis, Rutgers University, 1976), 17.

42 *PDN*, March 16, 1926; *New York Mirror*, March 16, 1926.

43 *PDN*, March 19, 1926.

44 *PDN*, March 10, 1926.

45 *PDN*, March 22, 1926.

46 *PDN*, March 27, 1926; *PDN*, March 22, 1926.

47 *PDN*, March 22, 1926.

48 *NYDN*, March 23, 1926; *PDN*, March 24, 25, and 26, 1926.

49 *APEN*, March 29, 1926; *Long Branch* (NJ) *Daily Record*, March 29, 1926; *NYDN*, March 30, 1926.

50 *PDN*, March 30, 1926; *New York Daily Graphic*, March 30, 1926, in Walsh scrapbook 73.

51 *NYW*, April 10, 1926, and *New York Sunday News*, April 11, 1926, both in Walsh scrapbook 73.

52 *PDN*, April 10, 1926.

53 Alfred Wagenknecht to Hortense Wagenknecht, April 10, 1926, in Wagenknecht papers, box 1, folder 10; *NYDN*, April 19, 1926; ACLU memorandum, "Police Violence" (May 1926?), in ACLU papers, vol. 302; *New York Sunday News*, April 11, 1926; *New York Graphic*, April 13, 1926; *New York Sun*, April 13, 1926; clippings in Walsh scrapbook 73; *BER*, April 14, 1926.

54 *BER*, April 14, 1926. By 1926, martial law had been instituted in Idaho, Colorado, and West Virginia to break militant strikes, but always by the governor, not local police. See Charles Fairman, *The Law of Martial Rule* (Chicago: Callaghan, 1943), chap. 5.

55 *New York Graphic*, April 14, 1926, in Walsh scrapbook 73; *PDN*, April 14, 1926.

56 *BG*, April 15, 1926; *NYDN*, April 15, 1926; *PCN*, April 15, 1926; Harry Fleischman, *Norman Thomas: A Biography* (New York: Norton, 1964), 104–107.

57 Kamika Bennett, "Passaic Negro Workers Strike: The Passaic Strike of 1926 and the Making of a Radical and Multi-Racial Struggle" (master's thesis, Rutgers University Newark, 2020), 63. As Bennett shows, the strike leadership's commitment to include Black workers in the strike prevented the strike from breaking down along racial lines.

58 Newspapers usually Americanized his first name to "Frank" and changed his surname to Dito, Gido, or Deedo. I am grateful to Carol Luparella, parish secretary of St. Stanislaus Kostka RC Church, for the correct spelling of Dyda's name (correspondence with author, February 12, 2019).

59 Information from: *PDN*, April 14 and 15, 1926; *BER*, April 14 and 15, 1926; *DHN*, April 14, 1926; *NYDN*, April 15 and 18, 1926; *BG*, April 15, 1926. The Bergen County Medical Examiner does not keep autopsy reports from before 1946 (Debra A. Trentacosta, correspondence with author, May 15, 2019).

60 *BER*, April 17, 1926; *NYDN*, April 18, 1926; *TSB*, April 21, 1926.

61 *NYHT*, April 17, 1926, in Walsh scrapbook 74; *NYW*, May 26, 1926, ACLU papers, vol. 313; lists of contributors, April 19 and 24, 1926, in AFPS papers, reel 16. See also David L. Rosston to Oswald Garrison Villard, April 21, 1926, in Villard papers, MS AM 1323, folder 2975; [Morris Ernst?] to Miss Winifred Chapel, June 9, 1926.

62 For a listing of bonds issued in March and April 1926, see letter from National Surety Company to Morris Ernst, June 24, 1924; for First National Bank stock, see Morris Ernst to Robert N. Nugent, National Surety Company, November 12, 1926; both in "American Fund for Public Service, Correspondence re: Bail," in Ernst papers.

63 *New York Sun*, April 17, 1926, Walsh scrapbook 74.

64 *PDN*, March 3, 26, and 30, 1926. For the anti-injunction law, see NJL (1926), chap. 207; *NYW*, August 14, 1926, in ACLU papers, vol. 304; *Gevas v. Greek Restaurant Workers' Club*, 99 NJ Eq. 770 (1926).

65 On the early injunctions, see *PDN*, February 10, 1926.

66 Forstmann and Huffmann's bill of complaint and the injunction are in the Vorse papers, box 116. The names are not in alphabetical order, and some seem to be alternate spellings of the same name. *NYDN*, April 17, 1926.

67 *NYHT*, April 17, 1926, Walsh scrapbook 74.

68 *NYHT*, April 18, 1926, *NYDN*, April 19, 1926, and *NYW*, April 19, 1926, all clippings in Walsh scrapbook 74.

69 "I.L.D. to Gather All Resources for 'Free Weisbord' Campaign," ILD press release, April 17, 1926, in Comintern, 515:1:915.

70 *NYW* April 20, 1926,in Walsh scrapbook 74; *Sheboygan* (Wisconsin) *Press*, April 20, 1926; "A.C.L.U. Endorses I.L.D. Passaic Drive," *I.L.D. News Service*, April 21, 1926, in Comintern, 515:1:915; *DW*, May 24, 1926.

71 *NYW*, April 20, 1926, in Walsh scrapbook 74.

72 J. P. Cannon, memorandum on defense committee, April 22, 1926, in Comintern, 515:1:915; Cannon, "The United Front at Passaic," *LD*, June 1926.

73 *BER*, April 26, 1926. On Nelkin, see his obituary in the Hackensack *Record*, June 17, 1979; *New York Mirror*, April 27, 1926, in Walsh scrapbook 74.

74 *NYT*, May 31, 1941, *NYW*, April 26, 1926, and *NYEP*, April 26, 1926, all clippings in Walsh scrapbook 74. On Vanderbilt, see Nelson Johnson, *Battleground New Jersey: Vanderbilt, Hague, and Their Fight for Justice* (New Brunswick, NJ: Rutgers University Press, 2014).

75 *BER*, April 30, 1926; *New York Graphic*, May 1, 1926, in Walsh scrapbook 74; *LL*, May 5, 1926; Irwin, "Conflict Resolution," 2; Siegel, "Passaic Textile Strike," 218; *LL*, May 5, 1926.

76 *New York Sun*, April 29, 1926, in Walsh scrapbook 74; *BER*, April 30, 1926.

77 *NYDN*, May 6, 1926; Irwin, "Conflict Resolution," 55; *Forstmann & Huffmann Co. v. The United Front Committee of Textile Workers*, 99 NJ Eq. 230 (1925–1926); *NYEP*, May 7, 1926, in Walsh scrapbook 74.

78 *NYW*, May 12, 1926, in Walsh scrapbook 74; Irwin, "Conflict Resolution," 55. Irwin states that Bentley allowed up to ten picketers; *New York American*, May 15, 1926, in Walsh scrapbook 74.

79 *NYDN*, May 24, 1926.

80 Irwin, "Conflict Resolution," 56; *NYT*, June 3 and 4, 1926.

81 *NYW*, July 7, 1926, in ACLU papers, vol. 314; *NYT*, July 8, 1926; *PDH*, July 8 and 9, 1926.

82 On the use of detectives and provocateurs, see Robert Dunn, "National Labor Blacklist Agency Forming," *Federated Press Eastern Weekly Letter*, August 25, 1926; Dunn, "Labor Spies and Company Unions in Same Family," *Federated Press Eastern Weekly Letter*, September 8, 1926; Dunn, "Frame-Up Artists at Work: How Labor Spies Operate," *Labor Age*, January 1928; all in Dunn papers, box 8, "Material on Labor Spies" folder. *PDH*, July 18, 1926; July 27, 1926; *Paterson News*,

July 23, 1926; *Long Branch Daily Record*, July 26, 1926. On Sam Elam, see Bennett, "Passaic Negro Workers Strike," 6–7.

83 *NYT*, July 28, 1926. According to a UFC press release, this was "a huge bologna knife, which the cop was able to produce from his pocket [and] declared to be the property of Weisbord." News release, July 28, 1926, AUF 6046, box 389, folder 1.

84 *PDH*, July 2 and 19, 1926; *APEN*, July 22, 1926; *NYDN*, July 22, 1926. On Nosovitsky's history as an agent provocateur, see Theodore Draper, *Roots of American Communism* (New York: Viking, 1957), 227–228.

85 *PDH*, August 23, 1926. On the number of arrests, see Simon, "The Passaic Strike," 61.

86 *NYW*, April 19, 1926, in Walsh scrapbook 74; *APP*, April 19, 1926; *NYDN*, May 25 and 28, 1926; *APEN*, May 7, 1926; *New York Mirror*, May 25, 1926, in Walsh scrapbook 74; *DHN*, May 27, 1926; *Long Branch Daily Record*, May 27, 1926; *Evening* (Wilmington, DE) *Journal*, June 14, 1926; *The Bee* (Danville, Virginia), June 14, 1926; *BER*, June 17, 1926; *NYE*, June 17, 1926, in Walsh scrapbook 74; *BDE*, June 19, 1926; *NYDN*, August 30, 1926.

87 *NYDN*, September 23, 1926; *Camden Evening Courier*, September 22, 1926; *PCN*, September 24, 1926; *Newark Evening News*, September 25, 1926. To the extent possible, the names are presented here spelled according to information found in government directories using Ancestry.com.

88 For an example of this hysteria, see *PDH*, June 21 and July 17, 1926; *NYDN*, September 23, 1926; *NYEP*, June 20, 1926; *NYW*, September 24, 1926, clippings in ACLU papers, vol. 314.

89 On Bellene, see *DW*, September 27, 1926; *APEN*, March 16, 1926; *BER*, April 14, 1926; *PDH*, June 25, 1926, clippings in ACLU papers, vol. 314.

90 *Long Branch Daily Record*, September 23, 1926; *DW*, September 27, 1926; "Passaic in Danger," *LD*, November 1926; *LL*, September 29, 1926; *LL*, October 13, 1926; *PDH*, June 18, 1926.

91 C. E. Ruthenberg to James P. Cannon, October 4, 1926, and Ruthenberg to Cannon, October 8, 1926, both in Comintern, 515:1:715; Hollace Ransdell, "Greasing the Rails for Passaic Strikers," *LD*, January 1927.

92 Hollace Ransdell, *Prisoners of the Passaic Strike* (New York: Joint Committee for Passaic Defense, 1926), 4.

93 *PDH*, January 26, 1927. See also *TSB*, June 25, 1926, which has a front-page photograph of Toth's bruises. *NYW*, September 24, 1926, in ACLU papers, vol. 314; John J. Ballam, "Report by National Textile Organizer—Passaic Situation," October 29, 1926, in Comintern, 515:1:815.

94 Minutes of ILD Executive Committee, November 26, 1926, in Comintern, 515:1:915; "Passaic's Frame-Up Victims," *LD*, March 1927; *BER*, January 20 and April 8, 1927. Wisnewski was elected justice of the peace in Garfield while he was in jail (*LL*, November 10, 1926); Hollace Ransdell, "Guilty! Of What? Add Eight More Political Prisoners to the List," *LD*, May 1927; Hollace Ransdell, "The State versus Thomas Regan, Textile Worker," *LD*, April 1927; *LL*, March 16, 1927; see also news release by Textile Council of Passaic and New Jersey, March 11, 1927, AUF 6046, box 389, folder 1.

95 Briggs, "Rally Labor for the Passaic Strike Prisoners," *LD*, May 1927; *PDH*, May 9, 1928.

96 See the correspondence in the file "American Fund for Public Service, Correspondence re: Bail," in Ernst papers.

97 Hollace Ransdell to AFPS, May 15, 1927, in AFPS papers, reel 16; *BER*, March 3 and October 26, 1928; *PDH*, October 26, 1928.

98 *NYEP*, December 18, 1926, in ACLU papers, vol. 304; *BER*, May 23, 1927, February 16, 1928; *PMC*, May 25, 1927; *PDH*, July 16, 1928; Anna Marnitz to Morris Ernst, January 11, 1930, in AFPS papers, reel 16.

Chapter 7 Building Relief and Solidarity

1 Benjamin Gitlow to C. E. Ruthenberg, March 4, 1926, and Ruthenberg to Gitlow, March 9, 1926, both in Comintern, 515:1:713. Thomas L. Sakymster, "A Communist Newspaper for Hungarian-Americans: The Strange World of the *Új Elöre*," *Hungarian Studies Review* 32, nos. 1–2 (2005): 47.

2 TUC minutes, February 3, 1926, Draper papers, box 29; Wagenknecht to "Dear Hortense," February 5, 1926, in Wagenknecht papers, box 1, folder 9; minutes of the CEC Textile Committee, February 13, 1926, in PRL.

3 In the 1920s the IWA affiliate in the United States changed its name several times, starting as Friends of Soviet Russia then becoming Friends of Soviet Russia and Workers' Germany in 1923, Workers' International Relief in 1924, International Workers' Aid in 1926, and Workers' International Relief again in 1927. I am grateful for Russell Campbell for clarifying the evolution in the group's name.

4 For recent scholarship on Münzenberg and the IWA, see Kasper Braskén, *The International Workers' Relief, Communism, and International Solidarity: Willi Münzenberg in Weimar Germany* (Basingstoke: Palgrave Macmillan, 2015); Holger Weiss, ed., *International Communism and Transnational Solidarity: Radical Networks, Mass Movements and Global Politics, 1919–1939* (Leiden: Brill, 2017); Sean McMeekin, *The Red Millionaire: A Political Biography of Willi Münzenberg, Moscow's Secret Propaganda Tsar in the West* (New Haven: Yale University Press, 2003). On the IWA Irish campaign, see Adrian Grant, "Workers to the Rescue: Workers' International Relief in Ireland, 1925," *History Ireland* 19, no. 1 (January/February 2011): 38–41.

5 Basic biographical information on Wagenknecht taken from obituary and statement by the CP in *DW*, August 27, 1956. In a letter to his wife, Wagenknecht recalled a discussion among Communist organizers in the strike who "began talking about funny things relating to the antics of some of the comrades in sex matters, when Vorse said all of a sudden, that altho all other comrades had been related to this or that woman in or out of the party, and had had their episodes, I seemed to remain a mystery in this regard, not a faintest rumor having been passed to now connecting me with any such matters" (Wagenknecht to Hortense Allison, March 8, 1926, in Wagenknecht papers, box 1, folder 3). On Wagenknecht's arrest during the war, see *Guilty? Of What? Speeches before the Jury in Connection with the Trial of C. E. Ruthenberg, Alfred Wagenknecht, Charles Baker* (Cleveland: Socialist News, 1917). Along with Baker and Ruthenberg, Wagenknecht was convicted for hindering selective service registration by persuading Alphonse J. Schue not to register; they were sentenced to one year in jail. The Supreme Court upheld their conviction a year later in *Ruthenberg v. U.S.* (1918); Theodore Draper, *American Communism and Soviet Russia* (New York: Random House, 1986 [1960]), 88.

6 Draper, *American Communism*, 176; *Labor Unity*, June 1928; Wagenknecht's letters to his wife during the strike give a sense of his routine. They are in the Wagenknecht papers, box 1, folder 9. Sara Fanny Simon, "The Passaic Strike—A Study in Left Wing Leadership" (master's thesis, Columbia University, 1928), 33.

7 Jacob A. Zumoff, "Hell in New Jersey: The Passaic Strike, Albert Weisbord, and the Communist Party," *Journal for the Study of Radicalism* 9, no. 1 (Spring 2015): 146; *TSB*, March 3, 1926; Simon, "The Passaic Strike," 35–38.

8 *DW*, January 22, 1927; Annick Des Roches, "Women United in Defense of the Family: The Public Battle for Improved Domestic and Workplace Conditions during the Passaic Textile Strike of 1926" (master's thesis, Hunter College, 2006); *PDN*, March 27, 1926.

9 *TSB*, March 15, 1926.

10 Bruce Watson, *Bread & Roses: Mills, Migrants, and the Struggle for the American Dream* (New York: Penguin, 2005), 186; Steve Golin, *Fragile Bridge: The Paterson Silk Strike of 1913* (Philadelphia: Temple University Press, 1988), 181.

11 "Two Important Last Minute Messages!," draft appeal, Comintern, 515:1:913.

12 Siegel, "Passaic Textile Strike," 289–292.

13 Siegel, "Passaic Textile Strike," 304; "A Call for a Conference to Support the Passaic Strike," Comintern, 515:1:913; *Textile Workers Bulletin*, June 4, 1926; minutes of the Support the Passaic Strike Conference, June 25, 1926, in AUF 646, section 7, box 388, folder 1.

14 *DW*, July 8, 20, and 27, 1926, and August 5 and 18, 1926; Siegel, "Passaic Textile Strike," 293.

15 *DW*, July 26, 1926; *TSB,* July 22, 1926; Siegel, "Passaic Textile Strike," 273, 302; Clarina Michelson for the Emergency Committee for Strikers' Relief, to "Dear Friend," May 8, 1926, in Dana papers, box 72, folder 1.

16 Local merchant quoted in Steven R. Irwin, "Conflict Resolution and the Development of Law: The Passaic Textile Strike of 1926 and the New Jersey State Riot Act" (bachelor's thesis, Rutgers University 1976), 14; *TSB*, March 22, 1926.

17 "Statement of National Textile Organizer Ballam on the Present Status of Relief Work for Passaic and Disposition of Passaic Strike Film," January 29, 1927, Comintern 515:1:1197; Siegel, "Passaic Textile Strike," 308–309; Simon, "The Passaic Strike," 39.

18 William Z. Foster, *Strike Strategy* (Chicago: Trade Union Educational League, 1926), 49; Mary Heaton Vorse, "The Battle of Passaic," *NM*, May 1926; Simon, "The Passaic Strike," 83; Siegel, "Passaic Textile Strike," 230–231.

19 Wagenknecht to "Dear Family," May 12, 1926, in Wagenknecht papers, box 1, folder 10.

20 Louis Zukofsky, "During the Passaic Textile Strike of 1926," in *Complete Short Poetry* (Baltimore: Johns Hopkins University Press, 1997), 26; Mary McAvoy, "The Variegated Shoots: Hazel MacKaye and the Advent of Pedagogical Drama at Brookwood Labor College, 1925–1926," *Youth Theatre Journal* 29 (2015): 55–56; Leslie Fishbein, "The Paterson Pageant (1913): The Birth of Docudrama as a Weapon in the Class Struggle," *New York History* 72, no. 2 (April 1991): 222–223; *DW*, July 15, 1926. On the Workers' Theater Alliance, see Federal Writers' Project, *Philadelphia: A Guide to the Nation' Birthplace* (Philadelphia: William Penn Assoc., 1937), 228.

21 Vorse, "Battle of Passaic," *NM*, May 1926; "A Passaic Symposium: Snapshots of the Textile Strike," *NM*, June 1926.

22 Andrew Hemingway, *Artists on the Left: American Artists and the Communist Movement, 1926–1956* (New Haven: Yale University Press, 2002), 12. Hemingway is specifically referring to *New Masses*; Michael Denning, *The Cultural Front: The Laboring of American Culture in the Twentieth Century* (London: Verso, 1997).

23 *Hell in New Jersey: Story of the Passaic Textile Strikers Told in Pictures* (Passaic, NJ: General Relief Committee of Textile Workers, 1926); Alfred Wagenknecht to "Dear Hortense," March 26, 1926, in Wagenknecht papers, box 1, folder 9; Eugene Lyons, *Assignment in Utopia* (New Brunswick: Transaction, 1991 [1937]), 42.

24 Minutes of the Support the Passaic Textile Strike Conference, Methods of Raising Money Suggested by Alfred Wagenknecht, June 25, 1929, in AUF 6046, section 7, box 388, folder 1; *LL,* June 30, 1926; *TSB,* June 25, 1926; Lyons, *Assignment in Utopia,* 42.

25 J. Takacs, letter to editor, *South Bend Tribune,* July 17, 1926; *DW,* July 16 and August 12, 1926; *DW,* August 17, 1926.

26 *PDH,* July 7, 1926; *PDN,* July 31, 1926.

27 This section borrows heavily from Jacob A. Zumoff, "The Passaic Strike Documentary: The Role of Film in Building Solidarity," *American Communist History* 18, nos. 3–4 (2019): 269–295. Much of what scholars know about the film come from Kevin Brownlow, *Behind the Mask of Innocence* (New York: Knopf, 1990), 498–508; and Steven J. Ross, *Working-Class Hollywood: Silent Film and the Shaping of Class in America* (Princeton: Princeton University Press, 1998). There is also a section on the strike in Steven A. Krinsky, "Media as an Organizing Tool: The Use of Film and Video in Social Movements" (PhD diss., University of Texas at Austin, 1990).

28 Ross, *Working-Class Hollywood,* 162.

29 Fishbein, "Paterson Strike Pageant," 197–233.

30 On earlier labor films, see Ross, *Working-Class Hollywood.* On previous Communist film efforts, see Alexander Schwarz, "A Selection of Documents: Workers' International Relief and the Origins of Left-Wing Independent Film and Social Documentary in the U.S.A.," *Studies in Russian and Soviet Cinema* 12, no. 2 (2018): 153–174.

31 Gus Deak to Kevin Brownlow, November 1983, quoted in Brownlow, *Behind the Mask of Innocence,* 500.

32 *DW,* May 10, 1927.

33 A continuity script, divided into reels, is in the archives of the Comintern, 515: 1:913.

34 Continuity script, Comintern, 515:1:913.

35 Continuity script, Comintern, 515:1:913.

36 Continuity script, Comintern, 515:1:913.

37 *DW,* October 12, 1926.

38 *DW,* October 18, 1926; *PDN,* October 9, 1926.

39 *TSB,* August 6, 1926; *TSB,* August 18, 1926; statement by Gustav Deak, September 14, 1926, in *LL,* September 22, 1926.

40 *DW,* October 18, 1926; *LL,* October 20, 1926; C. E. Ruthenberg to J. J. Ballam, August 27, 1926, Comintern, 515:1:713.

41 *DW,* August 26 and September 3, 4, and 14, 1926. *NYT,* August 29, 1926.

42 *DW,* September 18, 23, 25, and 30, 1926.

43 News releases, nos. 3, 77, 99, 102, and 145 in AUF 6046, box 389, folder 2; *DW,* October 21, November 5 and 6, and December 16, 1926; *Englewood Times,* October 29, 1926; *LL,* December 1, 1926; *Petaluma Argus,* March 10, 1927; "Statement of National Textile Organizer Ballam," January 29, 1927, Comintern, 515:1:1197.

44 *DW,* March 2 and 10 and April 2, 1927.

45 Mary Anne Trasciatti, "Elizabeth Gurley Flynn, the Sacco-Vanzetti Case, and the Rise and Fall of the Liberal-Radical Alliance, 1920–1940," *American Communist History* 15, no. 2 (2016): 191–216; Asher, who was the state chairperson of the

Communist Party in New Jersey until 1959, recalled in her interview with Brownlow that there was a copy in the New Jersey CP office.

Chapter 8   Women, the Family, and the Passaic Strike

1 *DW*, July 29, 1926; *DHN*, April 13, 1926; *NYDN*, June 5, 1926; *Chicago Tribune*, May 2, 1926.

2 *NYT*, April 9, 1926; *BER*, August 18, 1927. I am spelling Sandosky's name as it appears in the *Garfield City Directory* (1927), accessed on Ancestry.com; she is listed as a member of the employees' strike committee in *TSB*, March 22, 1926; *Fifteenth Census of the United States* (1930), accessed on Ancestry.com. She is listed as Shedosky in the Census; *PHN*, June 11, 1926.

3 Mary Heaton Vorse, *Passaic Textile Strike, 1926–1927* (Passaic, NJ: General Relief Committee of Textile Workers, 1927), 14, 34.

4 *DHN*, April 1, 1926; *TSB*, March 22, 1926; *Sixteenth Census of the United States* (1940), accessed on Ancestry.com; Find-A-Grave index on Ancestry.com.

5 Figures on arrests taken from AFPS papers, reel 16. Several people, including women, were arrested more than once. The injunction is in Vorse papers, box 116. Several of the names seem to be alternate spellings of the same name; Albert Weisbord, Report on the Passaic Strike, fall 1926, in Comintern, 515:1:815; Eloise Shellabarger, "The Shawled Women of Passaic," *Survey* 44 (July 3, 1920).

6 Alice Kessler-Harris, *Out to Work: A History of Wage-Earning Women in the United States* (Oxford: Oxford University Press, 1982), 237.

7 Philip S. Foner, *Women and the American Labor Movement: From the First Trade Unions to the Present*, 2nd ed. (Chicago: Haymarket Books, 2018), 276, 280–281; Annelise Orleck, *Common Sense and a Little Fire: Women and Working-Class Politics in the United States, 1900–1965*, 2nd ed. (Chapel Hill: University of North Carolina Press, 2017), 54–59; Mari Jo Buhle, "Socialist Women and the 'Girl Strikers,'" Chicago, 1910," *Signs* 1, no. 4 (Summer 1976): 1039–1051; Jennifer Guglielmo, *Living the Revolution: Italian Women's Resistance and Radicalism in New York City, 1880–1945* (Chapel Hill: University of North Carolina Press, 2010).

8 See Lawrence Cappello, "In Harm's Way: The Lawrence Textile Strike's Children Affair," in *The Great Lawrence Textile Strike of 1912: New Scholarship on the Bread and Roses Strike*, ed. Robert Farrant and Jurg Siegethaler (New York: Routledge, 2014); Melvyn Dubofsky, *We Shall Be All: A History of the Industrial Workers of the World* (New York: Quadrangle Books, 1969), 250–252; Bruce Watson, *Bread & Roses: Mills, Migrants, and the Struggle for the American Dream* (New York: Viking, 2005), chap. 8.

9 Orleck, *Common Sense*, 77.

10 Foner, *Women and the American Labor Movement*, 286, 294.

11 Siegel, "Passaic Textile Strike," 76; Arthur Harrison Cole, *The American Wool Manufacture* (Cambridge: Harvard University Press, 1926), 2:107–110.

12 "Wages and Earnings" memorandum [1926], in Vorse papers, box 118, reference materials folder; *PCN*, April 19, 1926; *The Family Status of Breadwinning Women: A Study of Material in the Census Schedules of a Selected Locality* (Washington, DC: U.S. Government Printing Office, 1922), 26.

13 The best English translation is "Communist International Theses on Work among Women: A New Translation," in *Spartacist* 62 (Spring 2011). See Elizabeth Waters, "In the Shadow of the Comintern: The Communist Women's Movement,

1920–1943," in *Promissory Notes: Women in the Transition to Socialism*, ed. Sonia Kruks et al. (New York: Monthly Review Press, 1989), 29–58.

14 Rosalyn Baxandall, "The Question Seldom Asked: Women and the CPUSA," in *New Studies in the Politics and Culture of U.S. Communism*, ed. Michael E. Brown et al. (New York: Monthly Review Press, 1993), 144, 146; Kate Weigand, *Red Feminism: American Communism and the Making of Women's Liberation* (Baltimore: Johns Hopkins University Press, 2001), 20; Linn Shapiro, "Red Feminism: American Communism and the Women's Rights Tradition, 1919–1956" (PhD diss., American University, 1996), 44; Beth Slutsky, *Gendering Radicalism: Women and Communism in Twentieth-Century California* (Lincoln: University of Nebraska Press, 2015). On the appeal of the Bolshevik Revolution among women's activists, see Julia L. Mickenberg, "Suffragettes and Soviets: American Feminists and the Specter of Revolutionary Russia," *Journal of American History* 100, no. 4 (2014): 1021–1051, and Mickenberg, "New Women in Red: Revolutionary Russia, Feminism, and the First Red Scare," *Journal of the Gilded Age and Progressive Era* 18 (2019): 56–80.

15 Elsa Jane Dixler, "The Woman Question: Women and the American Communist Party, 1929–1941" (PhD diss., Yale University, 1974), 31; Kate Gitlow to Mary Waters, September 1, 1926, in Comintern, 515:1:782. The UCWCH was originally called the United Council of Working-Class Women; Shapiro, "Red Feminism," 62.

16 Van Gosse, "'To Organize in Every Neighborhood, in Every Home': The Gender Politics of American Communists between the Wars," *Radical History Review* 50 (Spring 1991): 109–141; Kathleen A. Brown, "The 'Savagely Fathered and Un-Mothered World' of the Communist Party, U.S.A.: Feminism, Maternalism, and 'Mother Bloor,'" *Feminist Studies* 25, no 3 (Autumn 1999): 554; Baxandall, "The Question Seldom Asked," 141, 148.

17 *DW*, March 7, 1925; October 27, 1925.

18 Albert Weisbord, *Passaic: The Story of a Struggle against Starvation Wages and for the Right to Organize* (Chicago: Daily Worker, 1926), 43–44.

19 For the demands, see Weisbord, *Passaic*, 28.

20 "Synopsis of Testimony regarding the Passaic Textile Strike," ACLU papers, vol. 302.

21 Sonya Michel, "The Limits of Maternalism: Policies toward American Wage-Earning Mothers during the Progressive Era," in *Mothers of a New World: Maternalist Politics and the Origins of Welfare States*, ed. Seth Koven and Sonya Michel (New York: Routledge, 1993); Anne Durst, "'Of Women, by Women, and for Women': The Day Nursery Movement in the Progressive-Era United States," *Journal of Social History* 39, no. 1 (Fall 2005): 141; Kathleen M. Canning, "Class, Gender, and Working-Class Politics: The Case of the German Textile Industry, 1890–1933" (PhD diss., Johns Hopkins University, 1988), 375–380.

22 *TSB*, April 21, 1926; May 7, 1926.

23 *TSB*, June 11, 1926.

24 Vorse, *Passaic Textile Strike*, 17–18.

25 Mary Anne Trasciatti, "Sisters on the Soapbox: Elizabeth Gurley Flynn and Her Female Free Speech Allies' Lessons for Contemporary Women Labor Activists," *Humanities* 7, no. 69 (2018): 5–7; Rosalyn Baxandall, "Pioneer and Aunt Tom: Elizabeth Gurley Flynn's Feminism," *Rethinking Marxism* 1, no. 1 (1988): 77; Lara Vapnek, *Elizabeth Gurley Flynn: Modern American Revolutionary, 1890–1964* (Boulder, CO: Westview Press, 2015), 51–52; Kate E. Wittenstein, "The Heterodoxy Club and American Feminism, 1912–1930" (PhD diss., Boston University, 1989), 33; Judith Schwarz, *Heterodoxy: Radical Feminists of Greenwich Village,*

1912–1940 (Lebanon, NH: New Victoria, 1982), 33–34; *NYT*, February 15, 1926; *Tampa Bay* (Florida) *Times*, February 17, 1926 (quote); *LL*, February 24, 1926; Mary Anne Trasciatti, "Elizabeth Gurley Flynn, the Sacco-Vanzetti Case, and the Rise and Fall of the Liberal-Radical Alliance, 1920–1940," *American Communist History* 15, no. 2 (2016): 191.

26 *NYDN*, March 4, 1926. On her speaking regimen, see Trasciatti, "Elizabeth Gurley Flynn," 193–194. In a letter to Vorse in September 1926, Flynn wrote of meeting with leaders of the Communist Party in Chicago during the convention of the ILD, but she is vague about whether she joined or not, stating, "My status was still undetermined" (Flynn to Vorse, September 11, 1926, in *Words on Fire: The Life and Writing of Elizabeth Gurley Flynn*, ed. Rosalyn F. Baxandall (New Brunswick, NJ: Rutgers University Press, 1987), 143. James Allen's editor's note to the second edition of her autobiography states that Flynn had corrected the draft manuscript to indicate she had applied to join the CP in the fall of 1926 instead of 1937; Elizabeth Gurley Flynn, *The Rebel Girl, an Autobiography: My First Life, 1906–1926* (New York: International, 1973), 11. Lara Vapnek, Flynn's most recent biographer, responded that "either Flynn had not tried very hard or someone had rejected her" (Vapnek, "The Rebel Girl Revisited: Rereading Elizabeth Gurley Flynn's Life Story," *Feminist Studies* 44, no. 1 [2018]: 31).

27 Vapnek, *Elizabeth Gurley Flynn*, 90. On Vorse, see *The Reminiscences of Mary H. Vorse*, Columbia University Oral History, 1957; Dee Garrison, *Mary Heaton Vorse: The Life of an American Insurgent* (Philadelphia: Temple University Press, 1989).

28 Gitlow to Ruthenberg, February 23, 1926, in Comintern, 515:1:713; Shapiro, "Red Feminism," 55–57.

29 See Patricia R. Campbell, "Portraits of Gastonia: 1930s Maternal Activism and the Protest Novel" (PhD diss., University of Florida, 2006), chap. 2.

30 Mary Heaton Vorse, "The War in Passaic," in *Rebel Pen: The Writings of Mary Heaton Vorse*, ed. Dee Garrison (New York: Monthly Review Press, 1985), 106–107; *LL*, March 17, 1926; *New Masses*, May 1926.

31 See the short biography of Lowell at the website of the Illinois Labor History Society, http://www.illinoislaborhistory.org/biographies-s#esther; see Buch's obituary in *NYT*, September 13, 1987; her life is detailed in her memoirs, Vera Buch Weisbord, *A Radical Life* (Bloomington: Indiana University Press, 1977).

32 See Chernenko's obituary by Art Shields in the *Daily World*, February 15, 1979. I also want to acknowledge the assistance of Brian Chenesky, grandnephew of Chernenko, in fleshing out her biography. List of arrests in AFPS papers, reel 16; *Camden Courier-Post*, April 21, 1926; Vera Buch Weisbord, *A Radical Life*, 127–128, 131–132.

33 Vera Buch Weisbord, *A Radical Life*, 113; interview with Martha Stone Asher by Gail Malmgreen, October 16, 1988, in Tamiment Ephemera.

34 Orleck, *Common Sense*, 220; Anne Fishel, "Women in Textile Organizing: An Interview with Sophie Melvin Gerson," *Radical History Review* 14–15 (1977): 109–119; interview with Sophie Melvin Gerson by Annelise Orleck, February 17, 1989; Deborah A. Gerson, "Sophie Melvin Gerson: The Brooklyn Years," *American Communist History* 17, no. 2 (2018); *LD*, September 1929; *NYDN*, August 7, 1953.

35 *BDE*, April 27, 1926; information on Silverfarb is from her Petition for Citizenship (no. 204285), November 23, 1932, in *New York, Naturalization Records, 1882–1944*, accessed from Ancestry.com; minutes of the Political Bureau of the

Young Workers' League, June 7, 1926, in Comintern, 515:1:907; "How the Polcom Is Splitting the Party," 1929, in Comintern, 515:1:1821. I would like to thank William Zame, Silverfarb's son, for providing biographical information about his mother.

36 *People's Weekly World*, September 3, 1994; *People's World*, December 22, 2001. Interview with Helen Winter by Joan Lockwood, January 29, 1993, pt. 2, in Wagenknecht papers, box 3, folder 43.

37 Ella Reeve Bloor, *We Are Many* (New York: International, 1940), 400.

38 David Lee McMullen, *Strike: The Radical Insurrection of Ellen Dawson* (Gainesville: University Press of Florida, 2010), chaps. 9–11.

39 *Barnard Bulletin*, April 30, 1926; *YC*, August 1926. On Gartenlaub, see *PDH*, November 25, 1925; Judith R. Ehrenfeld (Gartenlaub's daughter-in-law), email to author, August 16, 2019.

40 Vera Buch, "Organize the Women for Class Struggle," *DW*, November 26, 1926; Buch, "Report on the Work among the Women in Passaic & Vicinity (Beginning of June to end of Nov., 1926)," undated, in Comintern, 515:1:815.

41 Kate Gitlow to Mary Waters, September 1, 1926, and Gitlow, "What the Working-Class Women Have Done to Help Win the Passaic Strike," September 22, 1926, both in Comintern, 515:1:782. This article was printed in *DW*, December 7, 1926; *NYDN*, April 25, 1926; see also Annick Des Roches, "Women United in Defense of the Family: The Public Battle for Improved Domestic and Workplace Conditions during the Passaic Textile Strike of 1926" (master's thesis, Hunter College, 2006), 59–63. See notice in *TSB*, June 11, 1926, and a report on the conference in *TSB*, June 23, 1926.

42 Buch, "Report on the Work"; Vera Buch Weisbord, *A Radical Life*, 122; *DW*, September 14, 1926.

43 Vera Buch Weisbord, *A Radical Life*, 122–123. *TSB*, July 22, 1926; Piotrovska was married to Robert Dunn.

44 Buch, "Report on the Work."

45 Buch, "Report on the Work"; Vera Buch Weisbord, *Radical Life*, 135–136; interview with Vera Buch Weisbord by *Women and Revolution* (1978), PRL.

46 Interview with Sophie Melvin Gerson by Annelise Orleck, February 1989.

47 Buch, "Report on the Work."

48 Kate Gitlow to Jay Lovestone, September 22 and October 13, 1926, both in Comintern, 515:1:782; Kate Gitlow to C. E. Ruthenberg, November 27, 1926, and Ruthenberg to Gitlow, December 3, 1926, both in Comintern, 515:1:643; *DW*, December 7, 1926.

49 Sara Fanny Simon, "The Passaic Strike—A Study in Left Wing Leadership" (master's thesis, Columbia University, 1928), 43; Gustav Deak interview by Joe Doyle, January 13, 1986, in Tamiment Ephemera; Vera Buch Weisbord, *Radical Life*, 101.

50 *Women's Wear Daily*, April 10, 1926; *PDH*, September 16, 1926, February 3, 1927. In contrast, there were more than 1,000 children working in Paterson; *PCN*, April 19, 1926.

51 On Communist work among youth, see Paul C. Mishler, *Raising Reds: The Young Pioneers, Radical Summer Camps, and Communist Political Culture in the United States* (New York: Columbia University Press, 1999); *YW*, May 1, 1926.

52 *YW*, February 20, 1926; *YW*, March 6 and 27, 1926; *Young Pioneer*, March 1926; John J. Ballam, "Special Textile Report of Organizational Basis for Building Left

Wing and Party in Passaic under Conditions Obtaining thru Affiliation of Passaic to UTW," September 4, 1926, in Comintern, 515:1:913.

53 Ballam, "Special Textile Report"; Elizabeth Gurley Flynn, *I Speak My Own Piece: Autobiography of the "Rebel Girl"* (New York: Masses and Mainstream, 1955), 125–126; *Washington Post*, April 10, 1926.

54 *NYT*, April 9, 1926; *Women's Wear Daily*, April 10, 1926; *New York Evening World*, April 10, 1926, in Walsh scrapbook 73; *LL*, April 14, 1926; CEC Textile Committee, April 27, 1926, in Comintern, 515:1:814.

55 W. Jett Lauck telegram to Frank P. Walsh, April 15, 1926, Walsh papers.

56 *New York Evening World*, April 15, 1926, and *NYEP*, April 15, 1926, both in Walsh scrapbook 73; *LL*, April 21, 1926.

57 *TSB*, March 22, 1926; April 12, 1926.

58 *YW*, May 29, 1926.

59 *YC*, March 1926; *YC*, May 1926; letter from Henry R. Linville, president of New York Teachers' Union, March 5, 1926, in *TSB*, March 22, 1926.

60 The list of board members is from *Paterson Evening News*, October 26, 1926. Information on individual members is from: *PHN*, May 13, 1951 (Joseph M. Gardner); *PDN*, November 10, 1927 (Frederick E. Rohrbach); *PHN*, June 15, 1953 (John J. Breslawsky); *PHN*, November 7, 1951 (Mrs. George A. Terhune/ Katherine Conkling); *Paterson Evening News*, December 10, 1953 (Irving L. Werksman); *PHN*, June 4, 1953 (Joseph Naab); *PDH*, September 14, 1920; *PHN*, January 29, 1949; *PDH*, September 4, 1931; *PHN*, October 21, 1932; July 26, 1938; August 10, 1966; *PDH*, July 7, 1922; *BER*, June 8, 1926.

61 *NYT*, March 3, 1926; *PDN*, March 9, 1926; *Justice*, June 4, 1926; October 15, 1926.

62 Alfred Wagenknecht to Hortense Allison, May 12, 1926, in Wagenknecht papers, box 1, folder 9; *YW*, May 29, 1926.

63 *PCN*, July 16, 1926; *PDH*, July 19, 1926; Siegel, "Passaic Textile Strike," 307.

64 *YC*, August 1926; *DW*, July 3 and 19, 1926; Simon, "The Passaic Strike," 39; *YW*, June 15, 1926; *PDH*, August 9, 1926. Camp Victory is also described in *TSB*, July 22, 1926; Des Roches, "Women United," 59–63.

65 *PDH*, August 4, 1926; *PDN*, August 5, 1926, quoted in Des Roches, "Women United," 63; news release no. 44, August 1926, in AUF 6046, box 389, folder 2.

66 *DW*, July 3, 1926; *TSB*, July 15, 1926; *LL*, July 21, 1926; *Justice*, July 23, 1926; *Il Martello*, July 31, 1926.

67 On the Bolsheviks' attitude and the collectivization of family work, see, for example, Alexandra Kollantai, *Communism and the Family* (New York: Contemporary, 1920). Susan Levine, "Workers' Wives: Gender, Class and Consumerism in the 1920s United States," *Gender & History* 3, no. 1 (Spring 1991): 47–48; Caroline Waldron Merithew, "'We Were Not Ladies: Gender, Class, and a Women's Auxiliary's Battle for Mining Unionism," *Journal of Women's History* 18, no. 2 (2018): 63–94; Bryan Palmer, *Revolutionary Teamsters: The Minneapolis Teamsters Strikes of 1934* (Leiden: Brill, 2013), chap. 7.

68 Jack Rubenstein interview, February/March 1987; Mark Naison, "From Eviction Resistance to Rent Control—Tenant Activism in the Great Depression," in *The Tenant Movement in New York City, 1904–1984*, ed. Ronald Lawson (New Brunswick, NJ: Rutgers University Press, 1986); Joshua J. Morris, "Building a Movement: American Communist Activism in the Communities, 1929–1945," *American Communist History* 18, nos. 3–4 (2019): 215; Siegel, "Passaic Textile Strike," 305; *LL*, November 10, 1926. See news release no. 75, AUF 6046, box 389, folder 2.

69 *NYT*, March 11, 1926, quoted in Siegel, "Passaic Textile Strike," 288.
70 *NYDN*, June 16, 1928; *People's World*, May 18, 2002. I am grateful for Deborah Gerson for providing details about her father's early life; *PDN*, March 16, 1926; *Campus*, March 19 and 29, 1926; *YW*, April 17, 1926; *DW*, April 19, 1926.
71 Siegel, "Passaic Textile Strike," 288; *Columbia Spectator*, April 27, 1926; *Barnard Bulletin*, April 30, 1926; Hillman M. Bishop to Gustav Deak, undated letter, in *TSB*, May 21, 1926. These theses are Raymond H. Groff, "The Passaic Textile Strike of 1926" (master's thesis, Columbia University, 1927), and Simon, "The Passaic Strike" (1928). *BDE*, April 27, 1926.
72 Leaflet for Trades Council Hall, in Comintern, 515:1:913; *Yale Daily News*, March 18 and 19, April 9 and 10, 1926; *Harvard Crimson*, March 19, April 12 and 16, and November 16, 1926.
73 Rubenstein interview, February/March 1987; *PHT*, July 8, 1989; "How the Polcom Is Splitting the Party," 1929, in Comintern, 515:1:1821.
74 Mishler, *Raising Reds*, 3; Theresa Wolfson, "Trade Union Activities of Women," *Annals of the American Academy of Political Science* 143, no. 1 (1929): 127.

Chapter 9 The End of the Strike

1 William Z. Foster, *Strike Strategy* (Chicago: Trade Union Educational League, 1926). The *Daily Worker* began serializing the pamphlet on October 29, 1926. I am grateful to Edward Kartsen for emphasizing the importance of this pamphlet.
2 Foster, *Strike Strategy*, 45, 70–88.
3 See William Z. Foster to Morris L. Ernst, May 30, 1926, AFPS papers, reel 13.
4 American Commission at Sixth Plenum of the Executive Committee of the Comintern, quoted in Draper, *American Communism and Soviet Russia*, 228–229.
5 Foster, *Strike Strategy*, 27.
6 *WSJ*, September 25, 1926; *LL*, October 6, 1926; Stephen Wise to Hillman, June 5, 1926, and Stephen Wise to Justine Wise, June 8, 1926, both in Polier papers, box 1, folder 15.
7 TUC minutes, June 2, 1926, PRL.
8 *New York Graphic*, June 6 and 7, 1926, both in Walsh scrapbook 74; *BG*, June 7, 1926; Sara Fanny Simon, "The Passaic Strike—A Study in Left Wing Leadership" (master's thesis, Columbia University, 1928), 71.
9 *TSB*, June 11, 1926.
10 Quotations from letter from Clarina Michelson to William Green, July 2, 1926, in AFL Executive Council Vote Books, AFL papers. The full statement is available in minutes of AFL Executive Council, June 25–30, 1926, in AFL papers; see also the *American Federation of Labor Weekly News Service*, July 10, 1926.
11 *NYT*, July 4, 1926.
12 Alfred Weisbord and Gustav Deak to William Green, in *PDN*, July 15, 1926. See also *PDN*, July 9, 1926.
13 William Green to Clarina Michelson, July 10, 1926, in AFL Executive Council Vote Books, AFL papers.
14 See the advertisement in *PDH*, July 14, 1926; *PMC*, July 9, 1926; *PDH*, July 10, 1926; *PNC*, July 10, 1926.
15 Albert Weisbord, telegram to William E. Borah, July 22, 1926, in Borah papers, box 213, first Passaic strike folder; William E. Borah to Colonel Johnson, July 22, 1926, in Borah papers, box 213, second Passaic strike folder.

16 Charles F. H. Johnson, telegram to William E. Borah, July 26, 1926, in Borah papers, box 213, second Passaic strike folder.

17 *NYT*, July 24 and 25, 1926; *LL*, August 4, 1926; *TSB*, July 30, 1926.

18 *TSB*, August 6, 1926. A copy of the resolution is in Walsh papers, box 25, first Passaic strike folder.

19 See telegram from John J. Ballam to C. E. Ruthenberg, July 26, 1926, in Comintern, 515:1:714.

20 Telegram from C. E. Ruthenberg to J. J. Ballam, July 27, 1926, in Comintern, 515:1:714. I have edited the telegram slightly for clarity.

21 "Report on Textile Industry (Passaic Strike)," by John J. Ballam [?], early August 1926, in Comintern, 515:1:815; C. E. Ruthenberg to J. J. Ballam, August 27, 1926, in Comintern, 515:1:713. Ruthenberg was complaining that the Lauck Committee's statement contained an anti-Communist statement.

22 Membership figures from Robert R. R. Brooks, "The United Textile Workers of America" (PhD diss., Yale University, 1935), 53; minutes of AFL Executive Council, March 23–29, 1926, in AFL papers.

23 Henry T. Hunt to Frank P. Walsh, August 10, 1926, in Walsh papers, box 25, first Passaic strike folder.

24 Statement by Thomas F. McMahon, August 12, 1926, in Walsh papers, box 25, first Passaic strike folder. The correspondence between the UTW and the Lauck Committee is printed in *TW*, August 1926; W. J. Lauck, telegram to William E. Borah, August 12, 1926, in Borah papers, box 213, third Passaic strike folder; John [Ballam], telegram to C. E. Ruthenberg, August 12, 1926, in Comintern, 515:1:714; Albert Weisbord to W. Jett Lauck, August 13, 1926, in *TW*, August 1926. A carbon copy of the letter is in Comintern, 515:1:912.

25 W. J. Lauck, telegram to William E. Borah, August 12, 1926, in Borah papers, box 213, third Passaic strike folder; W. Jett Lauck, Henry T. Hunt, Helen Todd, and Frank P. Walsh to Charles F. H. Johnson and Julius Forstmann, August 14, 1926, in Walsh papers, box 25, first Passaic strike folder; *TSB*, August 18, 1926.

26 *PDH*, August 19, 1926. See also "A Statement of the Policy of Botany Worsted Mills in Its Relations with Employees," August 19, 1926, with covering note by Charles F. H. Johnson, August 21, 1926, in Borah papers, box 213, third Passaic strike folder.

27 *PDH*, August 20, 1926. This interpretation is based on Borah's letter to Julius Forstmann, September 2, 1926, and Borah's letter to Lauck, September 3, 1926, both in Borah papers, box 213, third Passaic strike folder.

28 W. Jett Lauck telegram to William E. Borah, August 19, 1926; Borah telegram to Lauck, August 20, 1926; Lauck telegram to Borah, August 20, 1926; Borah telegram to Lauck, August 21, 1926; Lauck to Borah, August 26, 1926; all in Borah papers, box 213, third Passaic strike folder.

29 *NYT*, August 27, 1926; *PDH*, August 27, 1926; *DW*, August 28, 1926; William Green to Stephen Wise, September 29, 1926, in Borah papers, box 213, third Passaic strike folder.

30 *DW*, August 14, 1926; TUC minutes, April 7, 1926, PRL.

31 On Weisbord's opposition, see his letter to Theodore Draper, September 8, 1958, https://www.marxists.org/archive/weisbord/Draper.htm. See also Morton K. Siegel, "The Passaic Textile Strike of 1926" (PhD diss., Columbia University, 1953), 249–251; John J. Ballam [?], "Supplementary Report on Textile (Passaic)," August 7, 1926, in Comintern, 515:1:815.

32 John J. Ballam, "Report of the National Textile Organizer on the Amalgamation Conference Held in NYC August 14 and 15, 1926 with the Federated Textile Union and Independents," August 23, 1926, in Comintern, 515:1:815.

33 Albert Weisbord, *Passaic: The Story of a Struggle against Starvation Wages and for the Right to Organize* (Chicago: Daily Worker, 1926), 58.

34 "Report of National Textile Organizer Ballam on Passaic Strike Situation," February 9, 1927, Comintern, 515:1:1197. This report indicates that Ballam had raised similar worries as early as September 1926; "Report on Textile Industry (Passaic Strike)," by John J. Ballam [?], early August 1926, in Comintern, 515:1:815.

35 Ballam, "Report on Textile Situation (Passaic)," August 21, 1926, in Comintern, 515:1:815.

36 John J. Ballam, "Report on Textile Situation (Passaic)," August 21, 1926, and Ballam, "Report on Textile Industry: Passaic Strike," September 4, 1926, both in Comintern, 515:1:815.

37 See TUC minutes, September 17, 1926, PRL; C. E. Ruthenberg to John J. Ballam, October 14, 1926, in Comintern, 515:1:713.

38 *PDH*, September 3, 1926; *PCN*, September 3, 1926. *LL*, September 8, 1926; W. Jett Lauck to William E. Borah, September 3, 1926, in Borah papers, box 213, third Passaic strike folder.

39 In 1929, when he was expelled from the Communist Party, Keller stated he had been a member "since 1926"; see Hearing of Central Control Commission, December 9, 1929, in Comintern, 515:1:1699.

40 *DW*, September 4, 1926; C. E. Ruthenberg to J. J. Ballam, September 24, 1926, in Comintern, 515:1:713; *PDH*, September 3, 1926. According to the Federated Press *Labor Letter* (September 8, 1926), Rubenstein also left Passaic; John J. Ballam, "Report on Textile Industry: Passaic Strike," September 4, 1926, in Comintern, 515:1:815. On Vera Buch, see Vera Buch Weisbord, *A Radical Life* (Bloomington: University of Indiana Press, 1977), 127–128, 131–132; C. E. Ruthenberg to J. J. Ballam and W. W. Weinstone, August 13, 1926, in Comintern, 515:1:713.

41 John J. Ballam, "Special Textile Report on Organization Basis for Building a Left Wing and Party in Passaic under Conditions Obtaining thru Affiliation of Passaic to UTW," September 4, 1926, in Comintern, 515:1:815.

42 *PHN*, August 8, 1952; Jay Lovestone to W. W. Weinstone, October 20, 1926, in Comintern, 515:1:746.

43 Emil Gardos, "Report on Party Work in Passaic," January 27, 1927, in Comintern, 515:1:1173; "Report of National Textile Organizer Ballam on Passaic Situation," February 9, 1927, in Comintern, 515:1:1197; Gardos to "Dear Comrades," August 17, 1927, in Comintern, 515:1:1046.

44 John J. Ballam to Herbert Benjamin, January 10, 1927, and Emil Gardos to "Dear Comrade," March 20, 1927, both in Comintern, 515:1:1197; Siegel, "Passaic Textile Strike," 234; Hilfers's speech on September 14, 1926, in *Official Proceedings of the Forty-Eighth Annual Convention of the New Jersey State Federation of Labor* (Newark: New Jersey State Federation of Labor, 1927), 45. On Weisbord's nickname, see David J. Goldberg, "Immigrant Workers and Labor Organizations, 1912–1926: Lawrence, Massachusetts, and Passaic, New Jersey," in *Work, Recreation, and Culture: Essays in American Labor History*, ed. Martin Henry Blatt and Martha S. Norkunas (New York: Routledge, 1996), 221.

45 *PDH*, September 13, 1926; Simon, "The Passaic Strike," 84.

46 *PDH*, September 13, 1926.

47 Local 1603 drew up a proposed plan of organization in Passaic, stressing an industrial union for all the mills, with local autonomy and democracy, but there is no evidence that the convention discussed it. See Gustave Deak and Eli Keller, "Memorandum on Form of Organization for Local #1603 Passaic and Vicinity," in Comintern, 515:1:912.

48 *TW*, December 1926.

49 In a report on the convention, Ballam wrote that McMahon "said that the present UTW local will be scattered within one year" ("Report on UTW Convention by Nat'l Textile Org. Ballam," September 18, 1926, in Comintern, 515:1:815). Such a statement is not in the proceedings printed in the *Textile Worker*. One delegate did state: "It has also been said by our chairman that if the organization goes along for a year, we will only have a skeleton organization of what we may take in at this particular time" (*TW*, January 1927).

50 *TW*, December 1926.

51 *TW*, December 1926; news release no. 3, September 20, 1926, AUF 6046, box 389, file 2.

52 *NYT*, October 12, 1926; Melvyn Dubofsky and Warren Van Time, *John L. Lewis: A Biography*, abridged ed. (Urbana: University of Illinois Press, 1986), 97. On the convention, see also Philip S. Foner, *History of the Labor Movement in the United States*, vol. 10 (New York: International, 1994), 1–10, 18–19.

53 *DW*, September 4, 1926; Gustave Deak to William Green, September 30, 1927 [*sic*], with cover note to Thomas F. McMahon, September 30, 1926, in Comintern, 515:1:912.

54 *DW*, October 7, 1926; John J. Ballam to C. E. Ruthenberg and William Z. Foster, September 29, 1926, in Comintern, 515:1:713; [C. E. Ruthenberg?] to J. Louis Engdahl, October 2, 1926, and Engdahl to Ruthenberg, October 4, 1926, both in Comintern, 515:1:640; C. E. Ruthenberg to J. J. Ballam, October 5, 1926, in Comintern, 515:1:713; "Ellen Dawson Speech on Passaic for AFL Convention," in Comintern, 515:1:912.

55 See [J. Louis Engdahl] to C. E. Ruthenberg, October 6, 1926, in Comintern; undated, unsigned report on convention, most likely Engdahl to Ruthenberg, both in Comintern, 515:1:640. For Green's offer to Wise to speak, see William Green to Stephen Wise, September 29, 1926, in Borah papers, box 213, third Passaic strike folder.

56 *Report of the Proceedings of the Forty-Sixth Annual Convention of the American Federation of Labor* (Washington, DC: Law Reporter Printing Co., 1926), 223–225. See also *NYT*, October 12, 1926. Wise's speech and Green's response are also printed in *TW*, October 1926.

57 See [J. Louis Engdahl] to C. E. Ruthenberg, October 6, 1926, and undated, unsigned report on the convention, most likely Engdahl to Ruthenberg, both in Comintern, 515:1:640.

58 *Passaic Textile Strikers Relief Bulletin*, October 26, 1926, AUF, section 7, box 388, folder 1; Cyril Briggs edited this paper. See also *DW*, October 8, 1926; Political Committee minutes, October 13, 1926, PRL.

59 John J. Ballam, "Report from National Textile Organizer—Passaic Situation," October 29, 1926, in Comintern, 515:1:815.

60 *PDH*, November 5, 1926. Sotak, a member of the Slavic Committee, was pastor of Saints Peter and Paul Greek Catholic Church; see his obituary in the *Pittsburgh Post-Gazette*, February 19, 1947; John J. Ballam, "Report from National Textile

Organizer—Passaic Situation," October 29, 1926, in Comintern, 515:1:815; *PDH*, November 5, 1926; split between companies was reported by Ballam in his October 29 report and by Lovestone in the Political Committee minutes, October 29, 1926, PRL.

61 "Tentative Agreement between W. W. Gaunt, Passaic Worsted Spinning Company and James Starr, United Textile Workers of America" [November 1926], BLSCBA, pt. 17, collection 6178/017, folder 20. The agreement is described in *TW*, November 1926. See also *PDH*, December 12, 1926; *LL*, November 24, 1926; Raymond H. Groff, "The Passaic Textile Strike of 1926" (master's thesis, Columbia University, 1927), 47–48.

62 News release, November 16, 1926, AUF 6046, box 389, folder 2; *DW*, November 13, 1926; John J. Ballam, "Report of National Textile Organizer," November 16, 1926, in Comintern, 515:1:815.

63 On the hospital strike, see Leon Fink and Brian Greenberg, *Upheaval in the Quiet Zone: 1199SEIU and the Politics of Health Care Unionism* (Champaign: University of Illinois Press, 2009), chap. 4.

64 John J. Ballam, "Report of National Textile Organizer," November 16, 1926, in Comintern, 515:1:815. At the September 1926 convention of the New Jersey Federation of Labor, Hilfers stated that "when the organization is perfected, they are going to issue a charter to each mill." See Hilfers's speech in *Official Proceedings of the Forty-Eighth Annual Convention*, 45.

65 News release, November 29, 1926, in AUF 6046, box 389, folder 2; *LL*, December 1, 1926. In his October 29 report, Ballam indicates that "the Botany Worsted mill and the New Jersey spinning have restored the 10% wage-cut in their mills" but "the mills have never made this public"; John J. Ballam, "Report of National Textile Organizer on Passaic Strike Situation: Settlement, Etc.," December 4, 1926, in Comintern, 515:1:815.

66 Telegram from John J. Ballam to C. E. Ruthenberg, November 26, 1926, in Comintern, 515:1:714.

67 See, for example, Lenin's "Report at the Meeting of the All-Russia C.E.C., February 24, 1918," in *Collected Works* (London: Progress, 1965), 27:43. Lenin also deals with the treaty in *"Left-Wing" Communism: An Infantile Disorder*, from 1920, in *Collected Works* (London: Progress, 1964), vol. 31.

68 *DW*, November 29, 1926.

69 John J. Ballam, "Report of National Textile Organizer on Passaic Strike Situation: Settlement, Etc.," December 4, 1926, in Comintern, 515:1:815.

70 Thomas F. McMahon to Dundee Textile Company, December 16, 1926, and Dundee Textile Company to Thomas F. McMahon, December 17, 1926, in BLSCBA, pt.17, collection 6178/017, folder 28. *LL*, December 22, 1926; news release, December 14, 1926, in AUF 6046, box 389, folder 1; Groff, "Passaic Textile Strike," 48.

71 News release no. 136, undated [December 1926], AUF 6046, box 389, folder 2. The statement was signed by Cyril Briggs; *Labor Unity*, January 1, 1927; John J. Ballam, "Report of National Textile Organizer," January 12, 1926 [1927], in Comintern, 515:1:1197.

72 *LL*, November 10, 1926; Julius Forstmann to John H. McGuire, W. C. Cabell, George H, Talbott, Thomas J. Kernan, and Michael Sotak, November 5, 1926, in *PDH*, November 5, 1926; Julius Forstmann to Thomas J. Kernan and W. Carrington Cabell, January 19, 1927, in *PDH*, January 20, 1927.

73 *PDH*, January 20, 1927.

74 Ballam, "Report on Passaic Situation," February 4, 1927, in Comintern, 515:1:1197.
75 News release, February 15, 1927, AUF 6046, box 389, folder 1; Groff, "Passaic Textile Strike," 48.
76 *LL*, February 23, 1927; Groff, "Passaic Textile Strike," 48; *LL*, March 9, 1927; Simon, "The Passaic Strike," 90–92; *BCN*, March 2, 1927; "Report of National Textile Organizer Ballam," March 1, 1927, in Comintern, 515:1:1197.
77 "Report of National Textile Organizer Ballam," January 14, 1926 [1927]. See Ballam's reports on Passaic of February 4 and 19, March 1, and July 15, 1927, all in Comintern 515:1:1197.
78 News release by Textile Council of Passaic and New Jersey, March 11, 1927, AUF 6046, box 389, folder 1.
79 *Passaic Chamber of Commerce Bulletin*, September 1927.

Chapter 10   After the Strike

1 James P. Cannon, *First Ten Years of American Communism: Report of a Participant* (New York: Lyle Stuart, 1962), 141.
2 Dieter Groh, "Intensification of Work and Industrial Conflict in Germany, 1896–1914," *Politics & Society* 8, nos. 3–4 (1978): 371–375.
3 Sara Fanny Simon, "The Passaic Strike—A Study in Left Wing Leadership" (master's thesis, Columbia University, 1928), 4.
4 James P. Cannon, *First Ten Years*, 142.
5 *Militant*, February 22, 1930, reprinted in James P. Cannon, *The Left Opposition in the U.S., 1928–31* (New York: Pathfinder Press, 1981), 243–244.
6 *LL*, March 2, 1927; news release, March 24, 1927, in AUF 6046, box 389, folder 1; "Report on National Textile Organizer Ballam on Developments in Passaic," July 15, 1927, in Comintern, 515:1:1197; *PHN*, June 2, 1953.
7 Paul L. Murphy, David Klaassen, and Kermit Hall, eds., *The Passaic Textile Strike of 1926* (Belmont, CA: Wadsworth, 1974), 167–168; news release, April 1927, AUF collection 6046, box 389, folder 1.
8 Emil Gardos to Jay Lovestone, April 1, 1927, in Comintern, 515:1:1025; news release, April 12, 1927, AUF collection 6046, box 389, folder 1; *Passaic Chamber of Commerce Bulletin*, May 1927.
9 *PDN*, April 13, 1928; *Labor Unity*, May 1928; *APP*, August 2, 1928.
10 Murphy, *Passaic Textile Strike*, 167–168; *DW*, December 25, 1929; *Labor Unity*, January 18 and February 1, 1930; *NYT*, August 20, 1935; *PHN*, June 2, 1953.
11 William Carlos Williams, *Life along the Passaic River* (Norfolk, CT: New Directions, 1938), 9.
12 *NYT*, November 27, 1977; Eric Wakin, "Professor James P. Shenton, '49: History's Happy Warrior," *Columbia College Today*, September 20, 1996, http://www.columbia.edu/cu/record/archives/vol22/vol22_iss3/Professor_Shenton.html.
13 Jacob Zumoff, *The Communist International and US Communism* (Leiden: Brill, 2014), chaps. 9–12.
14 *DW*, April 8 and 12, May 12, 1927; *PDH*, April 14, 1927; *Paterson Evening News*, April 14, 1927; *PMC*, April 15 and 18, May 10, 1927; *NYDN*, May 11, 1927. On the campaign, see Emil Gardos, "Passaic Political Campaign," May 5, 1927, and "Passaic Election Campaign," May 22, 1927, both in Comintern, 515:1:1173. See also *PHN*, April 18, 1947. Bambach's obituary is in *PHN*, September 16, 1965; Smelkinson's obituary is in *PHN*, May 23, 1969.

15 *PDN*, September 2, 1927; *DW*, September 15, 1927. For the results, see *PDN*, November 9, 1927. Deak had stood for Congress in November 1926 on "the labor party ticket" and polled 516 votes in Garfield; see news release, November 4, 1926, AUF 6046, box 389, folder 1.

16 "Resolution on the American Question," endorsed by the ECCI presidium, July 1, 1927, in Lovestone papers, box 207.

17 Michael W. Santos, "Communist and Communism: The 1928 New Bedford Textile Strike," *Labor History* 26, no. 2 (1985): 230–249; Daniel Georgianna with Roberta Hazen Aaronson, *The Strike of '28* (New Bedford: Spinner, 1993); *PDN*, April 18, 1928; David Lee McMullen, "The Elusive Ellen: Reconstructing the Life of Ellen Dawson and the World around Her" (PhD diss., University of Aberdeen, 2005), chap. 6; *Labor Unity*, August 1928; *PDN*, September 13 and 21, 1928; *BG*, September 24, 1928.

18 Paterson *News*, December 3 and 12, 1928; Robert R. R. Brooks, "The United Textile Workers of America" (PhD diss., Yale University, 1935), 258; "Report to the CEC on Work of the National Textile Workers Union for Month of February 1929," Lovestone papers, box 207; John A. Salmond, *Gastonia 1929: The Story of the Loray Mill Strike* (Chapel Hill: University of North Carolina Press, 1995).

19 For examples, see A. Lozovsky's speeches in the *Bulletin of the IV Congress of the Red International of Labour Unions*, no. 3, evening session, March 19 and 24, 1928, in Zimmerman papers, box 2; Call for New York and Metropolitan Area Conference of the TUEL, May 18 and 19, 1929, in ILGWU papers 5780/014, box 45, folder 7.

20 For depiction of the strike as a victory, see *DW*, November 13, 1926; news release no. 134, December 14, 1926, AUF 6046, box 389, folder 1; *The Communist International between the Fifth and Sixth World Congresses, 1924–28* (London: Communist Party of Great Britain, 1928), 342; Art Shields, *On the Battle Lines, 1919–1939* (New York: International, 1986), 157. For depictions of the strike as a compromise, see William Z. Foster, *History of the Communist Party of the United States* (New York: International, 1952), 250–251. Arthur Zipser, in the *Daily World* (April 24, 1986), wrote that "the strikers' victory proved to be not only partial but also temporary."

21 See Albert Weisbord, *Passaic Reviewed* (San Francisco: Germinal Press, 1976), 1–21; Engdahl at American Commission, June 17, 1927, in Comintern, 495:37:12; "K" [William Kruse?] to "Dear J" [Engdahl?], August 8, 1927, in Comintern, 515:1:946; Emil Gardos to "Dear Comrades," August 17, 1927, in Comintern, 515:1:1046.

22 On Lovestone, see Robert J. Alexander, *The Right Opposition: The Lovestoneites and the International Communist Opposition of the 1930s* (Westport, CT: Greenwood Press, 1981); Paul Le Blanc and Tim Davenport, eds., *The "American Exceptionalism" of Jay Lovestone and His Comrades, 1929–1940* (Leiden: Brill, 2015); Ted Morgan, *A Covert Life: Jay Lovestone, Communist, Anti-Communist, and Spymaster* (New York: Random House, 1999).

23 *RA*, December 15, 1929; October 1, 1930.

24 Minutes of Central Control Commission, December 12, 1929, Comintern, 515:1:1699; *RA*, January 15, May 1, October 10, and November 22, 1930; *Class Struggle*, August 1931, December 1931. The articles from *Class Struggle* are taken from www.weisbord.org.

25 Vera Buch Weisbord, "The Party Record of James P. Cannon" (1978?), on www.weisbord.org; Gustav Deak interviewed by Joe Doyle, January 13, 1986, in Oral

History; for Weisbord's correspondence with Draper, see http://www.weisbord
.org/Draper.htm.

26 See *NYT*, April 28, 1977, and September 13, 1987, for their obituaries. A more
substantial obituary for Vera Buch Weisbord is in the *Chicago Tribune*, September 9,
1987; much more detail about their lives is provided in her autobiography, Vera Buch
Weisbord, *A Radical Life* (Bloomington: Indiana University Press, 1977).

27 I have been unable to find any mention of Deak's leaving the Communist Party in
the *Daily Worker*. In 1927 the Lovestone faction claimed Deak supported them,
and his name does not appear in the *Daily Worker* after 1929, indicating that Deak
may have left in the wake of the Lovestone expulsions, but there is no evidence
that he joined Lovestone's group. In 1933 Weisbord reprinted the *Herald-News*
endorsement of Deak in his journal, *Class Struggle* (February 1933), and commented: "For a long time Gus Deak was the local leader of the Communist Party.
I have waited to read if there has been any statement made by the Communist
Party. To my great regret there has been none." The first mention of Deak's being
active in the taxpayers' association is in *PHN*, July 12, 1932. The group was
founded that January with the goal of eliminating the personal property tax.
Perhaps because of Deak's association with the group, it had to defend itself from
accusations of being affiliated with the Communist Party; see *PHN*, September 25, 1932, and January 9, 1933; *BER*, March 20, 1936; *PHN*, October 26, 1938;
BER, January 23, 1940, October 6, 1971, and February 22, 1974.

28 Paterson *News*, May 8, 1987; Hackensack *Record*, May 8, 1987; Paramus *Shopper
News*, May 13 and 20, 1987. For an overview of Deak's political career, written
when he became city manager, see Hackensack *Record*, February 22, 1974.

29 McMullen, "The Elusive Ellen," 53–61; Paterson *News*, April 18, 1967; *PHN*,
April 18, 1967.

30 For Rubenstein's expulsion, see *DW*, August 17, 1929. See his obituaries in *PHN*,
July 8, 1989; Hackensack *Record*, July 8, 1989; *NYT*, July 8, 1989. Because Rubenstein shared a name with the man who shot Lee Harvey Oswald—the latter
shortened it to Jack Ruby—his Communist past sometimes features in conspiracy
theories about the Kennedy assassination by people who do not realize they are
two different people.

31 Minutes of Central Control Commission, December 12, 1929, Comintern,
515:1:1699; *DW*, December 17, 1929.

32 *Workers Age*, September 15, 1934; Alexander, *Right Opposition*, 51; *PHN*, January 28, 1935; *PHN*, June 22, 1985; Vera Buch, *A Radical Life*, 115.

33 Anne Fishel, "Women in Textile Organizing: An Interview with Sophie Melvin
Gerson," *Radical History Review* 14–15 (1977): 109–119; interview with Sophie
Melvin Gerson by Annelise Orleck, February 17, 1989, in author's possession. I wish
to thank Professor Orleck for providing a copy of the transcript of this interview;
Deborah A. Gerson, "Sophie Melvin Gerson: The Brooklyn Years," *American
Communist History* 17, no. 2 (2018); *LD*, September 1929; *NYDN*, August 7, 1953.

34 Interview with Martha Stone Asher by Gail Malmgreen, October 16, 1988, in
Tamiment Ephemera.

35 *NYT*, September 7, 1949; *Congressional Record*, October 18, 1949; *NYT*, November 20, 1991; *People's Weekly World*, September 3, 1994; *People's World*, December 22, 2001. I am grateful to Carl Winter's daughter, Michele Artt, for
confirming his identity as Carl Weisberg.

36 For Chernenko's obituary, see *Daily World*, February 15, 1979; see also *Daily
World*, May 10, 1979.

37 See the folder "New Jersey Labor Leader Corruption," in Dunn papers, box 8, including clippings from *DW*, September 15 and 16, 1927; *Camden Morning Post*, September 15, 1927.

38 On the importance of overcoming ethnic divisions, see Sven Beckert, "Migration, Ethnicity, and Working-Class Formation: Passaic, New Jersey, 1889–1926," in *People in Transit: German Migrations in Comparative Perspective, 1820–1930*, ed. Dirk Hoerder and Jorg Nadler (New York: Cambridge University Press, 1995), 377–378; Lizabeth Cohen, *Making a New Deal: Industrial Workers in Chicago, 1919–1939* (New York: Cambridge University Press, 1990), 3–5; Gary Gerstle, *Working-Class Americanism: The Politics of Labor in a Textile City, 1919–1960* (Princeton, NJ: Princeton University Press, 2002). This process of what David Montgomery called "assimilation through opposition" was different from earlier strikes in which most strikers came from the same ethnicity, with class and ethnic identity fused. See David Montgomery, "Thinking about American Workers in the 1920s," *International and Labor and Working-Class History* 32 (Fall 1987): 18; John J. Bukowczyk, "The Transformation of Working-Class Ethnicity: Corporate Control, Americanization, and the Polish Immigrant Middle Class in Bayonne, New Jersey, 1915–1925," *Labor History* 25, no. 1 (1984): 53–82.

39 Irving Bernstein, *Turbulent Years: A History of the American Worker, 1933–1941* (Boston: Houghton Mifflin, 1971), 298–315; Clete Daniel, *Culture of Misfortune: An Interpretive History of Textile Unionism in the United States* (Ithaca, NY: Cornell University Press, 2001), chaps. 2 and 3; John Salmond, *The General Textile Strike of 1934: From Maine to Alabama* (Columbia: University of Missouri Press, 2002); Janet Irons, *Testing the New Deal: The General Strike of 1934 in the American South* (Urbana: University of Illinois Press, 2000). My analysis of the 1934 strike benefited much from Michael Goldfield, *The Southern Key: Class, Race, and Radicalism during the 1930s and 1940s* (New York: Oxford University Press, 2020), chap. 6, which professor Goldfield kindly allowed me to read in draft form.

40 Bernstein, *Turbulent Years*, 616–623; John W. Kennedy, "A History of the Textile Workers Union of America, C.I.O" (PhD diss., University of North Carolina, 1950), 44.

41 Daniel, *Culture of Misfortune*, 72–73; Goldfield, *Southern Key*, chap. 6.

42 *PMC*, October 24, 1933; *BER*, May 8, 1936; *NYT*, August 25, 1936; *BER*, August 26, 1936; *NYT*, April 26, 1937; *PMC*, September 30, 1944; Hackensack *Record*, July 8, 1989; Salmond, *General Textile Strike*, 135, 139–140.

43 Salmond, *General Textile Strike*, 134, 137–138.

44 *Botany Worsted Mills*, 4 NLRB 292 (1937); *Botany Worsted Mills*, 41 NLRB 218 (1942); *National Labor Relations Board v. Botany Worsted Mills*, 133 F.2d 876 (3d Cir. 1943); *Botany Worsted Mills*, 56 NLRB 370 (1944); *PMC*, May 9, 1944; *NYT*, June 8, 1944; *NYT*, August 22, 1944.

45 *PHN*, June 23, 1944; *BER*, August 15, 1944.

46 *BCN*, August 1, 1946; *PHN*, September 3, 1947.

47 *PHN*, January 16, 1952; *PMC*, March 17, 1952. Also in 1952, the TWUA split, with one faction, led by Emil Rieve, remaining in the CIO and another, led by George Baldanzi, rejoining the AFL as a reconstituted UTW. The TWUA-CIO and UTW-AFL fought over who should represent workers at the Passaic-area mills—a dispute that is beyond the scope of this book.

48 *PHN*, June 2, 1953; *NYT*, December 31, 1955. According to the National Labor Relations Board, the Botany workforce was reduced from 1,450 employees to 95.

See *Botany Mills and Local 68, International Union of Operating Engineers*, 115 NLRB 1497 (1956); *PMC*, December 1, 1965; *PHN*, February 5 and March 14, 1970.

49 *NYT*, October 19, 1957; Theodore Forstmann's obituary is in *NYT*, November 20, 2011.

50 *BER*, February 5 and May 23, 1957. I am grateful to Jayne St. George, of the Lodi Public Library, for helping to pin down the date of the final closure of the plant.

51 Beth H. Land, "Textile Industry Making a Comeback in the U.S. Southeast," *Area Development Online*, 2017, https://www.areadevelopment.com/Print /advanced-manufacturing/Q2-2017/textile-industry-making-comeback-in-US -southeast.shtml; Marty Moran, "2019 State of the U.S. Textile Industry," *Textile World*, May 15, 2019, https://www.textileworld.com/textile-world/features/2019 /05/2019-state-of-the-u-s-textile-industry/; Bureau of Labor Statistics, Occupational Employment and Wages, May 2017, "51-6099: Textile, Apparel, and Furnishings Workers, All Other," https://www.bls.gov/oes/2017/may/oes516099.htm.

52 *Passaic County Business Directory* (2013), 7.

53 Caleb Crain, "State of the Unions," *New Yorker*, August 19, 2019; *Vox*, February 13, 2019, https://www.vox.com/policy-and-politics/2019/2/13/18223211/worker-teacher -strikes-2018-record; Pew Research Center, "U.S. Income Inequality, on Rise for Decades, Is Now the Highest since 1928," https://www.pewresearch.org/fact-tank /2013/12/05/u-s-income-inequality-on-rise-for-decades-is-now-highest-since-1928/.

54 *Vox*, February 13, 2019.

Selected Bibliography

All sources used in writing this book are cited in the notes. What follows is a selected list of sources that will be useful for researchers of the strike.

Newspapers

An essential source for research into the Passaic strike is the array of daily newspapers published in New York City and northern New Jersey at the time of the strike. The Communist Party and groups aligned with it also had several publications. Also useful were labor newspapers and left-wing newspapers. Newspapers were consulted on microfilm, in electronic databases, and in scrapbooks in the American Civil Liberties Union and Frank P. Walsh collections.

Bergen Evening Record
Daily Worker
Federated Press Labor Letter
Jersey Journal
Labor Defender
New Masses
News Release
New Textile Worker
New York Daily News
New York Evening Post
New York Herald Tribune

New York Times
New York World
Passaic Daily Herald
Passaic Daily News
Passaic Herald-News
Paterson Morning Call
Progresso Italo-Americano
Textile Strike Bulletin
Textile Worker
Young Comrade
Young Worker

Archival Sources

American Civil Liberties papers, Mudd Library, Princeton University*
American Federation of Labor papers, Meany archives, Silver Spring, Maryland*
American Fund for Public Service papers, New York Public Library*
Archives Union File, Kheel Center, Cornell University
Daniel Bell papers, Tamiment Library, New York University
William E. Borah papers, Library of Congress

Bureau of Labor Statistics Collective Bargaining Agreements, Kheel Center, Cornell University
Communist International, Russian Institute for Contemporary History, Moscow (microfilm consulted at Tamiment Library, New York University) *
Consumers' League of New Jersey papers, Special Collections, Rutgers University
Calvin Coolidge papers, Library of Congress*
H.W.L. Dana papers, Longfellow National Historic Site, Cambridge, MA
Theodore Draper papers, Hoover Institution, Stanford University
Morris Ernst papers, University of Texas at Austin
International Ladies' Garment Workers' Union/Charles Zimmerman papers, Kheel Center, Cornell University
Labor Research Association papers, Tamiment Library, New York University
Jay Lovestone papers, Hoover Institution, Stanford University
Joseph Magliacano papers, Tamiment Library, New York University
David Lee McMullen papers, Tamiment Library, New York University
NAACP papers, ProQuest Digital History Vault*
Newark Evening News morgue, Newark Public Library*
Ordinances of City of Passaic, City Clerk's Office, Passaic City Hall
Passaic Strike Oral History Project, American Labor Museum, Haledon, NJ
Passaic Strike Vertical File, Forstmann Library, Passaic
Justine Wise Polier papers, Schlesinger Library, Harvard University
Printed Ephemera Collection, New York University
Prometheus Research Library, New York City
Socialist Party papers, Duke University*
Oswald Garrison Villard papers, Houghton Library, Harvard University
Mary Heaton Vorse papers, Walter Reuther Library, Wayne State University, Detroit
Wagenknecht/Winter family papers, Tamiment Library, New York University
Frank P. Walsh papers, New York Public Library
Stephen S. Wise papers, Brandeis University*
Charles Zimmerman papers, Tamiment Library, New York University
*consulted on microfilm or electronic copy

Oral History and Interviews

Martha Stone Asher by Kevin Brownlow, May 24, 1988
Martha Stone Asher by Gail Malmgreen, October 16, 1988, copy in Printed Ephemera Collection, Tamiment Library, New York University
Gustav Deak by Joe Doyle, January 13, 1986, copy in Printed Ephemera Collection Tamiment Library, New York University
Sophie Melvin Gerson by Annelise Orleck, February 17, 1989
Jack Rubenstein, February/March 1987, Passaic Strike Oral History Project
Mary Heaton Vorse, *Reminiscences of Mary H. Vorse*, Columbia University Oral History Collections, 1957
Vera Buch Weisbord by *Women and Revolution*, 1978, in Prometheus Research Library
Helen Winter by Joan Lockwood, January 29, 1993, in Wagenknecht/Winter papers, Tamiment Library, New York University

Articles, Books, Dissertations, Theses, and Pamphlets

While there is no published monograph about the Passaic strike itself, the interested reader is directed to the following sources. Many of the unpublished materials in this list are available in Special Collections at the Archibald S. Alexander Library at Rutgers University, the Botto House American Labor Museum, or, in the case of materials from Columbia University, Rare Books and Manuscripts at Butler Library.

Asher, Martha Stone. "Recollections of the Passaic Textile Strike of 1926." *Labor's Heritage* 2, no. 2 (April 1990): 4–23.

Beckert, Sven. "Migration, Ethnicity, and Working-Class Formation in Passaic, New Jersey, 1889–1926." In *People in Transit: German Migrations in Comparative Perspective 1820–1930*, edited by Dirk Hoerder and Jörg Nagler, 347–378. Cambridge: Cambridge University Press, 1995.

Bennett, Kamika. "Passaic Negro Workers Strike: The Passaic Strike of 1926 and the Making of a Radical and Multi-Racial Struggle." Master's thesis, Rutgers University Newark, 2020.

Brooks, Robert R. R. "The United Textile Workers of America." PhD diss., Yale University, 1935.

Cannon, James P. *First Ten Years of American Communism: Report of a Participant.* New York: Lyle Stuart, 1962.

———. *James P. Cannon and the Early Years of American Communism.* New York: Prometheus Research Library, 1992.

Des Roches, Annick. "Women United in Defense of the Family: The Public Battle for Improved Domestic and Workplace Conditions during the Passaic Textile Strike of 1926." Master's thesis, Hunter College, 2006.

Draper, Theodore. *American Communism and Soviet Russia: The Formative Years.* New York: Viking, 1960.

Ebner, Michael H. "The Fiftieth Anniversary of the Passaic Textile Strike." *International Labor and Working-Class History* 11, no. 9 (1977): 9–10.

Fishel, Anne. "Women in Textile Organizing: An Interview with Sophie Melvin Gerson." *Radical History Review* 14–15 (1977): 109–119.

Foner, Philip S. *History of the Labor Movement in the United States*, vol. 10. New York: International, 1994.

Goldberg, David J. *A Tale of Three Cities: Labor Organization and Protest in Paterson, Passaic, and Lawrence, 1916–1921.* New Brunswick, NJ: Rutgers University Press, 1989.

———. "Immigrant Workers and Labor Organizations, 1912–1926: Lawrence, Massachusetts, and Passaic, New Jersey." In *Work, Recreation, and Culture: Essays in American Labor History*, edited by Martin Henry Blatt and Martha S. Norkunas, 201–232. New York: Routledge, 1996.

Groff, Raymond H. "The Passaic Textile Strike of 1926." Master's thesis, Columbia University, 1927.

Hell in New Jersey: Story of the Passaic Textile Strikers Told in Pictures. Passaic: General Relief Committee of Textile Workers, 1926.

Irwin, Steven R. "Conflict Resolution and the Development of Law: The Passaic Textile Strike of 1926 and the New Jersey State Riot Act." Bachelor's thesis, Rutgers University, 1976.

Liberman, Esther E. "The Influence of Left-Wing Radicalism in the Paterson Silk Strikes of 1912–1913, and Passaic Woolen Strike of 1926." Unpublished undergraduate paper, Brooklyn College, 1965.

McMullen, David Lee. *Strike! The Radical Insurrections of Ellen Dawson*. Gainesville: University Press of Florida, 2010.

Murphy, Paul L., David Klaassen, and Kermit Hall, eds., *The Passaic Textile Strike of 1926*. Belmont, CA: Wadsworth, 1974.

Palmer, Bryan D. *James P. Cannon and the Origins of the American Revolutionary Left, 1890–1928*. Urbana: University of Illinois Press, 2007.

Siegel, Morton K. "The Passaic Textile Strike of 1926." PhD diss., Columbia University, 1953.

Simon, Sara Fanny. "The Passaic Strike—A Study in Left Wing Leadership." Master's thesis, Columbia University, 1928.

Vorse, Mary Heaton. *The Passaic Strike of 1926–1927*. Passaic: General Relief Committee of Textile Workers, 1927.

Weisbord, Albert. *Passaic: The Story of a Struggle against Starvation Wages and for the Right to Organize*. Chicago: Daily Worker, 1926.

———. *Passaic Reviewed*. San Francisco: Germinal Press, 1976.

Weisbord, Vera Buch. *A Radical Life*. Bloomington: University of Indiana Press, 1977.

Zumoff, Jacob A. *The Communist International and US Communism, 1919–1929*. Leiden: Brill, 2014.

———. "Hell in New Jersey: The Passaic Strike, Albert Weisbord, and the Communist Party." *Journal for the Study of Radicalism* 9, no. 1 (Spring 2015): 125–170.

———. "The Passaic Strike Documentary: The Role of Film in Building Solidarity." *American Communist History* 18, nos. 3–4 (2019): 269–295.

Index

Page references in *italics* refer to illustrative material.

About the Author

JACOB A. ZUMOFF is the author of *The Communist International and U.S. Communism, 1919–1929*. He is an assistant professor of history at New Jersey City University.